A History of French Louisiana

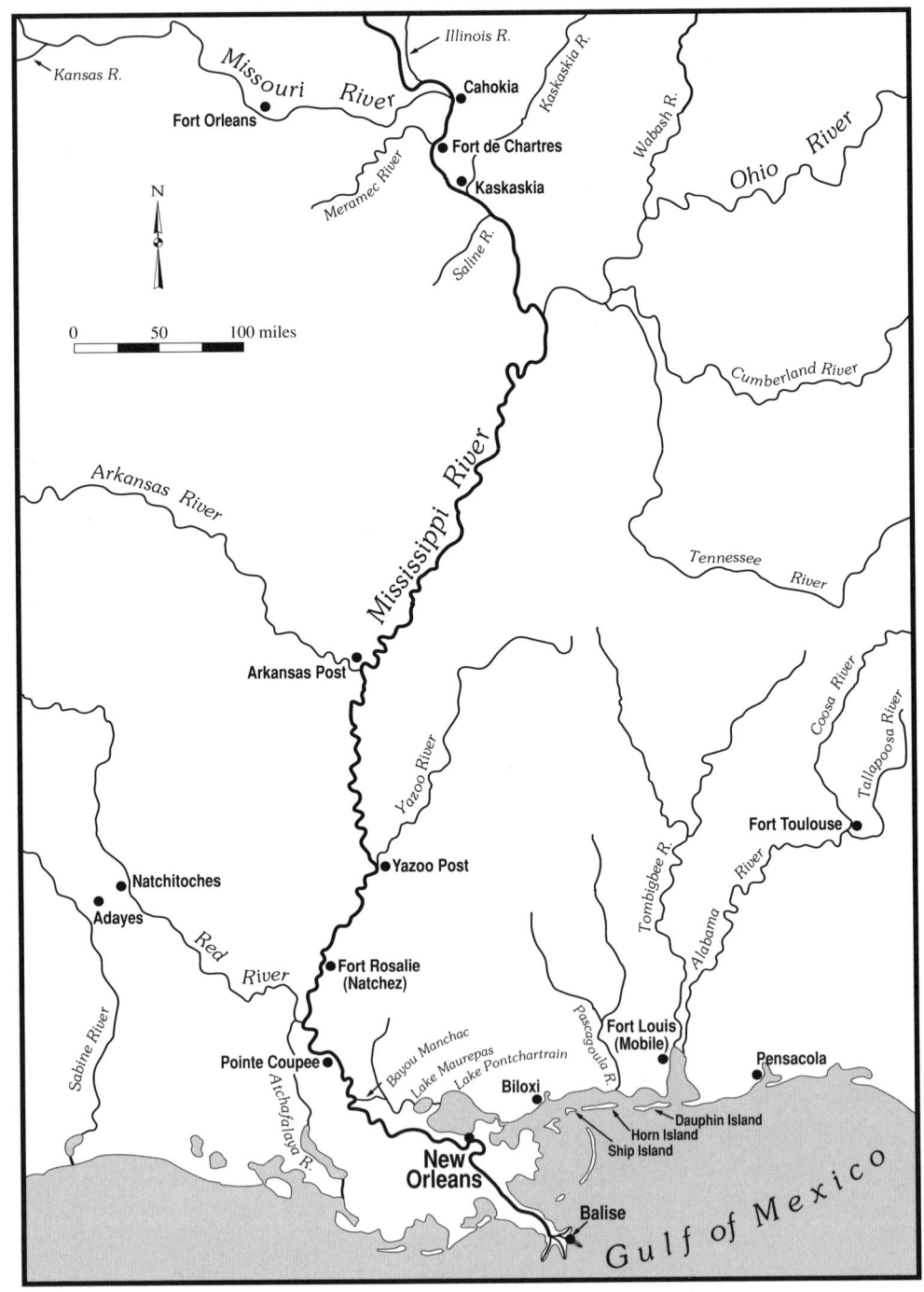

French Colonial Louisiana   Map by John Snead

A HISTORY OF FRENCH LOUISIANA

Volume Two
Years of Transition, 1715–1717

MARCEL GIRAUD
Translated by Brian Pearce

Louisiana State University Press
BATON ROUGE AND LONDON

Copyright © 1958 by Presses Universitaires de France
Originally published as *Histoire de la Louisiane française*, Tome Second: *Années de transition (1715–1717)*.
Translation copyright © 1993 by Louisiana State University Press
All rights reserved
Manufactured in the United States of America
First printing
02 01 00 99 98 97 96 95 94 93   5 4 3 2 1

Designer: Laura Roubique Gleason
Typeface: Palatino
Typesetter: Graphic Composition, Inc.
Printer and binder: Thomson-Shore, Inc.

Library of Congress Cataloging-in-Publication Data

Giraud, Marcel, 1900–
  A history of French Louisiana.

  Translation of Histoire de la Louisiana française.
  Includes bibliographical references and index.
  Contents: v. 1. The reign of Louis XIV, 1698–1715, translation by Joseph C. Lambert—v. 2. Years of transition, 1715–1717, translated by Brian Pearce—
  —v. 5. The company of the Indies, 1723–1731, translated by Brian Pearce.
  1. Louisiana—History—To 1803.   I. Title.
F372.G513   976.3   71-181565
ISBN 0–8071–0058–7 (v. 1)

Translation of this volume has been made possible through the generous assistance of the French Ministry of Culture.

The paper in this book meets the guidelines for permanence and durability of the Committee on Production Guidelines for Book Longevity of the Council on Library Resources.⊗

Contents

Introduction   ix
Abbreviations   xi

   I   The Council of the Navy and Some New Personalities   1
  II   Louisiana and Scientific Opinion   11
 III   The New Tendencies   27
 IV   Crozat's Views and Influence   38
   V   Financial Difficulties   50
 VI   The End of Crozat's Monopoly   56
VII   The Government and Its Personalities   72
VIII   The Defense of the Colony   100
 IX   Emigration and Colonial Society   115
   X   Economic Stagnation   132
 XI   Occupation of the Hinterland   151
XII   Native Policy and the Conflict with the British   162
XIII   Tension Between France and Spain   180

Bibliography   203
Index   207

Maps

French Colonial Louisiana *Frontispiece*
Native Peoples of Southern Louisiana 166–67
Native Peoples of the Missouri Country 194

Introduction

THE FIRST YEARS of the Regency were not a period of fresh achievements in Louisiana. No fundamental changes took place in the internal life of the colony, which was still subject to Antoine Crozat's debilitating regime.

However, the interest that Louisiana had aroused in France at the end of Louis XIV's reign became both greater and more focused, and the numerous suggestions put forward in relation to the colony seemed to show that it was on the eve of innovations. The ruling personages expressed new ideas and tendencies from which Louisiana was soon to benefit. Scientific curiosity, quickening in the home country, spread increasingly to the Mississippi colony and raised questions that went beyond the concerns dominant at the beginning of the century. Inclinations toward active measures were even shown in this connection. To be sure, they led to no decisive results, largely because of the country's financial situation, but these dispositions and the movement of ideas that underlay them implied a presumption that the future of Louisiana would be different from its past. With the coming of the Regency, in fact, the colony entered a brief period of transition in which, beneath a seeming immobility, the need for a new regime made itself felt, while, in the home country, conditions were being created that prepared the way for the Company of the West. It fell to the latter, helped by the new tendencies and profiting from the suggestions advanced during these few years, to provide a foundation for the peopling and the economy of Louisiana that it had not managed to acquire under the rule of Pontchartrain.

Abbreviations

AE	Archives Etrangères (Archives du Ministère des Affaires Etrangères, Quai d'Orsay, Paris)
Mem. & Doc.	Mémoires et Documents
AN	Archives Nationales
AC	Archives des Colonies*
AHM	Archives Hydrographiques de la Marine
AM	Archives de la Marine*
BN	Bibliothèque Nationale, Paris
FF	Manuscripts, Fonds Français
FFNA	Manuscripts, Fonds Français, Nouvelles Acquisitions
LSHM	Louisiana State Historical Museum, New Orleans
La Rochelle, Rivière and Soullard	Notarial files of the practice of Rivière and Soullard (Archives de la Charente-Maritime, La Rochelle)
PRO	Public Record Office, London
Sem.	Archives du Séminaire Laval, Québec

*All letters in the series AC, C 9A, C 11A, C 13A, C 13B, C 13C, and AM, B 1, B 3, and B 7, when given without indication of addresses, are addressed to the Council of the Navy. Those in AC, B, and AM, B 2, unless otherwise indicated, emanate *from* the Council of the Navy.

A History of French Louisiana

The Council of the Navy and Some New Personalities

1

AFTER THE DEATH of Louis XIV, councils took the place of secretaries of state, and the direction of colonial affairs was removed from the comte de Pontchartrain, who had been in charge of them since the birth of Louisiana. Henceforth, the colonies came under the Council of the Navy and also, to a certain extent, under the Council of Trade, an organ standing between "state finance and the navy" that the Regent set up at the beginning of 1716 "on the model of what existed under the late king."[1] Where Louisiana was concerned, the Council of the Navy formed the essential cog in the administration, because Crozat's monopoly deprived the Council of Trade—in which Louis Béchameil, the sieur de Nointel, ordinary state councillor, was responsible for the direction of the colony's economy—of any possibility of direct action. Neither the Regency Council, in which Marshal d'Estrées oversaw naval affairs, nor the Council of Finance intervened except to ratify the decisions of the Council of the Navy and assign the credits required to carry them out. The composition of the Council of the Navy reflected a certain concern for competence, since, besides the heads of the council and its chairman, Louis Alexandre de Bourbon, the comte de Toulouse, and Marshal d'Estrées, respectively—whose positions as Admiral and Vice-Admiral of France meant that they performed these functions "as of right"—the council included several persons who were familiar with maritime and colonial matters, such as Alain-Emmanuel, the marquis de Coëtlogon, Antoine Bochard, the comte de Champigny, and Bernard Renaut. The council's secretary, Henri de Besset de La Chapelle, had acquired his experience under the ministry of Pontchartrain, whom he served for many years as private secretary.[2]

1. AE, Mem. & Doc., France, 1213, f. 7–11, Ordinance to serve as regulation for the Council of Trade, Jan. 4, 1716; BN, FF 7220, f. 135, Declaration of Sept. 15, 1715; Saint-Simon, *Mémoires*, ed. A. de Boislisle (Paris, 1879), XXIX, 334.

2. BN, FF 7221, f. 49, Ordinance by the king to serve as regulation for the Council of the Navy; Saint-Simon, *Mémoires*, XXIX, 74, 153; Philippe de Coucil-

Years of Transition, 1715–1717

Judging by the great number of reform projects put forward at this time, the country hoped for important changes from this new regime. Memoranda flooded in, coming from the most diverse sources and encouraged by the duc d'Orléans himself. To examine them and extract suggestions that could contribute to "the good of the state," the Regent set up a special commission consisting of state councillors and masters of requests.[3]

Most of these memoranda sought solutions for the kingdom's financial weakness.[4] Some, however, criticized religious intolerance, which was so harmful to the country's economic life, condemned the ways in which savings were invested in France, and pointed out the mistake made in not "honoring" the "profession of merchant" as it was honored in England and Holland. By encumbering merchants with administrative hindrances, the state prevented the formation of a class of rich businessmen capable of large-scale enterprises and turned the trader's interest instead toward the acquisition of public offices, thus diverting him from trade with the colonies. In this way, the state paralyzed the growth of its American possessions.[5]

The duc d'Orléans was considered intelligent—more intelligent than industrious, perhaps—and his mind was curious, open, liberal, and concerned with problems of finance and foreign policy. It was logical for many people openly to denounce religious intolerance, something to which he was not at all in-

---

lon, marquis de Dangeau, *Journal du marquis de Dangeau, avec les additions inédites du duc de Saint-Simon,* ed. E. Soubie and L. Dussieux (Paris, 1858), XVI, 184.

3. AE, Mem. & Doc., France, 1219, f. 109v, Jean Chaperon, Mémoire pour le rétablissement . . . du commerce de France, Oct. 28, 1715; 1228, f. 63–63v, Mémoire pour les trois ordres du royaume; 1229, f. 204–205, Anonymous letter in the name of the nobility . . . ; AM, A 1 51, Decision of the king's Council of State, April 25, 1716.

4. AE, Mem. & Doc., France, 1208, f. 340, Anonymous letter, October, 1715; 1209, f. 11–12, Demicourt, lieutenant-colonel in the Royal Bavière regiment, Nov. 15, 1715; f. 34–41, Abbé Servien, November, 1715; f. 64ff., Mémoire sur le change des monnaies, November, 1715; f. 155–57, Mémoire sur les monnaies, end of 1715; f. 162–63, Mémoire au Régent pour acquitter les dettes de l'Etat, 1715; f. 176ff. Mémoire (pour) l'établissement d'une subvention . . . ; 1212, f. 46v–49, Mémoire présenté à Mgr de Duc d'Orléans . . . ; 1219, f. 109v–10, Chaperon, Mémoire pour le rétablissement . . . ; f. 115–16v, De Malon, Mémoire au Duc d'Orléans, March 7, 1716.

5. AE, Mem. & Doc., France, 1208, f. 265–66, Mémoire tendant à l'acquittement des dettes du Roy . . . ; f. 278v, Mémoire de M. Fosse, October, 1715; 1209, f. 366–67, to M. de Cély, intendant of Béarn; 1212, f. 300v–301, Extract from a memorandum by M. de Fougerolle; 1219, f. 105v–109, Chaperon, Mémoire pour le rétablissement. . . .

clined.⁶ The confidence that the Regent inspired was justified, if we are to believe the duc de Noailles, by the sincerity of his intentions and in particular by his desire to alleviate the inequality and arbitrariness of the taxation system in the interest of the "traders, craftsmen and . . . plowmen, who have always been made to bear the burden of what was not taken from the privileged orders." The country expected too much of him not to suffer rapid disappointment, which was echoed in the *Gazette de la Régence* as early as January, 1716. Thereafter, opinion regarding the Regent underwent frequent switches between approval and open blame, depending on the measures he decreed and the results he obtained.⁷

In a narrower context, great hopes were placed in the Council of the Navy, especially in the comte de Toulouse, who was its leading member, more so than Marshal d'Estrées. The latter's principal qualification to be chairman of the council was his position as Vice-Admiral of France and his personal knowledge of the West Indies, to which he had made several voyages.⁸ It was to the comte de Toulouse that everyone turned, in France and in Louisiana, who wished to see a more vigorous effort made in the colonial sphere. Crozat, who knew about the comte's earlier career and relied upon the interest he had long shown in the navy and the colonies, sent Toulouse lengthy memoranda about the Mississippi colony and obtained his promise to look after the affairs of Louisiana. The *ordonnateur* Marc-Antoine Hubert and the missionary François Le Maire also believed that from now on the colony would be given greater consideration.⁹

The comte de Toulouse, a very different man from the Regent, was no brilliant personality. His qualities were those of a hard-working individual, capable of application to a task, "regular,"

---

6. Saint-Simon, *Mémoires*, XXVI, 272, 289–94, XXIX, 127; La Mothe (known as la Hote), *La Vie de Philippe d'Orléans, petit-fils de France* (London, 1736), I, 223; Jean Buvat, *Journal de la Régence*, ed. Compardon (Paris, 1865), 118; M. G. Brunet, trans., *Correspondance complète de Madame, duchesse d'Orléans* (Paris, 1904), I, 25.

7. Jean Buvat, *Gazette de la Régence* (Paris, 1887), 47, 49, 52–53, 131–32; BN, FF 23672, f. 183–85v, Regency Council, session of June 21, 1717; FF 23673, f. 2–3, 8–9v, Regency Council, sessions of June 23 and 26, 1717; BN, FFNA 9640, f. 129–29 v, Mémoire pour les trois ordres du royaume, June 23, 1717.

8. BN, FF 11332, f. 127, Letters patent of August, 1718, granting the island of St. Lucia to Marshal d'Estrées; D. Neuville, *Etat sommaire des Archives de la Marine antérieures à la Révolution* (Paris, 1898), 328–32.

9. AE, Mem. & Doc., America, I, f. 147–47v, Crozat, Mémoire sur la Louisiane, 1716; AC, C 13A 5, f. 143, Hubert, October, 1717; f. 297v, Mémoire à S.A.S Mgr l'Amiral [1715 ?]; BN, FF 12105, f. 13, Le Maire, Mémoire sur la Louisiane, March 1, 1717.

and "exact." In his administrative career he was distinguished by a methodical mind and a concern for well-ordered management, which he also applied to the regulation of his household and which showed itself even in his favorite recreations, such as hunting, where he had the "rules and ordinances" affecting venery codified so as to establish "some sort of order and rule in the functions of the office of *Grand Veneur*."[10] During the War of the Spanish Succession, he had run the Council of Prizes in the same spirit. There he had shown great activity, much conscientiousness and "attention," and had devised a certain number of practical measures aimed at regularizing the recording in the Admiralty registry of judgments handed down in Paris, simplifying the procedure relating to prizes—the complexity of which was a source of pointless expense and malpractice—and making it easier for advocates and shipowners to understand this procedure. In everything he undertook, we observe this constant care for methodical regulation. The legal costs to which privateering gave rise were also subjected to codification, for which the comte de Toulouse "caused to be collected together all the regulations and decisions" in existence, so as to reduce the expense borne by shipowners and facilitate their undertakings.[11]

This background, together with his disinterestedness and honesty, fitted the comte de Toulouse for the dominant role he was given in the Council of the Navy. He was prepared for it by his knowledge of maritime law and the administrative side of the navy, which he owed to the instruction of Jean-Baptiste du Trousset de Valincourt, his colleague in the Council of Prizes and secretary-general of the navy. Merchants and shipowners could not fail to welcome the news of Toulouse's appointment to the post he was to occupy for several years. During the war he had, on a number of occasions, intervened in their interest against the hindrances that Pontchartrain, in full accord with Louis XIV, put in the way of freedom of trade, and he had reproached the minister of the navy for following a policy which, as he saw it, risked discouraging "new discoveries."[12] Conse-

---

10. BN, FF 22816, f. 177, L.-A. de Bourbon to M. de Harlay, April 25, 1715; Saint-Simon, *Mémoires*, XXIX, 93–94, 109; Buvat, *Gazette de la Régence*, 129; Dangeau, *Journal*, XVI, 199–200.

11. BN, FF 16731, f. 42–43v, 46, 48–49, 120, Correspondence of the comte de Toulouse; FF 16732, f. 198–99, the comte de Toulouse to marshal de Marillac, July 1, 1703.

12. BN, FF 16731, f. 57–60, 70, 73, 143, Correspondence between Valincourt and the comte de Toulouse; FF 11329, f. 3–4, (composition of the Council of the

quently, the advocates of French expansion in Louisiana saw in him a most valuable helper toward the accomplishment of their aims. And since the Regent, despite the "reserve" he showed toward the comte de Toulouse, took an interest in colonial matters—which fitted in with his scientific tastes—and since the duc de Noailles, the comte's brother-in-law and chairman of the Council of Finance, looked with a sympathetic eye upon the Mississippi colony,[13] people had every reason to believe that under the guidance of these men, Louisiana would at last enter a new phase of existence.

It really seemed that changes for the better were about to be made in colonial policy. The decisions of the Council of the Navy constantly manifested a desire to regularize the administration of the overseas provinces, subduing them, no less than the king's navy, to the methodical spirit that inspired all the initiatives of the comte de Toulouse. After ordering that all the "ordinances, regulations and decisions relating to the navy, the colonies and trade"[14] be collected together, so as to find in them the information needed for realizing a program of reforms, he meanwhile applied to France's colonial possessions measures calculated to improve and standardize the way they were governed. He established in the colonies, just as in France itself, Admiralty courts whose officers, appointed by the Admiral of France, would take "cognisance of the maritime cases" that until then had been left to judges who were not competent to deal with them.[15] He assimilated, as was appropriate for "all countries subject to the same authority," the rate of exchange of colonial currencies to that of France's money—with the sole excep-

---

Navy); Marquis de Villette, *Mémoires* (Paris, 1844), xxxi; AM, B 3 216, f. 12–13, 15–18, 22–22v, Pontchartrain to the comte de Toulouse, July–August, 1713; M. Giraud, "Tendances humanitaires à la fin du règne de Louis XIV," *Revue historique* (April–June, 1953), 226; M. Giraud, "Crise de conscience et d'autorité à la fin du règne de Louis XIV," *Annales* (April–June, 1952), 185.

13. AE, Mem. & Doc., America, I, f. 138ff., Hubert, Mémoire au sujet de l'établissement de la colonie de la Louisiane, envoyé par ordre de Mgr le duc de Noailles, 1717; f. 182v, Crozat, Mémoire sur la Louisiane, 1717.

14. AC, B 40, f. 583, to M. d'Albon, Jan. 10, 1718.

15. AC, B 38, f. 194v, to Vaudreuil and Bégon, Nov. 3, 1715; f. 285–86, to La Mothe and Duclos, Nov. 3, 1715; AC, B 39, f. 235v, to Vaudreuil and Bégon, June 26, 1717; f. 310–310v, Regulation concerning the local offices of the admiralty, Jan. 12, 1717; AM, B 1 2, f. 5–7, Distribution of activities of the Council of the Navy; AC, F 3 10, f. 1–7; Regulation concerning the local offices of the admiralty, Jan. 12, 1717.

tion of the rate for Spanish currency, which governors were allowed to raise in value in order to attract it into their local market.[16] To prevent embezzlement and injustices at the moment when he was endeavoring to suppress the practice of private trade in the king's navy, he subjected colonial administrators to more effective supervision, either by encouraging denunciations by their subordinates or by requiring that ships' captains record in their logbooks the conditions under which justice was administered in the colonies they visited.[17]

Accepting, moreover, the principle that "enlarging" the colonies was one of the essential aims of its policy, the Council of the Navy made an effort to become informed about the state of France's empire, so as to be in a position to take action appropriate to the empire's needs. Concerned about the condition of agriculture in its provinces, especially in Louisiana, the council urged officers posted to the Mississippi to ascertain what products might accord with the soil and climate.[18] The council required exact accounting for expenditures incurred in the colony, so that the amount of the annual subsidy, which it wished to pay more regularly, might no longer be decided by guesswork, and so that an end might be put to the disorder that made nonsense of Louisiana's accounts. Looking forward perhaps to the future possibilities of Mississippi trade mentioned in Crozat's correspondence, the council required from the *ordonnateur* Hubert "detailed memoranda" on the movement of shipping at Dauphin Island, on the exchange effected by the colony with France and the Spanish provinces round the Gulf of Mexico, on the

---

16. AM, B 1 2, f. 367–71v, Du Quesne, Martinique, Jan. 10, Feb. 17, 1715; AM, B 1 9, f. 214, Projet de mémoire du Roy au Sr de la Varenne, August, 1716; AM, B 1 20, f. 34–34v, Mémoire des habitants des îles au sujet de la monnaie, observations du Conseil des Finances; AC, B 38, f. 370v, to the marquis de Chateaumorant, July 13, 1716.

17. AC, B 38, f. 85, to the marquis de La Gallissonnière, March 3, 1716; f. 86, to Beauharnais, March 3, 1716; f. 88, to Lépinay, March 3, 1716; f. 136v–37v, Order to the midshipmen . . . ; f. 195v, to Vaudreuil and Bégon, Nov. 3, 1715; f. 311, Mémoire pour servir d'instruction au Sr de Lépinay, Oct. 20, 1716; f. 322, Mémoire du Roy au Sr Dusault, Oct. 20, 1716; f. 407–408, to the marquis Duquesne, Nov. 27, 1715; AC, B 39, f. 314v, Regulation concerning the local offices of the Admiralty . . . , Jan. 12, 1717; AM, B 1 9, f. 456v, Projet de mémoire pour . . . le Sr du Sault.

18. AC, B 38, f. 325v, Mémoire du Conseil de Marine au Sr Artus, Oct. 26, 1716; f. 432v–33, Instructions to Sr de La Varenne . . . , Aug. 17, 1716; f. 447v, Instructions to Sr de Ricouart, Aug. 25, 1716; f. 513v, Mémoire du Roy pour servir d'instruction à M. Dorvilliers, May 4, 1716; AM, B 1 9, f. 449v, Draft of instruction to Sr de Lépinay.

quality of the cloth and fabric received from the home country, on any defects he might notice in these goods that could hinder their sale in "the Spanish Indies," and on the local prices of foodstuffs and merchandise—doubtless an allusion to the council's intention to subject the prices charged by Crozat and the inhabitants to a supervision never before exercised.[19]

At the same time, the council intended to ensure a better supply of goods to Louisiana and the colonies generally. To put an end to the uncertainties that had proved so harmful to the inhabitants and garrison of Mobile and Dauphin Island, the council considered it of primary importance to restore the confidence of suppliers in the home country. It therefore offered the merchants, instead of payment in full on the spot, which it could not contemplate, payment "half at once and the other half three months after delivery" for the foodstuffs and commodities they supplied, and assured them that "this will be punctually performed."[20] Then, with a view to lessening the risk of spoilage that was so constant in the case of flour despatched to hot countries, the council ordered that foodstuffs be inspected more strictly and greater care be taken in packing them, and it laid down a scale of penalties for neglectful inspectors, the most effective of which was the obligation to pay for any flour that "may become spoiled through not being cleansed of bran."[21]

Finally, since regular supply presupposed more frequent fitting out of ships, and since Crozat had made only limited arrangements in this regard, the council decided to send out two frigates at once to the Mississippi. Thanks to this, Louisiana was to benefit in 1717 from the arrival of the largest number of ships that had visited it up to that time. The council's choice fell first on the *Samslack* and the *Paon,* but when the *Samslack* received an unfavorable evaluation from the officers of the port of Rochefort, it was replaced by the *Ludlow,* which, though in better condition, nevertheless needed, owing to its long "anchorings" in warm

---

19. AC, B 38, f. 309v, Mémoire . . . pour servir d'instructions au Sr Hubert, Oct. 20, 1716; f. 346v, to Hubert, Nov. 30, 1716; f. 498v–500, Instructions to the administrators of the islands; AC, C 13A 4, f. 903–906, Hubert, Dec. 7 and 10, 1716.

20. AC, B 38, f. 13, to Lempereur, Feb. 11, 1716; f. 72–72v, to Beauharnais, Feb. 4, 1716; AC, B 39, f. 151v, to Lusançay, July 19, 1717.

21. AC, B 38, f. 177v, 182v, to Beauharnais, Sept. 30, Oct. 19, 1716; AC, B 39, f. 3, 22v–23, to M. Pajot, Jan. 16, March 20, 1717; f. 124v–25, to M. Marin, April 21, 1717; AM, B 1 9, f. 3, La Gallissonnière, June 23, 1716; f. 45, Beauharnais, July 21, 1716; BN, FF 7220, f. 156, Decision by the council, Feb. 1, 1720.

seas, burdensome careening and repairs, and also complete renewal of its fittings, ropes, and gear, at a total cost of 30,000 livres.[22] This was a heavy charge on the naval budget. However, the council ordered that the necessary work be undertaken and that arrangements be made without delay for the recruitment of crews and organization of the command. To the hundred sailors who were to form the personnel of the two frigates the council added a pilot from the port of Rochefort, Chaviteau, who was already familiar with the coast of Louisiana. Command was entrusted to the sieur de Lépinay, who was going out to the colony as its governor. For the return voyage he would be succeeded in the *Ludlow* by the chevalier du Sault, while Gotteville Bellisle would be in charge, under his orders, of the *Paon*. Food supplies were estimated for a long absence—nine months—owing to the stopover that the vessels would have to make at Dauphin Island, and it was decided that the crews would receive their wine ration "half in brandy," so as to avoid the risk of its deterioration through heat. The officers and sailors were to be given three months' pay in advance.[23]

In fact, the Council of the Navy interested itself in all aspects of the colonial problem. As regards the peopling of the colonies, it did not propose to depart in any way from the principles of its predecessors. Being convinced of the usefulness of the system of indentured servants, the council kept in force the obligation that the Crown had imposed on merchants since 1698, to transport men to the colonies in numbers calculated according to the tonnage of their vessels, and it made no concession to merchants who, backed by the port commissioners, requested a mitigation of this duty.[24]

---

22. AC, B 38, f. 71v, 78v, 83v, 86, 102v, to Beauharnais, Feb. 4, Feb. 19, Feb. 29, March 3, April 6, 1716; AM, B 1 8, f. 478, Beauharnais, April 25, 1716; AM, B 1 9, f. 16–16v, Beauharnais, July 5, 1716; AC, C 13A 4, f. 817–20, 821, L'Epinay, June 4, June 27, 1716.

23. AC, B 38, f. 48v, to Sr Buisson, Aug. 11, 1716; f. 133, 151v, 161v–62, 168–68v, 174v, 182v, 184, to Beauharnais, June 15, July 14, Aug. 11, Sept. 5, Sept 14, Oct. 19, Oct. 28, 1716; f. 294–94v, to Sr Buisson, Sept. 14, 1716; f. 312, 344–44v, to L'Epinay, Oct. 20, Nov. 21, 1716; AM, B 1 9, f. 107v, Beauharnais, Aug. 1, 1716; f. 332v–33, Council of the Navy, Sept. 1, 1716 (petition from M. du Sault); f. 454–55v, Projet de mémoire pour . . . le Sr du Sault.

24. AC, B 38, f. 8, to Dorvilliers, Jan. 4, 1716; f. 16v, to Lusançay, Feb. 26, 1716; f. 456v, Instructions to Sr de Ricouart, Aug. 25, 1716; f. 495ff, Regulation regarding the indentured servants; f. 505, to M. Dorvilliers, Jan. 4, 1716; AC, B 39, f. 152, to Sr Michel, July 21, 1717; AM, B 1 20, f. 402v–403v, Lusançay, July 10, 1717.

The military defense of the colonies also engaged the council's attention. In France's American possessions, the council began to carry out works of fortification aimed at preventing any further loss of territory that would worsen the consequences of the losses already suffered during the War of the Spanish Succession.[25] Engineers were sent out to draw up plans for the works to be undertaken and to compile explanatory memoranda that would enable the council to make the appropriate decisions. So that the works might be executed rapidly and be permanent, the council recommended that stone be used instead of wood in the new fortifications, and that the work be done "on a piecework basis" or "on contract," since this would ensure greater productivity than when the work was entrusted to indentured workmen.[26]

Since the protection of the empire required, furthermore, reinforcement of the colonial garrisons, the comte de Toulouse intended to provide the military companies with their full official complement of fifty men, to improve their quality by finding recruits preferably among "men with trades" and "young and able-bodied" men, and to spare them, so far as possible, the unpleasantness that made service in the colonies so unpopular. Consequently, he was concerned to provide the soldiers with a suitable uniform. At their departure from the home country, when the men of the "new levy" often arrived at the embarkation point in a state of destitution that might result in their falling ill during the voyage, he arranged for clothing, smocks, hammocks, and blankets to be supplied. In the colonies where, as was especially the case in Louisiana, the troops were often without uniforms, he ordered that the companies, which henceforth would be dressed like the naval units, were to receive, in

---

25. AC, B 38, f. 65–65v, 66, to Beauharnais, Jan. 4, 1716, Jan. 10, 1716; f. 363–63v, to the marquis de Chateaumorant, July 13, 1716; f. 427v, Instructions to Sr de La Varenne, Aug. 17, 1716; AC, B 39, f. 266, to Sr de Verville, June 3, 1717; AC, B 40, f. 494v–95, to Vaudreuil, July 6, 1718; f. 514v, to Saint-Ovide and Soubras, April 27, 1718; AM, B 1 20, f. 154–55, Lefèvre d'Albon, Feb. 15, 1717; f. 321v–22, Chateaumorant and Mithon, March 25, 1717.

26. AC, B 38, f. 214v–15, to Vaudreuil and Bégon, June 23, 1716; f. 488–89, to Sr de La Roulaye, Oct. 13, 1716; AC, B 39, f. 228–30, to Sr Chaussegros, June 26, 1717; AC, B 40, f. 269–69v, to Sr de La Roulaye, March 15, 1718; AM, B 1 20, f. 67–68v, Instructions concerning the fortifications of Capt Breton Island; f. 345v, to M. de Montholon, June 24, 1717; AC, F 3 68, f. 102–102v, Mémoire du Conseil de Marine sur le Service que le Sr de Verville . . . ; f. 206v–207, Mémoire du Roy au Sr de Costebelle et au Sr de Soubras. . . .

one year, a "major set of apparel" made of wool and, in the following year, a "minor set" made up of lighter articles.[27]

All these initiatives and projects show that the members of the Council of the Navy sincerely desired to remedy the worst examples of neglect and feebleness on the part of the previous administration. Under the stimulus of the comte de Toulouse, an effort was being made to "provide the colonies with the help they need"; and the Council of the Navy did not disguise its pride in doing this.[28]

---

27. AC, B 38, f. 69v, to La Gallissonnière, Jan. 17, 1716; f. 90v, to La Gallissonnière, March 17, 1716; f. 130v, to La Gallissonnière, June 9, 1716; f. 406v, to Duquesne, Nov. 11, 1716; f. 520, to D'Orvilliers and d'Albon, May 12, 1716; AC, B 39, f. 159v–60, to Lusançay, Aug. 25, 1717; f. 282, to M. de Soubras, June 26, 1717; AM, B 1 8, f. 92–92v, Council of the Navy, session of Jan. 17, 1716, marginal notes; f. 184v–85, Council of the Navy, session of March 14, 1716; f. 200, Beauharnais, March 14, 1716; f. 666, Barrailh, June 30, 1716; AM, B 1 9, f. 235, Mesnier, March 27, 1716; AM, B 1 19, f. 120v–21, Mesnier, Dec. 5, 1716 (observations by the Council of the Navy); f. 214v–15, Pajot, Feb. 19, 1717; f. 315v–16, La Varenne, Jan. 11, 1717; AM, B 1 20, f. 329–30, La Varenne and Ricouart, April 7, 1717; AM, B 1 30, f. 53v, Draft of instructions for Sr Mézy; AM, B 3 243, f. 336v–37, 353v, Lusançay, Aug. 17, Sept. 7, 1717.

28. AC, B 38, f. 41, to M. Le Couturier, June 14, 1716; f. 85, to La Gallissonnière, March 3, 1716; f. 86v, to Beauharnais, March 3, 1716; AC, B 39, f. 136, to M. Le Couturier, June 12, 1717; f. 268, to Sr de Verville, June 3, 1717; f. 383v, to M. d'Orvilliers and d'Albon, Dec. 22, 1717.

Louisiana and Scientific Opinion II

THE SCIENTIFIC movement then under way in France gave the Council of the Navy an additional reason for concerning itself with colonial questions. This movement was not confined to scientists. It was encouraged, as we know, by the heads of the government—by Marshal d'Estrées, who was a member of the Académie Française and of the Académie des Sciences and as much interested in science as in literature, and above all by the Regent, who, faithful to the tradition of the Orléans branch of the royal family, promoted French cultural influences abroad, rewarded with jobs in the administration persons who were learned in the sciences, gave active support to the academies, and took interest in all forms of learning, in Paris and in the provinces.[1] The Regent's taste for geography and travelers' stories, which resulted perhaps from the teaching he had received from Claude de l'Isle and the affection he retained for him, spread to the wider field of the applied sciences, in which such remarkable activity was going on at that time.

Increasingly, the idea was getting about that theory alone could do no more than satisfy curiosity, and that experimental data were essential for the future of science.[2] Hence the impor-

---

1. BN, FF 22229, f. 245, Philippe d'Orléans to M. Guynet, intendant at Caen, Nov. 24, 1716; FF 22230, f. 27–32, Saint Jean Portal to the Regent, 1717; FF 22803, f. 7–8, Bégon to Cabart de Villermont, Jan. 10, 1693; BN, FFNA 5151, f. 107, to Rev. Fr. Feuillée, April 30, 1718; FFNA 7487, f. 513, Mémoire pour le Conseil de Marine; f. 514–15, comte de Toulouse and Marshal d'Estrées to Renaudot, Nov. 13, 1719; Address by the marquis de Dangeau at the reception of Marshal d'Estrées into the Académie Française, March 23, 1715; Dangeau, *Journal*, XVI, 184; M. Druon, "Philippe d'Orléans, Régent. Sa jeunesse, l'influence que son éducation eut sur sa vie," *Mémoires de l'Académie Stanislas*, 5th ser., XII (1894), 138. On Marshal d'Estrées and his scientific qualifications, see D. Neuville, *État sommaire des Archives de la Marine antérieure à la Révolution*, 163n1.

2. BN, FF 22225, Papers of Abbé Bignon, f. 7–8; Claude de l'Isle, Preface to Vol. I, *Abrégé de l'histoire universelle* (Paris, 1731); *Journal des Savants* (1716), 401; II (1718), 249; Druon, "Philippe d'Orléans."

tance attached by the Council of the Navy to the teaching of hydrography and the system of regular observation of the tides that it established in ports under the direction of pilots and hydrographic experts.[3] Hence also the interest aroused by observations in physics and astronomy in which distinction was won by, among others, the Minime father Louis Feuillée, who was soon to be entrusted with a mission to the Canary Islands to "determine there the first meridian, with astronomical precision," and whose work would inspire Joseph-Nicolas de l'Isle.[4] Concern was focused to a great extent, then, on geography and the natural sciences. The natural history of the West Indies was the object of a study-voyage backed by the Regent, while in Canada Sieur Michel Sarrazin, the king's doctor, was ordered to collect the "curiosities" of the country. He sent from Québec to Paris numerous plant specimens that enriched the collections in the Royal Garden, and the Regent rewarded him with gratuities and increases of salary.[5]

Geography was brought all the more to the attention of the government and the savants by the fact that, Guillaume de l'Isle having been raised to the dignity of First Geographer to the King, the subject assumed a place of honor in the curriculum of the young sovereign. Geography was considered not merely in its descriptive aspect but also from the strictly scientific angle. In the *Journal des Savants*, works devoted to "practical geography," to its usefulness in navigation, to the study of cartography, to "the way of knowing the location of places by means of geometrical and astronomical observations," actually replaced accounts of voyages.[6] It was at this time that the councils and the Académie des Sciences arranged for extensive land-survey operations

---

3. AM, B 1 4, f. 371v, Lusançay, May 21, 1716; f. 373v, Champigny, May 27, 1716; f. 427, Abbé Bignon, June 16, 1716; AM, B 2 245 (I), f. 40v, 70v, to Abbé Bignon, Jan. 29, Feb. 12, 1716; AM, B 3 236, f. 546ff., Letters to the Council of the Navy on the teaching of hydrography at Nantes; B 3 237, f. 480, Clairambault, Oct. 23, 1716; B 3 244, f. 114, Clairambault, April 5, 1717.

4. *Journal des Savants* (1716), 401, 438; BN, FFNA 5151, f. 102, Louis Feuillée to the Regent, Nov. 30, 1715; f. 107, to Rev. Fr. Feuillée, April 30, 1718; BN, FF 22227, De l'Isle to Abbé Bignon, June 26, 1720; AC, F 2C 1, f. 274, Hocquart, Toulon, Nov. 17, 1718.

5. AM, B 1 5, f. 178–78v, Champigny, Le Havre, Aug. 20 and 24, 1716; B 1 29, f. 1–1v, Lusançay, Nantes, Dec. 16, 1717; AC, B 39, f. 254v, to Vaudreuil and Bégon, July 7, 1717; AC, B 40, f. 83, to Lusançay, Jan. 7, 1718; AM, B 3 235, f. 339, Champigny, Aug. 24, 1716; BN, FFNA 5151, f. 148, Académie des Sciences to M. Sarrazin, Paris, March 2, 1717.

6. *Journal des Savants* (1715), 620; (1717), 25, 55, 219.

that would make possible a definitive work of cartography in full accord with the conception of Dominique-Jean Cassini and the two de l'Isles. In France, the Council of the Navy made the engineers Nicolas and Jean Magin responsible for "compiling maps and plans of the coasts of the realm." In Guyana, Captain Gabaret de Lerondière completed a map of the principal river basins. In Canada, the engineers Jacques de L'Hermitte and Jean-François de Verville undertook, at the council's request, the task of drawing an exact map of Cape Breton Island, with its strategic points, and a similar project was contemplated for the Québec (St. Lawrence) River and for Sable Island, the precise location of which was not known at that time. The same work was done for the Windward Islands. And when Father Feuillée was entrusted with his mission to the Canaries, Abbé Jean-Paul Bignon, a member of the Académie des Sciences, proposed that he should be accompanied by the geographer Philippe Buache, so that a general map of these islands might be produced.[7] In this way, France strengthened the reputation that in 1715 had led the British Board of Trade to seek in Paris more reliable maps of America than it could find in England.[8]

In these two spheres, geography and the natural sciences, Louisiana was increasingly attracting the interest of learned men and of the Council of the Navy. The cartography of the colony concerned them all the more because this country, only recently brought within the French empire, had up to then been subjected only to some hasty prospecting limited by the immensity of the area to be covered. For the first time, the council, wishing to clarify its vague notions of the lands occupied by the French, sent to Dauphin Island the "instruments of mathematics" that would be indispensable for the initial work—a quadrant, a plane table with a telescope, a clock showing seconds, dividers, and a compass.[9] It also ordered the engineer Artus to draw an

    7. AM, B 1 5, f. 375, Sieurs Magin at Le Crotoy, Nov. 4, 1716; B 1 20, f. 175–75v, Dorvilliers, Jan. 15, 1717; AC, B 38, f. 253v, to Costebelle and Soubras, March 10, 1716; f. 487–89, to Sieur de La Roulaye, Oct. 13, 1716; AC C 11A 37, f. 46–49, La Galissonnière, Jan. 16, 1717; f. 72–74, Council of the Navy, Feb. 23, 1717, deliberations on the letter from Sieur l'Hermitte; AM, B 2 251, f. 24v, to marshal de Villeroy, Jan. 10, 1718; BN, FF 22226, f. 264, Mémoire de Bignon au Cardinal Fleury.
    8. PRO, CO 5, 324 (10), f. 74–75, the Lords' Commissioners to Secretary Stanhope, July 15, 1715.
    9. AC, C 13A 5, f. 181v, General inventory of all the effects . . . found in the king's storehouses . . . on March 1, 1718; AC, F 1A 19, f. 74, Payment by the Treasurer-General of the Navy for purchase of mathematical instruments.

exact map of Dauphin Island and its harbor, to add to this "an exact plan" of the buildings there "and of the surroundings, with cross sections of the terrain," and to do the same work for Fort Louis and the neighboring region. On his part, the naval officer Du Sault, during his voyage in 1717, "marked down with compasses all the points" on the island's coast, the outline of which he reproduced on a map to be sent to the Council of the Navy.[10]

In this way began a preliminary program of work that corresponded to what the engineer l'Hermitte was doing at Cape Breton Island. It provided Guillaume de l'Isle with new data for the completion of his map of Louisiana, which he was preparing, on the basis of documents from "the store of maps and maritime plans," with the help of his pupil Buache, who was already sufficiently well acquainted with the cartography of "the Gulf of Mexico and neighboring countries."[11]

De l'Isle had in addition a first-class informant in the person of Father François Le Maire. Profiting from his long experience of the country and its inhabitants and his direct contact with the explorers, the missionary reproduced the itinerary followed by Louis Juchereau de Saint-Denis in 1714–1715 and drew maps of the Missouri country, the Gulf of Mexico, and the coast of Louisiana, the Spanish part of which was as familiar to him as the French.[12] Since, however, he lacked skill in the technical side of cartography, he sought advice from Guillaume de l'Isle, and they collaborated. While Le Maire informed the geographer about the natural regions that could be distinguished in the colony and the location of the native tribes, which was often not the same as during the time of Pierre-Charles Le Sueur or Governor Iberville, de l'Isle subjected his correspondent's maps to a savant's critical examination, correcting the meridians and the courses of the rivers—carrying out, in short, a task of revision

---

10. AC, C 13C 1, f. 82v, Hubert, n.d.; C 13C 2, f. 149, Du Sault, on board the *Paon*, Aug. 29, 1717; AC, B 38, f. 325–25v, Mémoire du Conseil de Marine au Sr Artus, Oct. 26, 1716; AC, D 2C 51, f. 11v–12, March 3, 1716 (notes on the officers of the companies in Louisiana).

11. BN, FF 22226, f. 263v–264, Mémoire de Bignon au Cardinal Fleury; f. 273–74, Buache to Maurepas, June 22, 1732; AN, AHM 3 JJ 387, 26 A, Bobé to Delisle (1717).

12. AN, AHM 3 JJ 387, 26 B, Bobé to De Lisle, March 8, 1717; AC, B 38, f. 326, to Le Maire, Oct. 28, 1716. On the Saint-Denis expedition, *cf.* M. Giraud, *A History of French Louisiana*, Vol. I, *The Reign of Louis XIV, 1698–1715*, trans. Joseph C. Lambert (Baton Rouge, 1974), 365ff. Le Maire's map of "the route followed by Saint-Denis" can be found in BN, Ge D 7883.

that would enable him subsequently to use the missionary's work in his own research.¹³

Others too were interested in the cartography of Louisiana. Around Guillaume de l'Isle, whose role was central owing to his high position and the influence it enabled him to exert on the heads of the government, formed a group of men keen on the same subject, successors to the group that had originally supported Iberville's enterprise. The Lazarite father Jean Bobé, who was attached to the royal chapel at Versailles, was outstandingly active as a member of this group. He was particularly helpful to de l'Isle because, working steadily to assemble documents on the American colonies as a whole, he transcribed them for de l'Isle, suggested details that might enrich his map of Louisiana, and constantly supplied him with fresh data. Antoine-Denis Raudot, son of the intendant of Canada and himself intendant in charge of recruitment for the navy and a future director of the Company of the Indies, was also a member of this circle. A friend of Jean Bobé's, he followed Father Le Maire's research attentively. Like de l'Isle he enjoyed "credit" at court. Both were received by the comte de Toulouse and Marshal d'Estrées, to whom they presented, in all their freshness, the maps made by Le Maire and de l'Isle. A link between these learned men and the missionary was created by the latter's brother, "M. Le Maire," who worked at court as an agent for the navy. Through him, Guillaume de l'Isle was informed of the work done by François Le Maire, and Bobé was able to see the maps that arrived from Louisiana and to extract commentaries from them that he passed on to the royal geographer.¹⁴

It appeared, furthermore, that the colony was destined to become a field of study for the natural sciences. The correspondence of Le Maire, who shared the interest in botany that was general at the time, provided material to serve the curiosity of men of learning. It was full of details about the vegetation of

13. AC, C 13C 2, f. 155, Mémoire de Le Maire, 1718; AN, AHM 3 JJ 387, 26 A, Bobé to Delisle (1717); 26 B, Bobé to Delisle, March 8, 1717; 26 R, copy of a letter "from my brother" (F. Le Maire) to M. Bobé, 1718; 22 D, Le Maire to de L'Isle, Dauphin Island, May 19, 1719.

14. AN, AHM 3 JJ 387, 26 C, Bobé to De Lisle, Versailles, April 24, 1717; 26 G–H, Bobé to De l'Isle, Jan. 4, 1717, March 18, 1718; 26 B, Bobé to De Lisle, March 8, 1717; AM, B 1 9, f. 273, Le Maire, Ile Dauphine, Jan. 25, 1716; AC, B 38, f. 326, to Le Maire, Oct. 28, 1716; AM, 55, Laffilard, Liste générale des officiers de finances et de plumes . . . , f. 210v, 284v. On Raudot, AM, B 1 22, f. 187v, Sicard to the Council of the Navy, April 6, 1717; AC, B 40, f. 96v–97, Decision of Feb. 8, 1718; AC, C 13A 4, f. 723–28, Duclos to M. Raudot, July 12, 1716.

Louisiana, about the crops that could be acclimatized there, and especially about its plants of medicinal value, which the missionary considered extremely varied and "of wonderful properties": sassafras, sweet gum, "ginseng of Tartary," cassina, which he identified as Paraguay tea—to all of these he, along with Antoine de La Mothe, le sieur de Cadillac, and the *ordonnateur* Hubert, ascribed the same "depurant" effects. Coffee, tobacco, indigo, the olive, and the mulberry—a variety of which La Mothe claimed to have discovered that was similar to the Piedmont one—were, in Le Maire's view, destined to enjoy "marvelous" success in Lower Louisiana, not to mention the wax and honey that were the natural products of the forest.[15] Le Maire passed all this information on to the Council of the Navy and to his brother, who spread it among his associates at court. Raudot formed a project for introducing the growing of coffee into Louisiana; he even sent out some seeds in the *Dauphine*, but they were lost. The botanists of the Royal Garden were even more interested in these observations. For several years Le Maire had been in correspondence with Danty d'Isnard, Joseph Pitton de Tournefort's successor in the chair of botany, and in 1714 he promised to send Isnard "some medicinal plants" to help him reconstitute the Royal Garden's collections, which had been hard hit by the severe winter of 1709.[16] He was proud to have as friends "several illustrious French savants," who included, perhaps, Abbé Bignon, to whom the council assigned the task of testing the "fragments from the mines" that had been sent home from Louisiana. They all, Le Maire said, urged him to write a "natural history" of the colony, which would provide them with a general picture of its "animals, plants and minerals." But such a task was beyond Le Maire's competence, his opportunities for work, and the resources of his library, and he regretted that no professional botanist had visited Louisiana, where such a specialist would certainly be able to collect a great number of new plants. Instead of the study asked of him, he sent to Jean Bobé, and then to the Council of the Navy, a succinct analysis of the

15. BN, FF 12105, f. 15–16, F. Le Maire, Mémoire sur la Louisiane, Fort Louis, March 1, 1717; AN, AHM 3 JJ 200, 4, Le Maire, Mémoire sur La Louisiane, May 13, 1718; AC, C 13A 4, f. 561–62, La Mothe Cadillac, Ile Dauphine, Jan. 23, 1716; C 13A 5, f. 287, Hubert, April 25, 1719.

16. BN, FF 12105, f. 16, Le Maire, Mémoire sur la Louisiane; AC, C 13C 2, f. 120–20v, Le Maire, De Pensacola, Jan. 15, 1714.

natural wealth of the country, which he thus helped to bring to the knowledge of scientific and political circles.[17]

The native inhabitants of Louisiana were also of the greatest interest to cultivated people in France and, in order to respond to this curiosity, Le Maire set about preparing a dissertation on their origins, since this was the point that most intrigued scholars. His reply amounted, for the moment, to a few concise views in which he concluded that the natives were of dual origin, some coming from Africa and others from Greenland, but this was only the preface to a more detailed study that he aimed to publish later.[18]

It was the wish of "the Court and the savants" that Le Maire condense all this wealth of information, all the data he had acquired on Louisiana, into an account that could decisively enlighten the public.[19] Claude and Guillaume de l'Isle had begun this work at the beginning of the century—the former by writing the history of how the country was discovered, the latter by indicating the main outlines of its geography—in a memorandum designed to be read before the Académie des Sciences.[20] The council now wanted something both more general and more complete, covering all aspects of the colony. While waiting for an opportunity to carry out this plan, Le Maire compiled in 1717 a long memorandum that he hoped would give partial satisfaction to the persons who had asked for it. The missionary had become, in a way, the official correspondent of everyone who was interested in the colony, providing them, to the best of his ability, with the elements of documentation that Iberville's contemporaries had sought earlier. Thanks to Le Maire and Guillaume de l'Isle and his friends, Louisiana came, by virtue of the size and novelty of the field of observations it seemed likely to make available, to outclass the older colonies in the mind of the world of learning.

At the same time, moreover, the question of the Western Sea—the strictly scientific aspect of which was accompanied by

17. AC, B 40, f. 105v, to Abbé Bignon, March 6, 1718; AC, C 13C 2, f. 109, 120–20v, Le Maire, De Pensacola; f. 158v, Mémoire de Le Maire, 1718; BN, FF 12105, f. 5, 16, Le Maire, Mémoire sur la Louisiane.

18. AC, C 13C 2, f. 162v–264v, Mémoire sur la Louisiane, 1718.

19. *Ibid*, f. 153.

20. AN, AHM 3 JJ 388, 12 B, Claude de l'Isle, Sur la découverte que l'on a faite . . . de la rivière de Mississipi; 12 E, Des découvertes qui ont été faites dans l'Amérique septentionale. . . .

an economic one—strengthened the community of interest between savants and statesmen where Louisiana was concerned. This question had long been under discussion; the Jesuits had brought it up even before they reached the region of the Great Lakes. Then Claude de l'Isle, early on, concerned himself with the problem. Using accounts by Spanish and English historians since La Salle's time, reports on New France by the Jesuit fathers, and the testimony, written or spoken, of La Salle, Father Louis Hennepin, and above all Le Sueur, de l'Isle struggled to prove that there was a sea on the same latitude as the region that the Spaniards had named Quivira, where it was supposed that fabulous riches were to be found. This sea was situated to the northwest of New Mexico, toward the fortieth degree of north latitude, extending to the vicinity of New France. If the sea was little known, de l'Isle said, it was because the Spaniards had been "careful . . . to conceal its existence," and because the French in Canada had been unable "to discover the truth about it," or had neglected to do so. But that it existed could not be denied: it washed the coast of Quivira and of "the western part" of New France.[21] De l'Isle had no doubt that this sea "communicates with the great southern sea," that "pacific sea" the discovery of which had been, according to Father Hennepin, La Salle's principal objective. In other words, discovery of the Western Sea would offer France a new route for navigation to China and Japan, different from the one utilized by the Spaniards from Acapulco to the Philippines.[22] Between the coasts of the two seas, and separated from the mainland by the "Red Sea" or "Vermilion Sea," de l'Isle placed California, but without being able to say whether this was an island or a peninsula, and without accepting the hypothesis that there was a strait—the Anian Strait—between California and the shores of Asia. "There must be," he wrote, "a stretch of 1,000 or 1,200 leagues of either sea or land between the edge of California and the edge of Asia."[23]

21. AN, AHM 3 JJ 388, 12 A, Claude de l'Isle, Conjectures sur l'existence d'une mer dans la partie occidentale du Canada et du Mississipi . . . ; 12 C, Preuves du voisinage de la Nouvelle-France avec le Nouveau-Mexique et de l'existence d'une mer dans la partie occidentale de cette même Nouvelle-France.
22. Ibid.
23. AN, AHM 3 JJ 387, 17 B, Letter from Claude de l'Isle to Cassini. The letter, published in Jean-Frédéric Bernard, *Recueil de voyages au Nord* (1715), III, 268ff., proves that de l'Isle, despite what he had said in his earlier memorandum, was not absolutely certain of the existence of communication between the Western Sea and the South Sea. On the tenacity of the belief that Lower California was an

In subsequent memoranda, the most important of which dates from 1703, more thorough study of the evidence obtained by French explorers from the Indians strengthened de l'Isle's conviction that the location of Quivira and the Western Sea did indeed correspond to his original calculations. As for the route that would give access to this sea, de l'Isle placed its point of departure in western Louisiana. "The river of the Osages or the Missouris" seemed to him to be the shortest and surest route. However, in a more southerly latitude he believed there was doubtless also a possible route through the country of the Cenis.[24]

Although the problem of the Western Sea had already been clearly formulated at the beginning of the century, it did not receive full attention before the accession of the Council of the Navy. In the meantime, Claude de l'Isle continued to concern himself with it, and, helped by his son Guillaume, whom he increasingly involved in his research, he assembled fresh evidence and repeated his earlier arguments.[25] Eventually, in 1717, Guillaume, whose scientific position was now higher than that of his father, laid the latter's work before the Council of the Navy. Illustrated with a map and under the title "Conjectures Regarding the Existence of a Sea in the Western Part of Canada and the Mississippi Country," this treatise was none other than the one composed by Claude de l'Isle in 1703.[26]

By this time the question was of interest not to savants alone. For several years it had fascinated the indefatigable Father Bobé. He, in his turn, devoted to it "several memoranda" (now lost), in the hope of convincing the court of the necessity and the "facility of this discovery." These were documents in which, as he admitted, he gave much scope to his imagination, but they interested Crozat and Marshal d'Estrées and brought Bobé to their

---

island, *cf.* Peter Masten Dunne, "Lower California an Island," *Mid-America* (January, 1953), 37–66.

24. AN, AHM 3 JJ 387, 17 X, Claude de l'Isle, 1703; 3 JJ 388, 12 C, Claude de l'Isle, Preuves du voisinage. . . .

25. AN, AHM 3 JJ 387, 23, Guillaume de l'Isle, Extrait d'un manuscrit de voyage entrepris par quelques Français . . . ; 3 JJ 388, 12 D, Preuves de l'existence d'une mer à l'Occident de la Nouvelle-France et d'un détroit pour aller de la baye d'Hudson à la mer Pacifique; 3 JJ 388, 12 F, Preuves du voisinage de la Nouvelle-France avec le Nouveau-Mexique. . . .

26. AN, AHM 3 JJ 387, 26 A, Bobé to Delisle (1717); AE, Mem. & Doc., America, I, f. 241–52, G. de l'Isle, Conjectures sur l'existence d'une mer dans la partie occidentale du Canada et du Mississipi, 1717.

notice. Raudot also gave a sympathetic reception to Bobé's ideas. Bobé now applied himself to producing a more scientific work in which he would conform to the methods of the learned world of his time, examining, like de l'Isle, the accounts left by travelers of every nationality and consulting people who had first-hand knowledge of the American continent—Henri de Tonty, La Mothe Cadillac, and the Canadian Alexandre Turpin, who had been with Le Sueur and witnessed the establishment of Fort L'Huillier, or Fort Green, on the Green River in what is now Minnesota.[27] Bobé also used the notes that Nicolas Jérémie had collected at Fort Bourbon when he was its governor, Jérémie's account of Hudson's Bay, and the map he had made of that feature. This gave Bobé a fresh opportunity to approach Raudot and Guillaume de l'Isle, and these three men, enthusiasts on the same subject, embarked on numerous exchanges of ideas and documents.[28]

Since, however, the matter required the collaboration of someone who was actually in Louisiana, the three appealed once more to François Le Maire. Bobé had interested the missionary in the problem and urged him to "work at [this] discovery," and Le Maire had responded all the more readily because he had long since been collecting information about the areas to the west. He had already translated from Spanish, in order to send it to France, "an abridged account of the discovery of New Mexico," had questioned Spaniards at Pensacola in order to find out what they thought about the "great lake of salt water" and the inhabitants around it that the baron de La Hontan placed in the western part of the Continent, and had even noted in his "memoranda" some significant allusions to a sea extending "far to the West" from Canada.[29] To meet Bobé's request, Le Maire, in a long memorandum that he presented to the Council of the Navy in 1717, made an initial review of the question of the Western Sea. He did not think it could be reached from "the big bays

27. AN, AHM 3 JJ 387, 20, Extract from a letter from M. de Tonty concerning Fort Detroit, written to M. Bobé, Paris, May 22, 1716; 26 A, Bobé to Delisle (1717); AC, C 11E 16, f. 42–44v, Mémoire pour la découverte de la mer de l'Ouest, compiled and presented by Bobé in April, 1718. On Fort l'Huillier, cf. Giraud, *History*, I, 48–49.

28. AN, AHM 3 JJ 387, 26 D. Bobé to de Lisle, Versailles, July 2, 1717; 26 E, Bobé to de L'Isle, Versailles, Aug. 2, 1717; Nicolas Jérémie, Relation du Détroit et de la Baie d'Hudson, in Bernard, *Recueil de voyages au Nord*, V.

29. AC, C 11E 16, f. 64, Bobé, Mémoire pour la découverte de la mer de l'Ouest, April, 1718; C 13C 2, f. 160–62, Le Maire, Mémoire sur la Louisiane, 1718; BN, FF 12105, f. 7–8, Le Maire, Mémoire sur la Louisiane.

to the north of Canada," or from the Vermilion Sea, which the Spaniards guarded. Only land routes could be considered. Further, the higher latitudes had to be ruled out because of cold and ice, and exploratory activity confined to a "reasonable region" corresponding to the zone between forty-five and forty-eight degrees north latitude, where Le Maire thought, like Claude de l'Isle, that the Missouri might lead to "some navigable river" that would flow into the Western Sea. As regards the distance to be traveled, Le Maire maintained that one could pronounce precisely on that only if one knew the exact orientation of the seacoast. There was merely "a strong appearance" that this "runs northward to near the Arctic Circle." If this proved to be the case, the Western Sea would, as Claude de l'Isle had already said, fringe "the western part of New France."[30]

Less scientific, Bobé placed the Western Sea between the 44th parallel, which he considered the border of California, and the 48th or 50th parallel, where, as he saw it, the lands began that joined America to Asia—this meant eliminating almost the entire western frontage of New France.[31] But the fundamental idea, shared by all these men, persisted—namely, that the American continent, at a latitude still controversial, ended in a sea that was linked with the South Sea, and they all agreed that the Missouri or one of its tributaries would be the main route for access to it.

On the other hand, their views on the usefulness of discovering this Western Sea were not unanimous. For Le Maire, it was a task of no practical interest, from which only science would gain. "I find in this matter," he said, "more curiosity than utility." France would gain little by establishing a link with Asia over a route which, starting from the sources of the Missouri, would cover "some 1,440 leagues of land and sea," without counting the distance from the Missouri to Dauphin Island, and from there to France. Trade with the East Indies would be made neither easier nor less expensive, and Le Maire advised that the enterprise be put off until Louisiana had been solidly "established" and its geography was better known.[32] For Claude de l'Isle, who had nothing to say about the distance involved, the opening of a new seaway under French control would be an event of great consequence for the kingdom. As for Bobé, he

---

30. BN, FF 12105, f. 8–9, Le Maire, Mémoire sur la Louisiane.
31. AN, AHM 3 JJ 387, 26 A, Bobé to Delisle (1717); 26 C, D, Bobé to De Lisle, March 8, July 2, 1717.
32. BN, FF 12105, f. 8–9, Le Maire, Mémoire sur la Louisiane.

was particularly attracted by the idea of this "fine discovery." He made the distance shorter, considering the Western Sea to be less than four hundred leagues from the confluence of the Missouri and the Mississippi, and, while urging that the enterprise be preceded by the dispatch of a scientific mission that could clear away the uncertainties, he regarded it a priori as "an easy and a serious matter."[33]

Whatever these differences of opinion might be, the question of the Western Sea assumed, as a result of the discussions and studies it inspired, fresh significance in these years of transition. It was too important for men like Father Charlevoix or Jean-Baptiste Duché, the director of the service of supply at Rochefort, who corresponded with Le Maire and, having been associated with the early progress of the colony, was now helping the Council of the Navy with his advice,[34] not to keep in touch with the debate. Nor could the Académie des Sciences remain indifferent, since the subject involved the problem of communication between the continents at the time when the visit of Tsar Peter the Great to Paris in 1717, and his promise to the Académie to send a mission to Siberia to discover whether an "arm of the sea" separated Asia from America, testified to the interest and international implications of the matter.[35] The Regent had every reason to concern himself in a question that touched his scientific curiosity and might perhaps increase the country's economic potential.

In February, 1717, when the Council of the Navy put before him Governor Vaudreuil's proposal to attempt to discover the Western Sea through the interior of New France, the Regent gave his approval unhesitatingly. The possibilities of success looked good. Vaudreuil, misled by stories told by the natives, believed that a river rising in the chain of lakes beyond Lake Superior ran directly into the sea. He suggested that three posts be established, the farthest of which, on the Lake of the Assiniboins (Lake of the Woods)—which he thought was the source of this river—would serve as the base for the enterprise. As a result, France would possess, by prolonging the line of the St.

---

33. AN, AHM 3 JJ 387, 26 A, Bobé to Delisle (1717); 26 D, Bobé to de Lisle, Versailles, July 2, 1717.
34. P. 151f. below.
35. AC, C 11E 16, f. 55, Bobé, Mémoire pour la découverte de la mer de l'Ouest, April, 1718.

Lawrence and the Great Lakes, a continuous waterway to the sea, providing sure communication with China.[36]

It was thus from the territory of New France that the search for the Western Sea was to be undertaken. By agreeing to Vaudreuil's proposal, the Regent did not mean to reject the Missouri route, only to profit from a suggestion that seemed easily realizable. Bobé's activity certainly had something to do with the speed of his decision. The Lazarite claimed to have interested the court in the question through his memoranda and to have converted Marshal d'Estrées in 1716 to the idea of an expedition of discovery. In 1717 Guillaume de l'Isle's memorandum, benefiting both from its author's great prestige and from Bobé's preliminary work, clinched the decision of the Council of the Navy. Bobé counted now on the influence of the geographer and "the esteem that these great men have for [de l'Isle's] knowledge" to commit the Regent and the council to increasingly vigorous action.[37] At the moment when Louisiana was about to pass under the direction of the Company of the West, the search for the Western Sea was in its first phase of realization, and although, as a result of Vaudreuil's initiative, efforts were thereafter concentrated on Canadian territory, the discussions concerning the Missouri route finally brought out the importance of Louisiana in the scientific domain.

It is harder to say whether the colony evoked in France a more general curiosity not confined to savants and public personages. Le Maire's correspondence seems, indeed, to restrict this curiosity to a rather limited elite of scholars and men of science. To the names already mentioned, we can add that of Abbé Pierre Le Lorrain de Vallemont, doctor of theology, even though his numerous publications were little known in the world of science and he seems to have "made some stir in the republic of letters" only through the ecclesiastical censure incurred by his book on occult physics. Since he was a tutor in the household of the marquis de Dangeau and was well informed on Louisiana through Le Maire, it is possible that Vallemont may have helped to maintain in the Dangeau family the interest it had shown from the

---

36. AC, C 11E 16, f. 13–16. Mémoire joint à la lettre de Vaudreuil et Bégon of Nov. 12, 1716; f. 17–20v, Letter from Vaudreuil and Bégon, Quebec, Nov. 12, 1716; AM, B 1 19, f. 96–100, Vaudreuil and Bégon, Nov. 12, 1716; AC, C 11A 37, f. 376, Council of the Navy, proceedings of Dec. 7, 1717.

37. AN, AHM 3 JJ 387, 26 A, Bobé to Delisle (1717); 26 D, Bobé to de Lisle, Versailles, July 2, 1717.

start in the Mississippi enterprise, and he may thus have widened the circle of persons who paid attention to its progress.[38] But Vallemont's influence cannot have extended beyond this circle of cultivated men.

To what extent was public opinion interested in the colony? In principle, the attitude adopted by the Council of the Navy in openly showing "favor and protection" to Louisiana, and thereby indirectly combating the prejudices of which it had for so long been the object, was bound to make the colony more popular. Also, there were now in Paris a certain number of "Louisianians"—officers and administrators recently arrived from the Mississippi. Some of these had returned home for good, others had come to lobby for promotion and were now ready to go back. This was the case with the Basque Derigoin, former director of Crozat's company, *Major* Pierre Dugué de Boisbriant, Captain François Mandeville, and the commissioner Jean-Baptiste Martin d'Artaguiette Diron. These "Louisianians" met Bobé and Guillaume de l'Isle, had interviews with the members of the Council of the Navy, who consulted them on the state of the colony, and spread awareness of it. Their contacts with the population enabled many people to become acquainted with living conditions in Louisiana and with the colony's future possibilities.[39]

Unfortunately, while some spoke up for a country to which they were attached, there were others who voiced unfavorable opinions. When La Mothe Cadillac arrived in 1717, after having been relieved of his duties, he did not conceal the poor view he took of the colony. At a lower level, Jean Roy—who came back to reveal the "wretched state" to which, after fifteen years, he had been reduced by his pay as a gunner—had every reason to complain about the fate of minor employees. Faced with the lack of sympathy shown him by the Council of the Navy, despite his intention to end his career in Louisiana where his family had settled, Roy could not fail to discourage people who might be

---

38. AC, C 13C 2, f. 109, Le Maire, De Pensacola, Jan. 15, 1714. On Le Lorrain de Vallemont, see Moreri, *Dictionnaire historique* (Paris, 1759). Goujet, *Bibliothèque des auteurs ecclésiastiques du XVIIIe siècle* (Paris, 1736), III 459–60; Giraud, *History*, I, 17–18.

39. AN, AHM 3 JJ 387, 26 K, Bobé to de l'Isle, May 27, 1718; AM, B 1 8, f. 634–34v, Proceedings of the Council of the Navy, June 16, 1716; B 1 9, f. 388, Proceedings of the Council of the Navy, Sept. 21, 1716; f. 414, Proceedings of Oct. 9, 1716; Giraud, *History*, I, 275, 305–306, 309; p. 100 below.

inclined toward emigrating to the colony.⁴⁰ In fact, opinions about Louisiana were too divided for the presence of these "Louisianians" to suffice to wipe out the prejudices of earlier years.

Besides, although Louisiana was now beginning to be better known, it still lagged far behind the other colonies in America. Descriptive geography, more accessible to the general public and with wider scope than the scientific sort, assigned only a modest place to Louisiana. The several re-editions of the memoirs of Louis Hennepin were the only travelers' accounts devoted to it. The lists of contents of the *Journal des Savants* reveal a substantial body of writing about Africa, the Middle East, and the South Sea, but allusions to Louisiana are reduced to rare documents such as the account of the Illinois by Father Marest (1712), published in the *Lettres édifiantes et curieuses* in 1715, or, more technical than descriptive, the letters of de l'Isle on the Mississippi and California, taken from Jean-Frédéric Bernard's *Recueil de Voyages au Nord*.⁴¹ Louisiana lacked the extensive publicity that travelers' accounts had given to the older-established colonies. Certainly no active propaganda could be expected from the Seminary of the Foreign Missions, whose director, at the end of 1716, predicted the colony's collapse in the event of Crozat's death.⁴² Finally, the memoranda which, at the beginning of the Regency, called upon the government to favor colonial trade and to direct toward this outlet "young men of family" and the too numerous purchasers of official positions, made no mention of the Mississippi colony. If they spoke of France's American possessions at all, they confined their attention to the West Indies and Canada.⁴³ Consequently, until the Company of the West came on the scene, Louisiana remained largely a concern for the world of the learned. Among the general public, despite the slight progress made, knowledge of Louisiana was still less widespread and its reputation more uncertain than in the case

---

40. AM B 1 9, f. 517–17v, Proceedings of the Council of the Navy, Nov. 16, 1716.

41. *Journal des Savants* (1715), 321; (1716), 3, 22; Bernard, *Recueil de voyages au Nord*, III, 257, 268.

42. Sem., Missions, no. 45, M. de Brisacier, Paris, Oct. 31, 1716.

43. AE, Mem. & Doc., France, 1212, f. 59v–62v, Mémoire pour rendre l'Etat puissant et invincible; f. 157–161, Mémoire concernant les moyens d'établir le droit d'amortissement des gabelles . . . ; 1219, f. 105v–109, Jean Chaperon, Mémoire pour le rétablissement . . . du commerce de France, Oct. 28, 1715.

of New France and the Caribbean colonies. But the attention it was arousing in scientific and political circles constituted a pointer that was all the more favorable for the colony's future in that the new tendencies appearing at this time among the leaders of France seemed certain to offer Louisiana more extensive possibilities of growth.

The New Tendencies   III

FROM THE OUTSET, the members of the Council of the Navy expressed tendencies that differed from those of the previous administration The concern for regulation and methodical management that spread from the comte de Toulouse to his colleagues shows that these were persons with a more realistic outlook, less marked by ideology, than Pontchartrain. Under the latter's rule the comte de Toulouse was not classed among the humanitarians. He was interested above all in the expansion of trade and voyages of discovery, and he acted as defender of the merchants operating in the South Sea, without concerning himself with the deeply humane considerations that, as the minister saw it, required that the trade of these merchants be forbidden.[1]

Accordingly, the correspondence of the Council of the Navy became, under Toulouse's influence, more strictly administrative, its tone and emphases reflecting the "exact" mentality of the Admiral of France. It did not, however, entirely eliminate the humanitarian formulations of the previous reign, although these were less prominent, and it remained true to a certain number of principles that Pontchartrain had always proclaimed. The council still enjoined the administrators of the colonies to protect the "humble settler," to take care that he was not crushed by the powerful, to cause justice to be done with complete impartiality, without regard to wealth or social position, and to apply a policy of "mildness" in relation to the Protestants living in the West Indies.[2] Moreover, the council continued to assert re-

---

1. AM, B 3 216, f. 12–13, 15–18, 22, Pontchartrain to the comte de Toulouse, July 26, Aug. 16, Aug. 30, 1713; M. Giraud, "Tendances humanitaires à la fin du règne de Louis XIV," *Revue historique* (April–June 1953), 225–26.

2. AC, B 38, f. 433–33v, Instructions to Sr de La Varenne . . . appointed governor and lieutenant-general of the French Windward Islands, Aug. 17, 1716; f. 444v–45, Instructions to Sr de Ricouart, intendant of the Windward Islands, Aug. 25, 1716; AC, B 40, f. 251–51v, Mémoire pour le Sr de Silvecanne, March 15, 1718; BN, FF 11329 (Council of the Navy), Extended instruction given to M. de Blondel, intendant of Martinique.

spect for individual liberty as a maxim that was inseparable from monarchy. It forbade compulsory enrollment in the troops, either in France or in the colonies, and even made more severe, by an ordinance of July, 1716, the penalties risked by anyone who infringed this prohibition. Where the companies serving in Louisiana or the West Indies were concerned, the council insisted that there be only voluntary enlistments of private soldiers or of midshipmen. Where necessary—and this happened in Louisiana—it ordered the release of men who had been forced to serve. Nor did the council allow men to be given assignments differing from those agreed upon when they joined up, or permit force to be used against port workers who refused to resume work. From the principle, so often affirmed, that "a Frenchman is born free," there followed the determination not to "imprison the inhabitants" in a particular colony, to allow them freedom of movement, and the prohibition, formally included in the jurisprudence of Louisiana, against enslavement of the king's subjects as a punishment for criminal offences.[3] As regards the black slaves, the council was still inspired by Pontchartrain's ideal. It sought to spare them from the iniquity of corporal punishment inflicted without any "formality of justice" and to obtain from their masters assurance that they would provide the slaves "regularly with food and clothing, in conformity with the royal ordinances." As for soldiers serving in the colonies, finally, the council prescribed that discipline be made more humane, free from "harassment" and pointless cruelty. It even condemned the practice, established since 1706 in St. Domingue, of making deserters "work in chains, like convicts."[4]

Yet, while the formulations and principles remained unchanged, the tone of the official correspondence was no longer

3. AM, A 1 52, Royal ordinance, July 2, 1716; AC, B 38, f. 93v, to Beauharnais, March 20, 1716; f. 145v, to Beauharnais, June 27, 1716; f. 291v, to Sr Artus, July 18, 1716; AC, B 41, f. 36v, to M. de Champmeslin, Feb. 13, 1719; f. 80v, to Sr Marias, May 10, 1719; AM, B 1 8, f. 108, Beauharnais, Jan. 19, 1716; 9, f. 116v, Proceedings of the Council of the Navy, Aug. 11, 1716; AC, C 13A 4, f. 942, Mémoire pour Messieurs de la Compagnie d'Occident . . . ; AM, B 2 245 (I), f. 108v, to La Gallissonnière, March 14, 1716; B2 251, f. 197v, to Clairambault, March 16, 1718; AC, C 9A 13, Chateaumorant and Mithon, May 30, 1717; AC, F 2C 1, f. 155, Hocqart, Toulon, June 5, 1717 (marginal note).

4. AC, B 38, f. 314v, Mémoire pour servir d'instruction au Sr de Lépinay, Oct. 20, 1716; f. 370v, to the marquis de Chateaumorant, July 13, 1716; f. 524, to d'Orvilliers, May 12, 1716; AC, B 40, f. 527–28, to d'Orvilliers and d'Albon, January, 1718; AM, B 1 20, f. 372v–73v, Chateaumorant, March 8, 1717; B 1 30, f. 339–39v, d'Orvilliers, Cayenne, May 25, 1718.

the same. Violence against blacks no longer aroused the council's anger, and it is clear that the council ceased to enforce with Pontchartrain's conviction the laws that protected slaves, despite the warnings that reached it concerning abuses committed by the colonists and threats of revolt by their slaves. What interested the council in these violations of the royal ordinances was not so much the colonists' rejection of the duties of humanity as the disagreeable effects these abuses might have on the life of the plantations. For Pontchartrain's lofty notions the council substituted a utilitarian policy that looked above all to the interest of the colonies.[5]

The council's proceedings and the notes written by its secretary, La Chapelle, in the margins of documents describing the misery of the workers at the ports are indicative of this new state of mind. Here and there a certain concern for justice still finds expression, but manifestations of compassion and sympathy grow rarer and rarer. Instead of ordering immediate relief, the council calls for inquiries, consults the intendants, and often even washes its hands of responsibility by referring complaints to the officers of the Admiralty or replies to requests for help with considerations of an administrative nature that put off a solution indefinitely. Less and less does it excuse the impatience of workers who have not been paid, and it does not hesitate to dismiss those who refuse to accept the payment offered them. The dryness of La Chapelle's notes, the categorical refusal to agree to any relaxation of administrative regulations that might bring some benefit to the population of the ports, or to act upon suggestions put up by the intendants to introduce some activity into regions particularly afflicted by unemployment, make a painful contrast to the correspondence of the previous period, which had shown so much understanding.[6] Considerations of a

---

5. AC, B 38, f. 370v, to the marquis de Chateaumorant, July 13, 1716; f. 432v–33, to Sr de La Varenne, Aug. 17, 1716; f. 513v, 524, to d'Orvilliers, May 4, May 12, 1716; AC, B 40, f. 259, Mémoire pour le Sr de Silvecanne, March 15, 1718; AM, B 1 8, f. 523–24, Le Febvre d'Albon, Cayenne, Jan. 21, 1716; B 1 20, f. 436v–37, Robert, July 19, 1717; AC, F 3 82, f. 92–92v, Bénard, Mémoire concernant l'état présent des colonies du Vent de l'Amérique, Sept. 13, 1723; M. Giraud, "Tendances humanitaires à la fin du règne de Louis XIV," 233–34.

6. AM, B 2 245 (I), f. 67–67v, to Clairambault, Feb. 12, 1716; B 2 251, f. 229, to Robert, June 18, 1718; AM B 3 236, f. 164–64v, Bigot, Lorient, July 31, 1716; B 3 237, f. 139, Clairambault, Lorient, March 23, 1716; f. 523v, Clairambault, Lorient, Nov. 22, 1716; B 3 243, f. 156v, Bigot, Lorient, Jan. 22, 1717; f. 251–52, Lusançay, Nantes, March 4, 1717; B 3 244, f. 407, Clairambault, Nov. 22, 1717; AM, B 1 8, f. 84v–85, Duquesne, Martinique, Sept. 12, 1715; B 1 22, f. 280, Robert, Brest, May 3, 1717; AC, F 2C 1, f. 235–36, Beauharnais, Sept. 12, 1718.

practical order and administrative necessities take precedence over strictly human considerations, and although a certain wavering is sometimes observable in the council's dispositions because of the persistence of an official ideology, the measures it takes and the tendencies it expresses increasingly indicate that its concerns have switched to a new direction.

Thus, the council's decision to allow slaveowners to retain ownership of slaves they sent to France to "learn some skill or trade," or whom they wished to keep in their service during visits to the home country, was a direct breach of a principle on which Pontchartrain had always refused to compromise. He had several times declared that slaves "become free when they touch the soil of France." Now, on a proposal by Marshal d'Estrées, approved by the Regency Council, it was decided in 1716 that slaves would remain slaves while in France, that everything they might acquire "by their industry or their occupation" was to become their masters' property, and that, in the event of a master's death, a slave would become the property of the heir. There was, of course, no question of instituting slavery on "the soil of France." The edict of October, 1716, forbade the sale or barter of blacks in the home country and laid down that slaves were to remain subject to their condition for a limited period only, which their owners would determine by agreement with the governors of the colonies; after that period expired, the slave, if he or she remained in France, would become "entirely free." Despite these precautions, however, the council's decision doomed a principle that Pontchartrain had declared unchangeable, and its initiative was guided above all by concern to safeguard the interests of slaveowners, to protect them from the risk of losing their slaves, and to ensure for the colonies a work force from which they could "gain benefit."[7]

Nor did the Council of the Navy reveal any sign of ideology with regard to the natives of Louisiana. To be sure, François Le Maire left it with no illusions about the latter: his correspondence does not support the theme of "the noble savage." He blames the natives for having no "passion" but self-interest, and although he allows them some good qualities, he invariably neutralizes these with defects or vices that counterbalance them.

7. AM, A 1 53, October, 1716, Edict concerning Negro slaves . . . ; AM, B 1 9, f. 508–512v, Council of the Navy, Oct. 28, 1716, Draft of edict concerning Negro slaves in the colonies; BN, FF 23664, f. 68v, Regency Council, Aug. 25, 1716, Report by Marshal d'Estrées; Giraud, "Tendances humanitaires à la fin du règne de Louis XIV," 232.

The council concurred without difficulty in the missionary's views. It did not believe that one could find "in this new world" "some image of the simplicity and innocence of the earliest centuries." "Profit," there as everywhere else, was "the great motive."[8] Further, the council declared flatly against the principle of mixed marriages. Pontchartrain had looked at this question and submitted it to the director of the Seminary of Foreign Missions; although he feared "to mix, through these marriages, good blood with bad," he was caught between the opposing views of the missionary Henry Roulleaux de La Vente and the *ordonnateur* Jean-Baptiste du Bois Duclos and asked for more information. The reign of Louis XIV had ended without any decision having been made.[9] With the Council of the Navy all hesitation vanished. It accepted the *ordonnateur*'s opinion, which was corroborated by the unfavorable picture of the native women drawn by Le Maire, and ordered that "this sort of marriage" be prevented so far as possible, recognizing that in a country where encounters with Indian women were unavoidable and white women were few, the rule would be hard to enforce.[10]

Even more than in its attitude toward blacks and Indians, the council's tendency to break with the scruples and reserve of the previous reign was revealed in its attitude regarding the way the colonies were to be peopled. In another denial of the respect for individual freedom that it upheld in its correspondence, the council gave in on the principle of forced emigration, which Pontchartrain had always opposed. As we know, the idea had its supporters in Louis XIV's reign.[11] It was now the theme of a movement of opinion that grew stronger and stronger, encouraged by the more conciliatory attitude attributed to the heads of the government. From Nantes and La Rochelle came requests from merchants that the Council of the Navy cause to be arrested and transported to the American colonies the "young vagrants" who were cluttering up the seaports. The merchants

8. AC, C 13A 4, f. 78–80, Mémoire sur la colonie de la Louisiane porté au Conseil de Régence le 11 février 1716; C 13C 2, f. 136v, Le Maire, De Pensacola, Jan. 15, 1714; BN, FF 12105, Le Maire, Mémoire sur la Louisiane, March 1, 1717.

9. AM, B 1 9, f. 329–30, Proceedings of the Council of the Navy, Sept. 1, 1716; AC, C 13A 4, f. 977–78, Projet de mémoire du Roy à Lépinay et Hubert; Giraud, *History*, I, 278–79.

10. BN, FF 12105, f. 17, Le Maire, Mémoire sur la Louisiane; AC, B 38, f. 316v–17, Mémoire du Roy pour servir d'instruction au Sr de Lépinay, Oct. 20, 1716; f. 334, Joint instructions to Lépinay and Hubert, Oct. 28, 1716.

11. Giraud, *History*, I, 273–74.

would include these arrestees in the contingents of indentured servants whom they were obliged to take out to the colonies, and whom it was increasingly difficult to recruit. This measure would also serve as an effective remedy for the plague of beggars that was creating an ever more disturbing problem in the towns of the kingdom. The merchants put it to the comte de Toulouse that the measure would not be at all "contrary to public liberty," since ancient ordinances allowed for vagrants to be sent to the galleys, and the judge-consuls of La Rochelle adopted this view and defended it before the Council of the Navy.[12] At the same time, the idea became widespread that persons found guilty of cheating the salt monopoly, whose great numbers worried many people, could be used in the colonies either as workmen—this was the intendant Michel Bégon's wish for Canada—or as indentured servants, as the merchants of Nantes desired.[13] All these suggestions ran counter to previous policy and to Pontchartrain's expressed wish to select the emigrants.

The council at first received such proposals with some reserve. Soon, however, its decision to send to Rochefort, for incorporation into the troops in Canada, a group of vagrants who had been arrested near Paris, showed that it had accepted the idea of forced emigration.[14] The council hesitated more about letting the merchants take their indentured servants from among the vagrants or the "tramps" in the General Hospital (that is, the poor house),[15] but it did not sweep the suggestion aside, since it had first intended the previous recruits to be sent to the colonies as indentured servants. The council certainly did not intend to give the measure general scope by obliging all those who were a burden on the state to emigrate. It rejected,

12. AM, B 1 20, f. 404, Lusançay, Nantes, July 10, 1717; B 1 21, f. 318v, The judges-consuls of La Rochelle, Nov. 30, 1717; B 1 30, f. 5–5v., The merchants of La Rochelle, [May, 1718 ?]; AM, B 3 243, f. 308–308v, Mémoire des négociants de Nantes, July 19, 1717; AE, Mem. & Doc., France, 1220, f. 11v, Mémoire au Régent par le Sr Biet, procureur du roi au siège du Grenier à sel de Creil, 1716; f. 124–25, Sr Lautmer to the Regent, Paris, Jan. 23, 1717.

13. AM, B 1 8, f. 319, Bégon, Sept. 7, 1715; B 1 9, f. 550, Mémoire des négociants de Nantes, November, 1716; AC, C 11A 36, f. 97, Vaudreuil, 1716; BN, FF 6932, f. 50, duc de Noailles to marshal de Villars, Dec. 28, 1715; 11370, f. 151–52, the Intendant of Soissons to the Council of the Navy, July 11, 1717.

14. AM, B 1 20, f. 137–38v, Beauharnais, June 1, 1717; f. 393–93v, Beauharnais, July 6, 1717; AC, B 39, f. 46v, to Beauharnais, June 9, 1717; f. 65v, to La Gallissonnière, July 3, 1717; f. 76, to Beauharnais, July 21, 1717.

15. AM, B 1 9, f. 550, Mémoire des négociants de Nantes, November, 1716; B 1 19, f. 370, M. de Soubras, Jan. 8, 1717.

for example, the proposal advanced by the intendant Raudot to penalize by depriving of their half-pay any of the disabled old soldiers who were looked after by the Admiralty's representatives at Dunkirk who might refuse to go and settle in Cape Breton Island.[16] Nonetheless, it had taken the first step along a road that overturned Pontchartrain's notions and would soon leave the field open for the deportations to Louisiana that were to take place.

Signs are not lacking, moreover, of the council's propensity to expand recruitment for the armed forces and the population of the colonies without regard to the consequences for the reputation of these services that might result. Such was the decision it took, as early as the end of 1715, at the instigation of Marshal d'Estrées, to enroll a batch of foundlings aged from fourteen to fifteen each year in the overseas companies, so as to make up their numbers. Such also was the practice that became established of posting to the colonial garrisons soldiers guilty of offences, or deserters who had been caught: in July, 1716, seventy-two deserters, sixteen of whom were destined for Louisiana, were waiting at Rochefort for the ships to be fitted out that would distribute them among France's American possessions.[17] Such, again, was the greater tolerance shown by the Council of the Navy to the principle of forced exile for "young wastrels," at the request of their families. So as to avoid abuses, the council declined to make this an absolute rule and cancel the privilege these ne'er-do-wells had hitherto been allowed to depart of their own free will. Unlike Pontchartrain, however, on several occasions the council agreed to the parents' request and ordered that young men be "embarked" by authority, without consulting their wishes.[18] Finally, the recruitment of women for the colonies was less and less governed by concern for selection, and the

16. AM, B 1 19, f. 370–70v, M. de Soubras, Jan. 8, 1717.

17. AC, B 38, f. 5v, to d'Argenson, Paris, Nov. 30, 1715; AM, B 1 2, f. 405, M. de la Malmaison, Guadeloupe, Aug. 2, 1715; B 1 8, f. 614v–15, Beauharnais, Rochefort, June 9, 1716; B 1 9, f. 4v, 17–18, La Gallissonnière, June 27, July 2, 4, 7, 1716; f. 35v, 43–44, La Gallissonnière, July 14, 16, 19, 1716; B 1 19, f. 78–78v, La Gallissonnière, Jan. 16, 1717; AM, B 2 246 (I), f. 8v, to M. de Champmeslin, July 1, 1716.

18. AC, B 38, f. 161–61v, to La Gallissonnière and Lépinay, Aug. 11, 1716; f. 191v, to Beauharnais, Dec. 19, 1716; f. 501, to M. de La Varenne, Dec. 19, 1716; AC, B 39, f. 160v, to M. Michel, Sept. 1, 1717; AM, B 1 29, f. 120v–21, Council of the Navy, Feb. 1, 1718, request by Pierre Cahouet and Catherine Raimond; AC, C 13A 6, f. 8–8v, Council of the Navy, Nov. 19, 1720, representations by Sr Sielve.

foundling institutions and the poor houses were henceforth the principal sources. The council no longer worried about the women's morality. To the requests sent to it by the governors of Cayenne or St. Domingue the council offered invariably the same solution, which in any case fitted the wishes of the administrators, even though the results were not always satisfactory for the colonies.[19]

In this way a new policy came to be outlined, which was defined not by any well-established plan of action but by a set of tendencies that would ensure a broader basis of recruitment for the population of the colonies, and which, in the case of Louisiana, would attain full realization under the Company of the Indies. This did not in itself constitute an advance beyond the policy followed in previous years, and it is certain that the colonies that had reached a certain degree of maturity could obtain but few advantages from it. To a country so thinly populated and backward as Louisiana, however, the new policy could provide a way of bringing in elements which, though doubtless of debatable utility, would at least give the country a certain numerical substance without burdening the Crown's finances. In principle, it seemed capable of supplying a provisional solution to the colony's demographic problem and also to that of financing emigration. This was the view expounded by Crozat when he asked the council to send to Louisiana forthwith a batch of offenders against the salt monopoly, and he had no difficulty in obtaining support for a plan that corresponded to the new direction taken by the council's policy.[20]

It is surprising that, at a moment when the council was so obviously turning away from the notions of the previous reign, it retained and even strengthened its intransigence regarding emigration by Protestants. Here was a sphere of recruitment that might have notably enriched the population of Louisiana, and it seemed logical to expect that the Regent, with his more liberal outlook, would agree to consider that possibility. The governor and the intendant of St. Domingue requested permission to "receive . . . French Protestant refugees," while not allowing them to practice their religion. If they were "granted this favor," that would "very soon increase the population of the col-

19. AM, B 1 8, f. 362v, Dorvilliers, Cayenne, April 21, 1716; B 1 9, f. 320v–22, Chateaumorant, July 31, 1716; B 1 20, f. 149v, d'Orvilliers, Feb. 10, 1717; AC, B 38, f. 3, 29 to d'Argenson, Nov. 16, 1715, April 21, 1716; f. 111v, to Beauharnais, May 5, 1716; f. 520–20v, to d'Orvilliers and d'Albon, May 12, 1716.
20. See p. 43 below.

ony." Yet the Regency Council refused to yield on this point and, while advising that those Protestants who were already established in the colony be allowed to stay, and an attempt made to convert them by persuasion, it ordered that thenceforth "only Catholics" be accepted in St. Domingue.[21] Where Louisiana was concerned, the previous rule applied unchanged. The official religion was seen by the council as a guarantee of loyalty, and it was considered dangerous to introduce into a colony so vulnerable and so directly exposed to British aggression persons whose beliefs might incline them to treat with the enemy.

Inevitably, the Council of the Navy, which made so many concessions on matters of principle, showed itself more conciliatory where persons were concerned. It gradually forgot the resentment of which Iberville's family had so long been the object. If a certain distrust toward them persisted, this was partly due to the interminable case arising from the Nevis expedition. Verifications without number, ceaseless arguments between the contending parties, and the general disorder in the accounts continually put off conclusion of the affair, while the petty officers and sailors who had participated in the expedition waited in vain, victims of these delays, for their due share of the profits from the prizes taken.[22] The serious question of the ransom of the island of Nevis, fixed originally at 140,000 piastres—on which Pontchartrain had expressed doubt as to Iberville's honesty—was still in suspense and, despite many approaches by the French ambassador, the British court refused to pay, even in part, a debt that it declared to be contrary to the laws of war. There was no security now for this payment, because most of the hostages had escaped from Martinique, where they had been held. Only one remained in the hands of the colonial authorities, and the British government was not disposed to

---

21. AM, B 1 2, f. 379v, 406v, Proceedings of the Council of the Navy, November, 1715; B 1 9, f. 132v, Draft of instruction for Sr de La Varenne, August, 1716; AC, B 38, f. 357v, to Blénac and Mithon, Jan. 27, 1716; f. 425, to Sr de La Varenne, Aug. 17, 1716; AC, C 9A 12, Blénac and Mithon, July 1, 1716.

22. AM B 1 1, f. 80, Robert, Brest, Oct. 14, 1715; B 1 5, F. 231–31v, Petition from the comtesse de Béthune, September, 1716; f. 173, Beauharnais, August, 1716; f. 308, Borie, October, 1716; f. 446v, 503v, Robert, Brest, Nov. 23, Dec. 14, 21, 1716; B1 21, f. 1–6, Isaac de Sossa, September, 1717; B 1 22, f. 1–3, 28–28v, 144v–46v, Robert, Brest, January, March, 1717; B 1 23, f. 15–18v, Naurois to the Council of the Navy, July, 1717; f. 89–92, Proceedings of the Council of the Navy, Aug. 21, 1717; f. 217v, 218v, L'Hôtellier to the Council of the Navy, December, 1717; BN, FF 23663, Proceedings of the Regency Council, Nov. 19, 1715; Giraud, *History*, I, 112ff.

fulfil the conditions of the treaty in order to purchase his freedom.[23]

Furthermore, the charges previously brought against Bienville concerning his activities in Louisiana had not been completely forgotten. The *ordonnateur* Duclos had refrained from carrying out any investigation, "had done nothing to clear up the matter," and the self-interested views ascribed to Bienville by Le Maire and Crozat, with their allegation that he wanted to monopolise "all the trade" of the colony, seem to justify the statements made by La Salle—to such an extent that the Council of the Navy instructed the *ordonnateur* Hubert, who was getting ready to take over from Duclos, to carry out once for all a check on the irregularities that had so often been denounced.[24] Bienville did not conceal the bitterness he felt in face of this latent distrust. He saw no cause for it other than the ill will—inexplicable to him—of Pontchartrain toward Iberville, an ill will that he blamed for blocking his promotion, for keeping him stuck for years in a situation that did not correspond to the services he had rendered to the colony, and that had made the inhabitants and the natives believe that, being "not held in esteem" by the court, he could be of no use to them "in their establishments."[25]

Despite the reasons it might have had for lacking confidence in Bienville, the council did not in fact keep up the ill will he attributed to it. The events that had given rise to that attitude were now too far in the past, and increasingly the memory of them had been overlaid by the Crown's obvious reasons for being grateful to Bienville. Pontchartrain himself, as we know, had arrived toward the end of his career at a more favorable attitude. This process became more marked with the change of reign, and Bienville was sufficiently aware of it to ask of the "jus-

---

23. Giraud, *History*, I, 115–17; AM, B 1 9, f. 26, 28, Council of the Navy, July 14, 1716; B 1 20, f. 335, de La Varenne, April 8, 1717; B 1 22, f. 149–50, Council of the Navy, March, 1717; B 1 33, f. 587–87v, Naurois to the Council of the Navy, August, 1718; AM, B 7 274, Chamorel, April 12, 1718; AE, Correspondence politique, England, 294, f. 36, Petition from two English hostages held at Fort St. Pierre, Martinique, since 1706, April 20, 1716; 295, f. 142–43, L.-A. de Bourbon and Marshal d'Estrées, Paris, Oct. 11, 1717; PRO, CO 5, 323(7), f. 347, Instructions for Daniel Pulteney and Martin Bladen, H.My's Commissaries to treat with the Commissary . . . to be appointed (by the French king), November, 1719.

24. AC, B 38, f. 305v, Instructions to Sr Hubert, *commissaire ordonnateur* in Louisiana, Oct. 20, 1716; AM, B 1 9, f. 397v, Crozat to the Council of the Navy, September, 1716. BN, FF 12105, f. 20, Le Maire, Mémoire sur la Louisiane, March 1, 1717; Giraud, *History*, I, 124, 309–310.

25. AC, C 13A 5, f.60–62, Bienville, at Fort Louis, May 10, 1717.

tice" of the council that he be given a reward appropriate to his "services."²⁶ His brother Sérigny, so gravely compromised in the Nevis affair, had now been rehabilitated. He kept his rank of lieutenant-commander, the marquis de la Galissonnière held him in high esteem, considering him a "good officer" who had "done his duty well," and important commands were soon entrusted to him. In 1717, moreover, the Regent, acceding to a request from "the Sieurs le Moine," granted Iberville's brothers confirmation of the letters of nobility of their father, Charles Le Moine de Longueil, which had until then been registered only with the Chambre des Comptes, and he allowed them to have these letters registered "with the Parlement of Paris and the Cour des Aides." Finally, the Council of the Navy took measures to pay Bienville and Chateaugué their salaries for the war years, which had not yet been done.²⁷ Although the council did not wholly abandon Pontchartrain's reservations and still refused to give Bienville the "advancement" he wanted, it acknowledged his qualities, judged him to be capable of taking on additional responsibilities, and accorded him a testimony of indisputable esteem by accepting unreservedly his version of the attacks committed by the Natchez Indians. Through showing this more trustful attitude the council prepared the way for Bienville's promotion in the near future to a higher position.²⁸ Thus the leaders of the Council of the Navy freed themselves to a large extent, where both principles and persons were concerned, from the hindrances or prejudices of Louis XIV's reign, and thereby laid the first foundations for the new state of affairs that was to take shape at the end of these years of transition.

26. *Ibid.*
27. AC, B 39, f. 198–201, Letters patent giving permission to the Srs Le Moine to have registered with the Paris Parlement and the Cour des Aides the letters of nobility granted in March, 1668, to Charles Le Moine de Longueil; AM, B 1 19, f. 296, La Gallissonnière, March 23, 1717; f. 403–404, Request from the Srs de Longueil, April, 1717; B 1 23, f. 191v–92, 205–206, Requests from Sr Dauteuil, Paris, November, 1717.
28. AC, B 38, f. 288v–89, to Bienville, Feb. 15, 1719. See p. 80 below.

IV Crozat's Views and Influence

PROFITING BY THE change of regime and the accession of persons who seemed more open to new suggestions, Crozat now sought to bring up afresh, with amplifications, the projects he had submitted to Pontchartrain at the end of the War of the Spanish Succession. He hoped to succeed through support from the comte de Toulouse, who, "being henceforth [himself] involved in the details of naval and colonial affairs," could not refuse to second his efforts, and also through the consideration he enjoyed at the beginning of the Regency. Crozat had won esteem, in fact, by the advances of funds he had made to the Royal Treasury and by the loans he had granted to the Chevalier d'Orléans, the Regent's natural son, to enable him to purchase an office that he could not have acquired without the help of a silent partner. The Crown had rewarded him with "the office of commander and grand treasurer of the Order of the Holy Ghost."[1] This particularly striking "mark of honor" and his position as a wealthy man, which seemingly made him indispensable to the Regent, strengthened Crozat's authority in political circles. It gave him the opportunity to try to interest the Court in Louisiana, to prove the need for concrete measures, through a series of memoranda that he addressed to the Council of the Navy between 1715 and 1717.

In these documents, which it is often difficult to date precisely, Crozat always defends what he has done, emphasizing the expenditure he has undertaken in Louisiana, the losses he has suffered in order to improve the "wretched" condition of the country and to sustain a monopoly, the burdens and responsibilities of which exceeded by far the profits to be gained from it. When through the opposition of Nicolas Desmaretz he was blocked in his plans for peopling the colony, he said he would

---

1. *Mercure galant* (September, 1715), 295–98; Saint-Simon, *Mémoires*, XXIX, 48, Dangeau, *Journal*, XVI, 390; Buvat, *Gazette de la Régence*, 390.

have handed back his privilege to the sovereign, had the Council of the Navy not been set up. Encouraged by the change in the kingdom's leading personnel, Crozat was now determined not to sacrifice the "great hopes" that the colony offered.[2] Accordingly, he set forth at length to the comte de Toulouse the reasons that he believed made it necessary for France to hold on to Louisiana.

Crozat repeated the strategical argument he had already formulated in 1714: the need to "establish a line of communication" between Canada and Louisiana so that the two colonies might "support each other," and to oppose Britain's ambitions in relation to the Illinois country, which if realized would enable Britain, at the first conflict, to seize Canada, access to which by way of Acadia and Plaisance she already commanded, then to take over Louisiana and so to open up the road to the Spanish-ruled territory in the Southwest. Louisiana was no less necessary to the kingdom on economic grounds. Not only did it contain great natural resources in the form of silver deposits whose existence was implicit in the eastward prolongation of the mountains of New Mexico; it also made possible trade with New Spain and with New Mexico, where the richest mines of Spanish America were situated. And these ideas were no longer hypothetical: the expedition of Ensign François du Tisné from Quebec to the Gulf of Mexico had proved that linking Canada with Louisiana was feasible; La Mothe's journey to the Illinois country had facilitated a preliminary survey of the mineral resources of that region; and Saint-Denis, by making his way into Mexico, had traced the route for trade relations with the Spanish colonies.[3]

These basic ideas, which Crozat set forth at the end of 1715, he developed in subsequent memoranda, supporting them with new information that reached him from Louisiana. In 1716, and even at the beginning of 1717, when he told the king of his intention to surrender the monopoly, he emphasized again the colony's strategic importance and the twofold protection it offered to Canada and Mexico against the designs of the British.

---

2. Giraud, *History*, I, 259–66; AC, C 13A 4, f. 993, [Crozat ?] Mémoire sur la Louisiane, 1715; f. 1017–18, 1020–21, Mémoire de Crozat à son Altesse Sérénissime, [December, 1715 ?]; C 13A 5, f. 231, Crozat, Mémoire pour faire connaître de quelle importance il est de conserver et de fortifier la colonie de la Louisiane, January, 1717; f. 297–98, Mémoire à S.A.S. Mgr l'Amiral, [1715 ?].

3. AC, C 13A 4, f. 993–95, 996–98, [Crozat ?], Mémoire sur la Louisiane, 1715; f. 1019, 1025–26, Mémoire de Crozat à S.A.S., [December, 1715 ?]; Giraud, *History*, I, 355–56.

But the country was vulnerable and would possess no strategic utility unless it was solidly defended against the neighboring imperialisms, for news received in February, 1716, had revealed to Crozat the seriousness of British designs on the Mississippi Basin and the imminence of a Spanish offensive toward both the Red River and the "Baie du Saint-Esprit" (Matagorda Bay), where La Salle had tried to establish his colony.[4]

At the same time, Crozat returned to the theme of Louisiana's economic future and the consequences that Saint-Denis' expedition would have (regardless of the hostile reaction of the viceroy of Mexico) for trade with Spanish America. Magnifying the importance of the discoveries made, the initiative for which he claimed for himself, Crozat affirmed that the French, who controlled the sea approaches to Mexico, possessed also, through the tributaries of the Mississippi, several lines of access to New Mexico.[5] From now on, fine prospects would open up before Louisiana. Its buckskins would supply material for the footwear manufacture in France; the meat of its wild cattle would replace Irish beef in the West Indies market; and the production of raw silk, the cultivation of rice, tobacco, perhaps hemp, and the exploitation of the forests would make available to France a profusion of raw materials the diversity of which could not be rivaled by any other colony. Moreover, commerce between France and Louisiana would stimulate shipping and thereby the training of crews for the navy.

Above all, the country's minerals ought to attract the attention of the authorities, for this enormous region "seems to offer us" the last source of wealth still to be found in America. A report that arrived by the *Paix* in September, 1716, and which Crozat immediately passed to the duc de Noailles and the comte de Toulouse made possible an estimate of the scale of these resources. The Canadian Bourdon, who lived in the Kaskaskias' village and was familiar with the region, was convinced of the existence in a zone ten to twenty-five leagues west of the Mississippi, and at a short distance from the Meramec River, of deposits of gold, silver, lead, and copper. He had himself shown La Mothe where gold was to be found; he had participated in the

4. AC, C 13A 4, f. 907–909, Crozat, Mémoire, 1716; C 13A 5, f. 230, 232–32v, Crozat, Mémoire pour faire connaître . . . ; AE, Mem. & Doc., America, I, f. 182, Crozat, Mémoire sur la Louisiane (beginning of 1717); Giraud, *History*, I, 367–68.

5. AC, C 13A 4, f. 907–908, Crozat, Mémoire, 1716; C 13A 5, f. 232, Crozat, Mémoire pour faire connaître . . . ; AC, Dépôt des Fortifications des Colonies (hereafter cited as Fortifications records), Louisiana, 6, Mémoire du Sr Crozat.

prospecting work carried out by Spaniards, "experts on minerals," whom he had taken with him on his journey into the Illinois country and who had been able to judge the quality of the silver ore; and he knew about the use the natives were already making of the lead deposits.

In other words, Louisiana possessed resources that were incalculably great, both in itself and through the trade that it could develop with the Spanish establishments, which would bring in precious metals. If Britain, which in the last analysis was more to be feared than Spain, were to seize Louisiana, these resources would be lost beyond redemption. As mistress of these minerals, assured of inexhaustible financial means, Britain would thenceforth be able to wage endless war, which would compromise the "security" of France in Europe.[6]

Crozat was no longer looking on Louisiana with the narrow vision of a speculator. More vigorously than he had earlier, on the morrow of the Peace of Utrecht, he now estimated the role that the colony was destined to play in the French empire and in the national economy, and he expounded a set of sensible ideas about its future in which the central theme was that France must safeguard its hold on Louisiana at any price. "This establishment" was too promising and the "reasons of state" associated with it too imperative for the Crown to contemplate giving it up. The example of Britain showed that power in Europe was based upon colonial trade.[7]

Consequently, it was necessary to reinforce Louisiana and to occupy the country solidly, taking advantage of the years of peace from which nothing had so far been gained. The weakening of the British colonies as a result of the revolt of the Indians, and the temporary setback that this event meant for British designs on the Mississippi, favored immediate action.[8]

The program that Crozat wanted carried out entailed, fundamentally, an increase in the military garrisons of the colony. He advised that they be doubled in size, to start with. Then, in 1716,

---

6. AC, C 13A 4, f. 907–908, 913–16, Crozat, Mémoire, 1716; C 13A 5, f. 231–35v, Crozat, Mémoire pour faire connaître . . . ; AE, Mem. & Doc., America, I, f. 182v, Crozat, Mémoire sur la Louisiane; f 275–78v, Crozat to the comte de Toulouse, Paris, Sept. 28, 1716.

7. AC, C 13A, f. 997, Crozat, Mémoire sur la Louisiane [1715 ?]; f. 1030, Mémoire de Crozat à Son Altesse Sérénissime [December, 1715 ?]; C 13A 5, f. 229, Crozat, Mémoire pour faire connaître. . . .

8. AC, C 13A 4, f. 907–909, Crozat, Mémoire, 1716; Giraud, *History*, I, 327–30.

given the prospect of a fresh British offensive, the danger of which he thought was only temporarily removed, he asked for an increase of four hundred men, which would bring the forces of Louisiana up to a total of twelve companies.[9] If they were to be able to provide more effective defense for the country, it would also be important to distribute them more widely, among a larger number of posts, additional to those mentioned in the royal instructions of 1714. This would extend the zone of French occupation to the upper valley of the Mobile River, to the Red River Valley, and perhaps to the valley of the Arkansas, and strengthen the existing positions in the Illinois country and at Biloxi. Finally, the last-mentioned post, the embryo of New Orleans, situated "at the point where a small stream runs from the Mississippi River into Lake Pontchartrain," ought henceforth to have a regular garrison, which would enable it to command the lower course of the river and protect vessels coming from Dauphin Island which were entering the Mississippi via the short cut of Bayou St. John.[10] At the same time, France should make an effort to win the alliance of the natives, whose loyalty would safeguard the colony more surely perhaps than "our own forces" against the aggressions of the British.[11]

However, this plan of action would be effective only insofar as it was backed by a population policy, because whatever military forces might be assigned for Louisiana's defense, it was foolish to hope to maintain possession of a country with so few inhabitants. As he had in 1714, Crozat emphasized this point especially, and he again proposed to associate himself with the measures taken by the Crown to promote increased population in the colony. His ideas had not changed. Following the example set by the Crown of Portugal for the colonization of Latin America, Crozat considered that the principal effort should come from the sovereign and that he himself ought not to be involved beyond a limited extent. But he believed it would be possible to reduce to a minimum the Crown's expenditure on this program.

No longer having to reckon with Pontchartrain's scruples about how to populate the colony, the financier proposed to

---

9. AC, C 13A 4, f. 910, Crozat, Mémoire, 1716; f. 999, Crozat, Mémoire sur la Louisiane, [1715?]; f. 1021, Mémoire de Crozat à S.A.S. [December, 1715 ?].

10. AC, C 13A 4, f. 443, Proceedings of the Council of the Navy, Oct. 20, 1716; f. 499–506, Mémoire de Crozat, 1716; f. 1020–25, Mémoire de Crozat à S.A.S. [December 1715 ?]; Giraud, *History*, I, 349–55. The term *Biloxi* was, in fact, used in a wider sense: *cf.* p. 139 below.

11. AE, Mem. & Doc., America, I, f. 182, Crozat, Mémoire sur la Louisiane.

make use of offenders against the salt monopoly, sending to Louisiana each year a hundred who had not yet served in the galleys. In France, he said, these individuals were of no further benefit to the state. "Little use" was made of the galleys, and the number of convicts had grown so large that they could scarcely be fed. But they might make good recruits for the colony, provided care were taken to select offenders from the agricultural provinces—Anjou, Poitou, Touraine, Maine—since such men were familiar with "the cultivation of the soil" and were not professional smugglers—most of them had broken the law only through poverty. The Crown would have no cost to bear other than the expense of the voyage and the cost of outfitting the emigrants—say, a hundred livres per head.

This investment could be made the responsibility of the farmers-general who, being relieved of the burden of keeping these men for years as galley-slaves, would instead pay out 150 livres per man. From this sum the Crown could draw, if desired, the small capital needed at the outset, on the understanding that this money would later be paid back into the fund created by the farmers-general, the purpose of which was to support convicted dealers in contraband salt who settled in Louisiana. Repayment would take place only after three years. In the meantime, the offenders would be distributed among the inhabitants as "indentured servants." When their thirty-six months of service were completed, they would be allowed to settle down as inhabitants, and each would receive from his master, as reward for his work, the sum of 150 livres. These payments, added to the money from the farmers-general, would enable the emigrants to meet their initial expenses as settlers. In other words, the operation would cost the Crown very little. Not only would the Crown enjoy a period of three years in which to assemble what would be a very modest sum, but conveyance of the recruits to the ports of Nantes or La Rochelle would be carried out at the expense of the farmers-general, and Crozat would be responsible thereafter for their transportation to Louisiana and distribution among colonists in need of manpower.[12]

At the beginning of 1716 Crozat conceived a plan for relieving the Crown of all financial obligation by requiring the farmers-general to pay 250 livres per man. By reducing to 50 livres the

12. AC, C 13A 4, f. 999–1000, Crozat, Mémoire sur la Louisiane [1715?], f. 1026–27, Mémoire de Crozat à S.A.S., [December, 1715?]; AM, B 7 31, f. 149v, Sr du Verger, Lisbon, Jan. 25, 1717; AE, Mem. & Doc., America, I, f. 182v, Mémoire concernant l'établissement de la Louisiane.

cost of transportation and clothing, it would then be possible to allot to each immigrant, on the expiration of his years of service—and without the Crown having to find any money—a capital of 200 livres, which the masters' gift would bring up to 350 livres. Crozat himself would grant additional advances in order to facilitate the settlement of these new colonists. Imperceptibly, the offenders in the colony would acquire, or reacquire, the habits of a settled way of life, especially if they were enabled to establish households by being allowed, if married, to bring their wives with them (these women's rural backgrounds would be a guarantee of their usefulness). To the wives would be added about a hundred girls from the poor houses—less desirable recruits, to be sure, but with at least satisfactory bills of health.[13]

This emigration program, which in the last analysis committed the Crown to no expense beyond that involved in transporting the girls from the poor houses, Crozat saw as merely a "suitable expedient" for promoting the peopling of the colony without the Crown having to bear any appreciable financial responsibility. As he saw it, the scheme was no more than a brief preliminary phase that would prepare the way for the emigration of "persons of goodwill," which would happen spontaneously once Louisiana was better defended and supplied with a somewhat larger population, and when royal finances had recovered sufficiently to contribute without difficulty to the cost—10,000 livres was Crozat's estimate—of the annual passages of soldiers and settlers to the colony. No more than two or three years would be needed for this initial phase based on compulsory emigration to be completed. The population would then be substantial enough to ensure a regular link between Canada and Louisiana, and it would enjoy a sense of security that would encourage the arrival of new elements better adapted to the needs of colonization.[14]

Crozat did not restrict his concerns to the problem of population alone. His memoranda are filled with suggestions that reveal his increasing interest in Louisiana and his wish to inspire the rulers with a will to new activity. No detail regarding the

13. AC, C 13A 4, f. 73, Mémoire sur la colonie de Louisiane submitted to the Regency Council, Feb. 11, 1716; C 13A 4, f. 912, Mémoire de Crozat, 1716; f. 1027, Mémoire de Crozat à S.A.S., [December, 1715?].
14. AC, C 13A 4, f. 1026–28, 1030, Mémoire de Crozat à S.A.S. [December, 1715?].

colony's affairs escaped his attention: the clothing of the troops, the fortification of Dauphin Island, the work force and materials to be employed there, the recruitment of workmen for incorporation in the new companies—on all these matters the financier had views.[15] He particularly urged the Council of the Navy not to neglect the provisioning of the colony's garrison. In December, 1715, he pointed out to the council that the flour sent out in the *Dauphine* would soon be exhausted, and he pressed it to dispatch to the troops at Mobile and Dauphin Island food sufficient for at least a year, using the ships assigned for service to St. Domingue, since after calling at Cap Français they could easily go on to Louisiana.

Crozat himself seems to have wanted to introduce a degree of forethought into his administration of the colony. Thus in 1716 he proposed to send to Dauphin Island a supply of salt beef, so as to spare the soldiers and the passengers whose departure he was organizing a repetition of the trials of 1713.[16] To judge by the precision with which he calculated the increases in expenditure to be expected in the future, it appears that he intended that the colony's affairs should no longer be left to chance. He did not hide from the Council of the Navy his view that, to meet the country's military expenditure and the costs of the emigration of the colonists who were to follow the illegal saltmakers, the Crown would have to be ready to increase its outlay. The sacrifice, he thought, would be slight in comparison with the long-term advantage that it would bring to France and to the Crown's finances, and it would enable Louisiana at last to take, in the French empire, a place that corresponded to its resources and strategic position.[17]

Crozat was not mistaken when he expressed confidence that the innovating views that prevailed in the Council of the Navy would ensure a welcome for his suggestions. In February, 1716, Marshal d'Estrées recommended application of the financier's

---

15. AC, C 13A 4, f. 305, 307, Proceedings of the Council of the Navy, Sept. 8, 1716; f. 979, Projet de mémoire du Roy à Lépinay et Hubert, October, 1716; AM, B 1 9, f. 465, Proceedings of the Council of the Navy, Oct. 11, 1716.

16. AC, C 13A 4, f. 1028–30, Mémoire de Crozat à S.A.S. [December, 1715?]; AM, B 1 8, f. 635–35v, Proceedings of the Council of the Navy, June 16, 1716; Giraud, *History*, I, 271.

17. AC, C 13A, 4, f. 911, Mémoire de Crozat, 1716; f. 1029–30, Mémoire de Crozat à S.A.S. [December, 1715?]; AE, Mem. & Doc., America I, f. 146v–47v, Crozat, Mémoire sur la Louisiane, 1716.

main ideas in a "long memorandum for support to be given to the Mississippi colony called Louisiana," which the Regency Council approved in its entirety.[18]

The Council of the Navy was actively engaged in protecting the weakest of the colonies, especially those exposed to danger through the proximity of the British. It declared its determination not to abandon Louisiana: the country "has been on the mend during the last two or three years," and "we ought not to stint help to it now."[19] The council based its conviction on Crozat's own arguments. Like him, it invoked the strategic importance of Louisiana, "advanced guard against the British colonies," which provided the only sure means to defend Canada, since Britain could cut off France's direct access thereto by sea whenever it wished. And the council repeated the financier's views on the role of colonies in building up "the power of the greatest states," quoting "the example of the British and the Dutch."[20] The economic argument followed. Besides the colony's agricultural resources, the variety of which no one dreamt of doubting any longer, there were the unlimited possibilities of the mineral deposits, both on the territory belonging to the King of France and on that of Spanish America, which Saint-Denis's expedition had suddenly brought near to France's colonial domain.[21]

So, then, the Council agreed with Crozat that Louisiana should be fortified and firmly established. More moderate than the financier, however, the council considered that it would be sufficient to double the strength of the garrison, increasing this to eight companies.[22] It was more concerned with increasing the civilian population and was soon to give unreserved approval to a memorandum that argued the necessity of sending to Louisiana more settlers than soldiers, because settlers organized into militia units would be able to contribute both to the defense of

---

18. AE, Mem. & Doc., America, I, f. 301, Mémoire sur l'établissement d'une Compagnie d'Occident après la remise du privilège de Crozat; BN, FF 23664, f. 21, Regency Council, session of Feb. 11, 1716.

19. AC, B 38, f. 427–29v, Instructions to Sr de La Varenne, Aug. 17, 1716; AC, C 13A 4, f. 1041–42, Mémoire sur la colonie de la Louisiane, Feb. 11, 1716.

20. AC, C 13A 4, f. 61–62, 64, 1036–40, Mémoire sur la colonie de la Louisiane, Feb. 11, 1716; AE, Mem. & Doc., America, I, f. 54, Mémoire sur la colonie de la Louisiane, February, 1716.

21. AC, C 13A 4, f. 54–58, 1034–35, Mémoire sur la colonie de la Louisiane, Feb. 11, 1716.

22. Ibid., f. 74–75.

the country and to its development.²³ For the moment, however, the Council of the Navy considered that the colony, a victim of its remoteness from France, was still too little known in the home country for "private persons to be eager to go and settle there." It therefore concurred with Crozat's conclusion that an annual emigration of offenders against the salt monopoly would provisionally make up for the shortfall in the peopling of the colony, and it agreed with all the financier's suggestions in this connection, especially those concerning recruitment in the agricultural provinces and the establishment of a settling-in fund by the farmers-general and the colonists, independent of any intervention by the Crown. A hundred women would be selected from the "foundling hospitals." When the Council proceeded to active measures, it was guided even more completely by Crozat's proposals, in that it authorized the emigration to Louisiana of the wives of the illegal saltmakers.²⁴

Nevertheless, while responding positively to the financier's initiatives, the Council also sought to correct the shortcomings of his program. Crozat, despite the clearsightedness he showed, always remained a businessman with an ax to grind, and he was unable to change in any fundamental way a system which, since it left the settlers no opportunity to make a profit, was hardly capable of bringing about that emigration of "persons of goodwill" on which he considered the colony's future depended. It was to the credit of the comte de Toulouse and Marshal d'Estrées that they became aware of his mistake. In their report of February, 1716, they agreed that it was not possible to deny the settlers a margin of "profit" and that emigration would depend on the "facilities" offered them "to make their fortunes." The country would never become populated if, for the sake of "deriving petty advances," the authorities there hastened to introduce "taxes and customs dues." Not only should Louisiana be spared any fiscal burdens, "some exemptions should be given in France" from duties payable on the produce it sent to the home country, so as to facilitate its sale. "This is how the British and the Dutch act when establishing their colonies."²⁵ The repeated

23. AC, C 13A 4, f. 923–29, Mémoire sur l'importance d'envoyer des habitants à la Louisiane, Oct. 8, 1716.
24. AC, C 13A 4, f. 71–73, Mémoire sur la colonie de la Louisiane, Feb. 11, 1716; BN, FF 23664, f. 21, Regency Council, session of Feb. 11, 1716. See p. 115 below.
25. AC, C 13A 4, f. 70–71, 1041–42, Mémoire sur la colonie de la Louisiane, Feb. 11, 1716.

complaints about Crozat's regime that reached the council soon after this, on the iniquity of his price policy and the poverty it caused among the population, the indictments presented by Father François Le Maire and by Sublieutenant Granville on his return from Louisiana, the increasingly obvious signs of discontent among the inhabitants, and the sailors' refusal to remain satisfied with the pay they received from the financier, all combined to convince the Council of the Navy that concessions must be granted.[26]

Accordingly, the council negotiated with Crozat and got him to agree to reduce his selling prices and slightly increase the prices he paid for purchases in the colony. Crozat further promised to allow his agents to make on the spot such adjustments to the schedule of prices as they might find "appropriate." A new formula seemed about to be introduced into the way the colony was run, one that would reconcile the interests of the financier with those of the inhabitants. From the instructions sent to the *ordonnateur* Hubert it emerges, further, that the Council of the Navy, while not wishing to encroach on Crozat's monopoly, reserved for itself the power, where necessary, to restrict his freedom of action so as to prevent excessive increases in prices to the detriment of the population.[27]

In this way a certain community of view began to be established between the financier and the Council of the Navy. Crozat had succeeded in making the rulers of France share his confidence in the future of Louisiana and in the role it was called upon to play in the French empire, and he had got them to accept the necessity to provide immediate help to the colony. He had not only appealed successfully to the comte de Toulouse and Maréchal d'Estrées; his reports had caught the attention of the Regent, who unhesitatingly agreed to the program put forward by the Council of the Navy. And by emphasizing the colony's mineral wealth Crozat had managed to enlist the interest of the duc de Noailles, who had recognized the need to "strengthen (the colony) with troops and settlers" and even promised to try to secure additional credits for the colony, so as

---

26. AC, C 13A 4, f. 91–92, Mémoire de l'enseigne de vaisseau Granville, May 2, 1716; AM, B 1 9, f. 339, Duclos, Jan. 27, 1716; f. 423–24, Duclos, June 3, 1716; BN, FF f. 12105, f. 18–19, Le Maire, Mémoire sur la Louisiane, March 1, 1717.

27. AC, C 13A 4, f. 980, 987–89, Draft memorandum from the king to Lépinay and Hubert, October, 1716; AM, B 1 9, f. 424v–25, Duclos, June 3, 1716; AC, B 38, f. 308–309v, Mémoire du Roy pour servir d'instructions au Sr Hubert, Oct. 20, 1716. See p. 64 below.

to make up to some extent for the inadequacy of the means at the disposal of the Council of the Navy.²⁸ The activity with which Crozat defended his ideas and beliefs brings to the forefront an aspect of his personality that makes up, to some extent, for the negative side of his doings in the colony. At the same time, the heads of the Council showed their intention to improve the lot of the settlers by rendering more equitable the regime he had established in Louisiana. The financier's agreement to the concessions they required of him seemed to show that he was ready to run the country in a more conciliatory spirit.

28. AC, C 13A 5, f. 297v, Mémoire à S.A.S. Mgr l'Amiral [1715 ?]; AE, Mem. & Doc., America, I, f. 182v, Crozat, Mémoire sur la Louisiane, 1717; f. 275, Crozat to Monseigneur (the duc de Noailles), Paris, Sept. 28, 1716.

V Financial Difficulties

UNFORTUNATELY, THE FINANCIAL distress from which France was suffering continued to subject the Louisiana colony to the same difficulty. The situation was now exceptionally serious because of the heavy debit balance inherited from Louis XIV's reign. The first year of the Regency brought no solution to the country's problems. The bank of issue founded by John Law in May, 1716, had only a slight effect on the finances and economy of the realm. The inadequacy of its capital prevented it from taking over responsibility for the state's debts, especially those contracted in respect to the colonies, so that it affected the latter only to an insignificant degree.[1] In June, 1716, the duc de Noailles agreed with Law that the kingdom's finances, for a number of reasons all connected with the methods that the Regency had inherited from the previous reign, were in "a very bad state."[2]

Just as during the War of the Spanish Succession, this situation, which spared none of the principal administrative services, compromised above all the resources of the navy and the colonies. In principle, according to the regulation laid down at

1. BN, FF 6933, f. 85–86, 90–115, Noailles to the intendants of the *généralités* of the *pays d'élection*, March 3, March 4, 1716; f. 169, to M. Turgot de St. Clair, March 16, 1716; 11370, f. 86, The intendant of Soissons to the duc de Noailles; 11371, f. 43–44, 78–79, 85, The intendant of the *généralité* of Amiens to the duc de Noailles, Jan. 1, May 8, May 31, 1716; 11372, f. 57–58, The intendant of the *généralité* of Orleans to Noailles, Nov. 19, 1715; 11375, f. 5–6, 7–9, The intendant of La Rochelle to Noailles, Oct. 31, Nov. 2, 1715; 11378, f. 111–12, 125, The intendant of Caen, Nov. 17, 1716, Jan. 13, 1717; AE, Mem. & Doc., France, 140, f. 45–46, On Sr John Law, Scotsman . . . ; 1214, f. 145–47, 149, Letters patent of May 2 and May 20, 1716; P. Harsin, *Crédit public et Banque d'Etat en France du XVIe au XVIIe siècle* (Paris, 1933), 56–59; E. J. Hamilton, "Prices and Wages at Paris under John Law's System," *Quarterly Journal of Economics* (November, 1936), 45–46. Cf. p. 94 below.

2. BN, FF 1431, f. 18–24, 31, Law, Histoire des finances pendant la Régence de 1715; 23673, f. 8–10, Regency Council, session of June 26, 1717.

the beginning of the Regency, the navy should have received between September 1, 1715, and December 31, 1716, an annual sum of eight million livres, which a later edict increased to 16 million after January 1, 1717. However, "either because the Treasury lacked the necessary funds or because they had been spent on other services," the navy received only a small part of this sum. Neither in 1715 nor in 1716, nor especially in 1717, did the comte de Toulouse succeed in obtaining payment of the amounts promised. In 1718 the Council of the Navy asked in vain for the arrears that were owed to it, and which, for 1717 alone, came to over 4,500,000 livres. Hence there was a permanent deficit, a general embarrassment in the "ordinary expenditure" of the navy and the galleys, at a time when the council had begun to undertake fortification works in the colonies that depended for their completion upon a regular supply of funds.[3] In France the comte de Toulouse was unable with the resources at his disposal to carry through the program of restoration of the navy for which Pontchartrain had laid down the main lines shortly before the death of Louis XIV.[4] And in the overseas provinces the Council of the Navy, forced to renounce costly undertakings, had to be content with incomplete achievements that bore no relation either to its efforts or to its aims.

The recommendation by the comte de Toulouse and Marshal d'Estrées to the administrators of the port of Rochefort "to economize on all expenditures" relating to the colonies, and the need, when they fitted out ships for a long voyage, to provide for return cargoes that would reduce the total cost of the enterprise, testify to the difficulties that this penury inflicted on them.[5] In many cases they had to consider making reductions that nullified their best intentions. They were unable even to honor the arrangements for payment that they made with merchants. While they kept to them whenever they were able, the irregularity in receipts from the Treasury often imposed upon suppliers delays in payment that contradicted the promises

Financial Difficulties

3. BN, FF 6933, f. 83, The duc de Noailles to the comte de Toulouse and Marshal d'Estrées, March 1, 1716; AN, G 7 1830, L.-A. de Bourbon, Mémoire sur les fonds destinés pour la marine et pour les galères.

4. BN, FF 11329, f. lxv, Abstract of the activity of the Council of the Navy (1715–1723); AC, F 2C 4, f. 128–29, Pontchartrain to the comte de Toulouse, May 26, 1715.

5. AC, B 38, f. 86v, to Beauharnais, March 3, 1716; f. 92–92v, to La Gallissonnière, March 21, 1716.

made by the Council of the Navy and led these merchants to increase their demands.[6]

The council was thus not always able to fulfil all its plans. It was obliged to accept the principle that enterprises in the colonies could not, owing to the expense they entailed, be undertaken on the same scale as at home. It was not possible, the council acknowledged, "to fortify as thoroughly in the colonies as in Europe."[7] The work the council accomplished in the colonies was consequently doomed, despite initial promise, to remain uneven, fragmentary, and even incomplete, its inadequacy being all the more marked in the new colonies, such as Cape Breton Island and especially Louisiana, where only substantial investments would have made it possible to ensure the development of a territory so vast and so thinly populated.

The poor financing of the navy explains why the two Mississippi frigates, the *Ludlow* and the *Paon,* could not be fitted out as quickly as the comte de Toulouse wished. Arguments about the price of supplies and delay in providing the funds needed to pay the workmen, "raise the crews," buy provisions for the voyage, and furnish the advances of pay for the ships' officers held back preparations for the voyage. The fitting-out of the ships, begun in April, 1716, was not finished until November. Bad weather and an accident that occurred while the vessels were being towed in the "river of Rochefort" further delayed the work.[8] The frigates left the roadstead of the Ile d'Aix on December 21, 1716, and did not reach Dauphin Island, after calling at St. Domingue, until the beginning of March, 1717. Only then did the colony receive that "help" the imperative need for which Crozat had pointed out at the end of 1715. And the help received still fell short of the colony's needs because the dimensions of the ships had been inadequate to convey all the provisions and merchan-

---

6. AC, B 38, f. 43v, to M. de Luzançay, June 30, 1716; f. 150v–51, to Beauharnais, July 14, 1716; AM, B 1 8, f. 169, Beauharnais, Feb. 29, 1716; B 1 33, f. 185–87, Council of the Navy, March 13, 1718, representations from the treasurers of the navy; f. 287v, Council of March 28, 1718, representations from the supplier of foodstuffs to the navy; AM, B 3 236, f. 327–28, Lusançay, Nantes, March 3, 1716; f. 396, 464–65, 487, Lusançay, May 14, Aug. 8, Aug. 25, 1716; AM, B 3 243, f. 323–24, 336–37v, Lusançay, July 27, Aug. 17, 1717.

7. AC, F 3 68, f. 103v, Mémoire du Conseil de marine sur le service que le S. de Verville . . . à rendre dans le voyage qu'il va faire à l'île Royale, June 27, 1716.

8. AC, B 38, f. 118v–20, to Beauharnais, May 19, 1716; AM, B 1 9, f. 465v, 478, Lépinay, Oct. 3, Oct. 9, 1716; f. 481, La Gallissonnière, Oct. 10, 1716; f. 481v–82, Beauharnais, October 8, 1716; f. 563, 594, Beauharnais, Nov. 17, Dec. 1, 1716; f. 620v–21, La Gallissonnière, Dec. 12, 1716; AC, C 13A 4, f. 871–74, Lépinay, Nov. 7, 1716.

dise required. Neither the *Paon* nor the *Ludlow* wholly satisfactory for the service to which they were assigned. The *Paon* was not fit for a colonial voyage because it lacked accommodations and "carried sail badly." The *Ludlow,* shallow and narrower than the *Samslack,* was so constructed that this vessel could not cope with the load of munitions and passengers it was expected to carry. In order not to sacrifice too much of its cargo, the crew had to stow supplies "in the spaces between the decks, the cables, and the spare stores." An additional frigate should have been provided, but the council, through lack of funds, was not able to increase further the cost of equipping an expedition which, despite its inadequacy, was nonetheless greater than those of previous years.[9]

The same note of parsimony is observed in the "list of the funds" for the colony. The credits that the council allotted to Louisiana were certainly larger than in the past. In 1716, being obliged to provide for the maintenance of four additional companies, the council increased the colony's credits to 98,000 livres, but they still did not reach the level requested by Crozat (104,000 livres). In 1717 funding was still fixed at the same amount, although the financier was asking for another increase, and expenditures in anticipation of an increase had already begun in the colony.[10] Nor could the council contemplate the increases that the *ordonnateur* Duclos urged it to make for "gifts to the savages" and fortifications. These funds, which the *ordonnateur* asked be doubled, stayed at 4,000 and 10,000 livres respectively, which prevented any vigorous initiative in either sphere.[11]

9. AM, B 1 5, f. 476v, 479v, Beauharnais, Dec. 7, 12, 1716; B 1 9, f. 16–16v, Beauharnais, July 5, 1716; f. 101–101v, Lépinay, July 25, 1716; f. 403v, Beauharnais, Sept. 26, 1716; f. 459, Draft of instruction to Sr de Lépinay; f. 478, Lépinay, Oct. 9, 1716; f. 495–95v, Beauharnais, Oct. 20, 1716; f. 579v–80, Lépinay, Nov. 21, 1716; f. 594, Beauharnais, Dec. 1, 1716; f. 645v, Lépinay, Ile d'Aix, Dec. 15, 1716; B 1 19, f. 7, La Gallissonnière, Dec. 22, 1716; f. 495–95v, Dusault, at Cap Français, Feb. 4, 1717; AE, Mem. & Doc., America, I, f. 290, Mémoire servant à l'intelligence du compte que le Sr Crozat présente de l'estimation . . . de ce qu'il cède du Roy. . . .

10. AC, C 13A 4, f. 999, Crozat, Mémoire sur la Louisiane, 1715; f. 1029–30, Crozat, Mémoire à Son Altesse Sérénissime [December 1715?]; C 13A 5, f. 192–92v, Hubert, June 10, 1718, AM, B 1 30, f. 428v, Proceedings of the Council of the Navy, Dec. 10, 1718; AC, F 1A 19, f. 80, List of expenditure that the king . . . orders . . . (for Louisiana), Oct. 1, 1716; AE, Mem. & Doc., America, I, f. 146v–47, Mémoire sur la Louisiane; f. 438, Duché, List of advances from the Company of Louisiana to the king, repayment of which is due.

11. AC, F 1A 19, f. 70v, List of expenditure to be undertaken for Louisiana in 1716; f. 76–80, List of expenditure that the king orders for Louisiana, Oct. 1, 1716; AM, B 1 9, f. 465v, Proceedings of the Council of the Navy, Oct. 11, 1716.

Nor was it any longer possible to improve the salaries of the higher officers. Despite the complaints of the *ordonnateur*, who pointed out to the council the necessity for changing a situation that was in line neither with the cost of living nor with the expenditures their functions entailed, the higher officers were left to get by as in previous years.[12] The "plan of expenditure" drawn up by the council for 1717 contemplated an increase in salary for *Major* de Boisbriant and a gratuity of 600 livres for Bienville. But this was only a plan, and no change in their conditions was actually made during these years of transition. In the case of Duclos, the matter was made worse when the Regent ordered the abolition of certain offices in order to mitigate the Treasury's distress. At the same time, Duclos lost his uncle, Monsieur de Saint Sulpice, inspector of the navy at Dunkirk, who had just bought him an office as naval commissioner from which he derived additional income. Without this support, Duclos was no longer able to meet the cost of living in Louisiana,[13] and so in 1716 he requested permission to return to France.

Whatever the items of expenditure listed in the Louisiana budget, we always observe the same spirit of economy. Even in respect to so essential an article as medical aid the Council of the Navy was unable to meet the requests of Crozat and the surgeon–medical officer. The only "medicine chest" it sent out to the colony had been calculated for a garrison consisting of two companies and was inadequate for the new establishment of troops.[14] The medicines, besides being liable to deterioration through the effect of the climate, were not sufficient for the frequent use the men had to make of them against "sudden fevers, scurvy, chest inflammations, [and] dysentery." The amount of

---

12. The governor's salary remained fixed at 4,000 livres, that of the *ordonnateur* at 1,500, that of the *lieutenant de roy* at 1,200, and that of the surgeon–medical officer at 600 (AC, F, 1A 19, f. 76v, 78v, List of expenditure that the king orders for Louisiana, Oct. 1, 1716; AC, C 13A 4, f. 662, Plan of expenditure which Duclos considers essential for maintaining the colony, June 5, 1716; AM, B 1 9, f. 420, Petition from Sr des Lauriers, Council of the Navy, Oct. 9, 1716; f. 552v–54, Chateaugué, July 17, 1716).

13. AC, F 1A 19, f. 280–82, Plan of expenditure for Louisiana for 1717; AC, C 13A 4, f. 711–12, Duclos, Dauphin Island, June 26, 1716; Giraud, *History,* I, 314–15. His office of commissioner brought Duclos 1,800 livres in fees, his salary as *ordonnateur* in Louisiana 1,500 livres (AC, F 1A 18, f. 184–85, Increases in expenditure provided for in 1716; F 1A 19, f. 76v, List of expenditure that the king orders for Louisiana, Oct. 1, 1716).

14. See p. 101 below.

brandy supplied also fell short of the needs of the sick and wounded.¹⁵

In its desire to do better than its predecessors, the Council of the Navy had thought it would be able to promise that each year Louisiana would receive exactly the amount of money assigned to it and would also receive a certain contingent of ships and emigrants, but reality refuted its expectations.¹⁶ The council soon became aware of the inadequacy of its means and admitted an inability to "do anything more."¹⁷ Apparently, the hope that the duc de Noailles had allowed Crozat to entertain of receiving "extraordinary aid" for the colony was not fulfilled. Although the council approved the financier's program, it was unable, since it could not grant him the additional funds he regarded as necessary, to support him in actually putting his ideas into effect.

The Council of the Navy consequently made no change in the agreement of 1714, which obliged Crozat to advance, in the Crown's name, the credits needed for meeting current expenditures in Louisiana.¹⁸ The council's own responsibility was confined to exceptional expenditures, such as the cost of fitting out the two frigates in 1716, which did not figure in the annual list of expenses. As a result, the fate of the colony depended in the last analysis on the attitude of Crozat rather than on action by the government—on the regularity with which Crozat could pay out the sums he was supposed to provide and on his readiness to put up with the delay in payments from official sources. Because of the condition of the royal finances, Crozat retained until his resignation the same degree of authority over the colony as in the past. It was therefore difficult for the Council of the Navy to exercise effective supervision over the policy of a man whose personal resources alone sustained the Mississippi colony.

15. AM, B 1 8, f. 636–36v, List of shipments to be made to Louisiana for the royal storehouses; B 1 9, f. 420, Petition by Sr des Lauriers, October, 1716; AC, C 13A 5, f. 48–48v, Hubert, Dauphin Island, Oct. 26, 1717.

16. AC, C 13A 4, f. 905–906, Hubert, La Rochelle, Dec. 10, 1716; AM, B 1 9, f. 350–50v, Proceedings of the Council of the Navy, Sept. 2, 1716; AC, B 38, f. 310, Mémoire du Roy pour servir d'instructions au Sr Hubert, Oct. 20, 1716.

17. AM, B 1 9, f. 465v, Proceedings of the Council of the Navy, Oct. 11, 1716; AC, B 38, f. 327–28, to Lépinay and Hubert, Oct. 28, 1716; AC, F 1A 19, f. 77v, 80, List of expenditure that the king orders for Louisiana, Oct. 1, 1716; f. 282–82v, Plan of expenditure for Louisiana for 1717.

18. See p. 58 below.

VI The End of Crozat's Monopoly

WHEN CROZAT'S BRIGANTINE the *Paix*, under the command of Captain Elie Jappie, brought to Louisiana in May or June, 1716, the news of the establishment of the Council of the Navy, the population of Mobile and Dauphin Island saw some hope for transformation in the near future of the way the colony was run.[1] However, it soon became clear that there would be no modification of the monopoly. The leaders of the Council of the Navy were aware of the movement of opinion that had become widespread in France, directed against the monopolist companies, and in principle the background of the comte de Toulouse gave reason to suppose that he shared these prejudices.[2] A number of measures—the intention announced by the Regency Council in 1716 to remove the trade in beaver skins from the sphere of activity of the companies, whose management it criticized severely; the decision of the Council of the Navy to promulgate the letters patent drawn up at the end of Louis XIV's reign, opening the slave trade freely to all French merchants (January, 1716); the exemptions or reductions in dues payments that the comte de Toulouse granted to these merchants in order to favor their operations; and the authorization by which he freed them from the obligation to produce a passport for "permitted voyages"—all indicate, certainly, a concern among the leaders to support the interests of private trade.[3] But the Council

---

1. AM, B 1 9, f. 419–19v, La Mothe and Duclos, July 15, 1716; AC, C 13A 4, f. 723–28, Duclos to Raudot, July 12, 1716; f. 729–35, Duclos to the comte de Toulouse, July 6, 1716; La Rochelle, Rivière and Soullard, 1716, f. 120v, Commitment of Pierre Olliveau to serve Captain Elie Jappie, Nov. 7, 1716.

2. Giraud, *History*, I, 317.

3. BN, FF 11329, f. liii, Abstract of the activity of the Council of the Navy; 23664, f. 39v, Regency Council, session of April 28, 1716; AM, A 1 50, August, 1715, Letters patent for freedom of trade with Guinea; AC, B 38, f. 70v, to the marquis de Chateaumorant, Jan. 27, 1716; AM, B 1 1, f. 56v, 58v, Mémoire sur l'usage et l'abus des passeports, Council of the Navy, Oct. 19, 1715; B 1 8, f. 563v–64, Lusançay, May 9, 1716; f. 671, Mémoire des négociants de Nantes, Council of

of the Navy could not encroach on monopolies that were indispensable to it, especially Crozat's, which relieved the Crown of financial responsibilities that were beyond its means. Crozat and his associates consequently retained the exclusive privilege of trade with Louisiana, just as the Company of Saint-Domingue held on to its concession.[4]

In a sense, the financier's monopoly was even strengthened. On October 5, 1716, at his request, the council confirmed the letters patent of 1712 and reminded merchants of the ban, expressly formulated in the ordinance of 1714, on sending any "seagoing vessel" to Louisiana and engaging in any trade in the colony. Should a vessel, "through an accident at sea," put in at Dauphin Island, its cargo was to be bonded in Crozat's storehouse and all purchases of "foodstuffs and other necessities" that the crew might wish to make in the country were to be effected through his agents.[5] Soon after this, the Regency Council, confirming Crozat's "conclusions" concerning the incident of the *Notre-Dame-de-la-Trappe*, granted him an annulment of the decisions that the Conseil Supérieur of the colony had taken on that occasion against the monopoly as literally interpreted.[6] Crozat's complaint against Captain Jean Escoubet, whom he accused of fitting out a trading vessel at Cap Français for a voyage to Louisiana, and the request he addressed to the Council of the Navy to impose exemplary penalties on this man, show clearly

---

the Navy, June 30, 1716; B 1 9, f. 407v–408, Complaint by the merchants of La Rochelle . . . , Council of the Navy, Oct. 4, 1716; f. 600–602, Draft of declaration (on the Guinea trade); AM, B 2 249, f. 222–22v, to the duc de Noailles, Dec. 1, 1717; AM, B 3 235, f. 433–34, Petition of the shipowner Feray, Oct. 30, 1716; AC, B 39, f. 344, to MM. de La Varenne and Ricouart, June 2, 1717; AE, Mem. & Doc., France, 1213, f. 184–85, Edict of February, 1716 (on passports); BN, FF 7220, Letters patent of April, 1716.

4. AC, B 38, f. 390–90v, to Chateaumorant and Mithon, Sept. 20, 1716; AM, B 1 9, f. 374v–77, Proceedings of the Council of the Navy, Sept. 14, 1716.

5. AC, A 22, f. 21–21v, Ordinance for execution of the letters patent granted to Sr Crozat . . . , Paris, Oct. 5, 1716; BN, FF 23664, Regency Council, session of Oct. 5, 1716; AC, C 13A 4, f. 307, 375, Proceedings of the Council of the Navy, Sept. 8, Oct. 5, 1716; f. 966–67, Draft of memorandum from the King to Lépinay and Hubert, October, 1716; C 13C 2, f. 140–41, Ordinance for execution of the letters patent granted to Sr Crozat, Oct. 5, 1716; Giraud, *History*, I, 250, 315–16.

6. Giraud, *History*, I, 316; AC, B 38, f. 344, to Crozat, Nov. 14, 1716; AM, B 1 9, f. 396–97v, Proceedings of the Council of the Navy, Sept. 22, 1716; f. 514–16v, Draft of decision in Crozat's favor, Nov. 9, 1716; AC, A 22, f. 24–24 bis, Cancellation of decisions made by Conseil Supérieur of Louisiana; BN, FF 23664, f. 77, Regency Council, Oct. 26, 1716.

his determination to give up nothing of his privilege. Yet Escoubet's vessel, which was captured by the Spaniards before it could reach Dauphin Island, was loaded with foodstuffs for the settlers and soldiers, and its arrival would have alleviated the famine then prevailing in the colony.[7]

Crozat was confident of backing from the council, which was in a number of ways under obligation to him. At Court he enjoyed powerful protection—among others, from Jean-Baptiste Duché, who was very influential in naval circles. Marshal d'Estrées paid tribute to Crozat in a report to the Regency Council, saying that he had "overlooked nothing in sustaining the colony" and had not let himself become "discouraged" by the responsibilities he had assumed.[8] And when the Council of the Navy recalled the governor and the *ordonnateur* from Louisiana it ordered their successors to "provide every safeguard" for Crozat's monopoly and for his agents. This change in the leading personnel of the colony was itself made at the request of the financier, who hoped that it would bring in persons better disposed toward him. This was why he decided to give back to the Conseil Supérieur of Louisiana, in October, 1716, the power of cognizance in cases concerning violation of his monopoly, a power the Crown had granted him, at his request, in 1714.[9]

In exchange for the confirmation of this privilege, Crozat agreed to continue to make funds available. The procedure did not change. The financier remained guarantor of payment for all "supplies" destined for Louisiana, but since in the last analysis the Crown was responsible for such payments, the "receipts" were "sent, like those of the other colonies, in the name of the Treasurer of the Navy."[10] Crozat was thus committed to put at the disposal of the Crown the total amount of the sums included

---

7. AM, B 1 19, f. 39–39v, Proceedings of the Council of the Navy, Jan. 12, 1717; B 1 20, f. 418–19, Chateaumorant and Mithon, May 11, 1717; AC, C 9A 13, Petition from Gédéon Nolivos and Pierre Moret to the marquis de Chateaumorant, Léogane, Oct. 15, 1717.

8. BN, FF 23664, f. 21, Regency Council, Feb. 11, 1716; AC, C 13A, f. 67–68, Mémoire sur la colonie de Louisiane presented to the Regency Council, Feb. 11, 1716.

9. AC, B 38, f. 302v, Mémoire . . . pour servir d'instructions au Sr Hubert, Oct. 20, 1716; f. 313, Mémoire pour servir d'instructions au Sr de Lépinay, Oct. 20, 1716; AC, C 13A 4, f. 375, Decision of the Regency Council, Oct. 5, 1716; AC, A 22, f. 21–21v, Ordinance for execution of the letters patent granted to Sr. Crozat, October 5, 1716.

10. AC, B 38, f. 179, to Beauharnais, Oct. 6, 1716; AM, B 1 9, f. 285v–86v, Proceedings of the Council of the Navy, Aug. 29, 1716.

in the "list of funds." The council even expected him to provide the additional funds needed to pay off the colony's debt after 1714. Besides this, it asked Crozat to conform to the mode of payment agreed upon, by paying "immediately, half the cost of the supplies" and "the other half three months after delivery."[11]

It was on this basis, in fact, that Crozat began, in 1712, to make purchases of provisions for the garrison. He ordered his correspondent at La Rochelle, the merchant Paul de Pont, *seigneur* of Les Granges de Vilson, to make all the payments for which he was responsible.[12]

Most of the payments that Crozat had to make went to meet the current expenses of the colony, which reproduced unchanged those of the preceding years. As has been mentioned, there were no increases except in the military credits. Where the arms and clothing of the troops were concerned, especially, the council granted increases that were needed both on account of the reinforcement of the garrison and of the need to remedy the most obvious shortcomings of the service. As a result of an observation from the Sieur de Lépinay that, in a colony where locksmiths (who also repaired firearms) were few, weapons defective from long use might give serious trouble, the council decided to distribute new weapons to the four companies of the "new levy"—two hundred *fusils* (rifles) and two hundred bayonets with sockets, together with the same number of powder horns. With a view, no doubt, to lightening the weight of armaments as well as to adapting the weaponry to the nature of the country, the council also abolished the use of the sword, which had up to then been standard equipment in the Louisiana companies, and consequently did away with sword belts. Swords were henceforth to be replaced by "small hand axes."[13]

The council furthermore provided for regular issues of cloth-

11. AM, B 1 9, f. 332, Proceedings of the Council of the Navy, Sept. 1, 1716; AC, B 38, f. 139–139v, to Beauharnais, June 23, 1716.

12. AM, B 1 8, f. 635, Proceedings of the Council of the Navy, June 16, 1716; AM, B 3 248, f. 159v, Creil, La Rochelle, July 15, 1717; AC, B 38, f. 174v, 180v, to Beauharnais, Sept. 14, Oct. 13, 1716; La Rochelle, Rivière and Soullard, 1717, f. 171, Commitment of Félix Lurat to serve Depont, Seigneur des Granges de Vilson.

13. AM, B 1 8, f. 528v–30, Beauharnais, Rochefort, April 30, 1716; f. 553v–54, Beauharnais, May 12, 1716; B 1 9, f. 44v, Beauharnais, July 21, 1716; AC, B 38, f. 140v–41, to Beauharnais, June 23, 1716; AC, C 13A 4, f. 117, Proceedings of the Council of the Navy, June 23, 1716; f. 983, Draft of memorandum from the King to Lépinay and Hubert, October, 1716; Archives of La Rochelle, B 5591, L.-A. de Bourbon to the Admiralty officers of La Rochelle, March 19, 1716.

ing, in accordance with the principle it had laid down for the colonial troops generally, though this was slightly modified in line with Crozat's suggestions. It adopted his idea, which was to issue a "major set of apparel" only at three-year intervals, with a "minor set" in each of the two intervening years, and it approved the types and quantities of cloth that the financier proposed for the uniforms. The "major set of apparel" would comprise, for sergeants, a jerkin of "greyish white" cloth and blue serge, with large pewter buttons and sleeves decorated with "fine silver braid," plus a jacket and breeches of "blue stockinet"; for drummers, a jerkin of blue cloth with copper buttons and a "large galloon of the King's livery," a jacket and breeches of red stockinet, and a smock made of drill; and for the ordinary soldiers, a grey jerkin with copper buttons, a jacket of red stockinet, breeches of blue stockinet, and a smock of drill. All were to receive, in addition, a hat, two black cravats, a pair of gaiters, and a pair of Saint-Maixent stockings. The "minor set" consisted merely of an issue of "small clothes," with, in the case of the sergeants, two pairs of shoes.[14] All this entailed, for the four new companies alone, according to the terms of the "contract made by the Council of the Navy with Sr. Desplaces, merchant at Paris," an expenditure of nearly six thousand livres, almost all of which Crozat paid.[15]

Crozat thus did not confine himself to the role of furnisher of funds to the Crown. He was involved in the negotiations by the council or the intendants of the ports with suppliers, and he even undertook some of the purchases. He kept, of course, strictly within the limits of the credits authorized by the Council of the Navy, and inside that narrow framework he operated with constant concern for economy. He suggested to the council that they cease to invite bids from suppliers of clothing at Rochefort, where costs were higher than in Paris, and he himself began negotiations with Sieur Desplaces in Paris. For the same reason, he avoided buying flour in Rochefort for the garrison. Prices there were particularly high in 1716 because drought had interrupted the functioning of the flour mills at Saint-Jean-d'Angély

---

14. AC, C 13A 4, f. 153–54, Proceedings of the Council of the Navy, July 27, 1716.
15. AE, Mem. & Doc., America, I, f. 296–98v, List of what is owed to Sr Crozat for reimbursement of sums advanced by him (for the clothing of the four companies.)

and almost exhausted the possibility of obtaining provisions in the market at Marans. Crozat left this task to a Tours merchant named Desruaux-Hardouin, who placed his orders in the province of Anjou. Despite the expense of transport by water from Nantes to Rochefort, a quintal of flour so obtained cost only 9 livres 8 sous, as against the 14 livres asked by the merchants of Rochefort, which meant a saving for the Crown of 6,500 livres.[16]

However, it is obvious that Crozat, who since the agreement of 1714 had continually advanced money for Louisiana, felt increasingly impatient with the extreme slowness of his reimbursement. He did not hide his discontent from the council. In September, 1716, he pointed out to them that he had so far been repaid none of the money he had laid out and asked that a system of monthly repayments be inaugurated, threatening that if the duc de Noailles could not give him satisfaction, he would "no longer sustain this business." The Council of Finance had indeed promised to repay him the 80,986 livres he had advanced for the year 1714 alone, yet by the end of 1716 he had received only one installment of no more than 30,000 livres, and at that date, so he claimed, the amount advanced by him already came to 300,000 livres.[17] Duché, who fully sympathized with Crozat, was afraid that the financier would use up, "to pay His Majesty's expenses," the whole of the capital he had invested in the enterprise and consequently would sacrifice all his commercial operations and, with them, all hope of making a profit.[18]

Nevertheless, Crozat did not suspend his advances, but we notice increasing irregularity in these payments, such as had not occurred at the beginning. On several occasions the comte de Toulouse, who troubled himself little about the delays in his own administration, called on Crozat to "say promptly and definitely whether or not he will pay." The council accused Crozat of unfairness toward suppliers, because the financier's attitude

---

16. AM, B 1 9, f. 45, 47v–50v, Council of the Navy, July 27, 1716, correspondence of Beauharnais and Crozat; f. 586v, Desruaux to the Council of the Navy, Nov. 11, 1716, B 1 19, f. 468v–69, Sr des Ruaux to the Council of the Navy, March 22, 1717; AC, B 38, f. 150v, to Beauharnais, July 14, 1716; B 39, f. 106v–107, to the intendant Chauvelin, Jan. 11, 1717.

17. AM, B 1 9 f. 362–63, Council of Sept. 8, 1716, Crozat's correspondence; B 1 20, f. 410v–11, Crozat, July 12, 1717; AC, B 38, f. 39v, to M. Le Couturier, May 27, 1716. For the actual amount advanced by Crozat, see p. 70 below.

18. AE, Mem. & Doc., America, I, f. 428, Duché, Etat des avances par la Compagnie de Louisiane; Giraud, *History*, I, 123, 133–35, 294.

compromised fulfillment of the clause in the contracts providing for payment on the spot. "It is just," Crozat was told, "to keep one's word when . . . it has been given."[19]

Crozat even showed some negligence, leaving out with no reason some details from the list of "provisions and merchandise for Louisiana." He was particularly slow to provide the pay and salaries of recruits, officers, and civilian personnel from the Crown sent to the colony. Despite assurances given by the council to the governor and the officers that they would be paid from the day of their "commission," they had been waiting since June, 1716, for the salaries that would enable them to settle their debts and assemble the "stores" needed for colonial service. Crozat issued his order for payment only in mid-October. In the meantime it was, paradoxically enough, the Council of the Navy that had to find ways of getting the money needed to let the soldiers have their pay and to provide the officers with means of subsistence, in the hope of being reimbursed by the financier.[20]

Crozat showed particular reluctance where arms were concerned. Despite repeated requests from the Council of the Navy, he failed to pay for goods that a Tulle industrialist, the Sieur de La Combe, sent to Louisiana in 1714. In 1716 he delayed still further, so that at his resignation he had still not settled the debt of those two years, thus disappointing La Combe, who had hoped that he would be "paid better by Crozat than by the Treasurer of the Navy."[21]

This dilatoriness and irregularity annoyed the suppliers, brought deplorable confusion into preparations for arming the

19. AC, 38, f. 45, 47, 49, 51v, to Crozat, July 14, Aug. 4, Aug. 11, Aug. 29, 1716; f. 167, to Beauharnais, Aug. 29, 1716; B 39, f. 150v–51, to Beauharnais, July 14, 1717; AM, B 1 9, f. 15v–16, 98v, Beauharnais, June 30, July 23, 1716; f. 101–101v, Lépinay, July 25, 1716; f. 155v–56, Beauharnais, Aug. 15, 1716.

20. AM, B 1 8, f. 528v–30, Beauharnais, April 30, 1716; f. 562–63, De Lauze and Gauveret, May 4, 1716; f. 604, La Gallissonnière, May 26, 1716; f. 607, Lépinay, May 30, 1716; f. 634, Proceedings of the Council of the Navy, June 16, 1716; B 1 9, f. 15v–16, 259v, Beauharnais, June 30, Aug. 22, 1716; f. 414v, De Lauze, Sept. 18, 1716; f. 544, de Bonneville, de Lause and Gauvery, Nov. 5, 1716; f. 559, Hubert, November, 1716; AC, B 38, f. 47, to Crozat, Aug. 4, 1716; f. 51v, to Crozat, Aug. 29, 1716; f. 93v, to Beauharnais, March 20, 1716; f. 99–99v, to La Gallissonnière, March 31, 1716; f. 123, to de Lause and Gauverit, May 23, 1716; f. 130v, to La Gallissonnière, June 9, 1716; f. 132v, to Beauharnais, June 9, 1716; f. 180v, to Beauharnais, Oct. 13, 1716; f. 297–97v, to Hubert, Oct. 13, 1716.

21. AC, B 38, f. 45, 54v, to Crozat, July 14, Oct. 14, 1716; AM, B 1 4, f. 57–57v, Mémoire du Sr de La Combe, Council of the Navy, Jan. 27, 1716; B 1 20, f. 412–13, Proceedings of the Council of the Navy, July 27, 1716; AM, B 2 245 (I), f. 38, to Sr de La Combe, Jan. 29, 1716.

troops, and added more delay to that for which the Council of the Navy was itself responsible. Moreover, through his desire to save money, out of concern for the Crown's resources, and to increase his chances of reimbursement, Crozat too often failed to pay attention to the quality of the provisions and merchandise he sent out. The Anjou flour proved unsatisfactory when inspected. The *ordonnateur* at Nantes had to have it re-ground in order to extract the moisture, and Lépinay doubted that it would survive the voyage, because of the high proportion of sand it contained. The salt beef that Crozat sent to Dauphin Island for consumption by the soldiers and the passengers on the *Ludlow* and the *Paon* was even more defective and was packed in "ill-conditioned" casks. The clothing itself, bought at the lowest price according to the financier's instructions, was of mediocre quality, inferior to what had been supplied to the troops in Cayenne and Canada.[22]

Consequently, the arrival of the two frigates brought only a temporary and precarious solution to the still troublesome problem of feeding the troops in Louisiana. Not only were the provisions not of the required quality, but because some of the flour had been left behind at Rochefort (where it was made into biscuit), for lack of storage space on the ships, and because Crozat had been unable to obtain the hundred quintals of rice he had tried to find for the garrison, their quantity, too, fell short of the colony's needs.[23] In fact, where all the articles conveyed by the convoy of 1716–1717 were concerned, artillery and munitions included, considerable reductions had to be made at the start of the voyage because of the shortage of space on the ships, and this was made worse by "inevitable and constant" deterioration suffered during the voyage by the foodstuffs and clothing on board.[24] After the arrival in September, 1715, of the storeship the

22. AM, B 8, f. 635v, Proceedings of the Council of the Navy, June 16, 1716; B 1 9, f. 521v, La Gallissonnière, Oct. 31, 1716; f. 522v–23, Beauharnais, Nov. 3, 1716; f. 545v, Lépinay, Nov. 10, 1716; f. 579v–80, Lépinay, Nov. 21, 1716; AM, B 3 236, f. 518–19, Lusançay, Oct. 3, 1716; AC, C 13A 4, f. 447–50, Lépinay, Oct. 31, 1716; f. 879, Lépinay, Nov. 17, 1716.

23. AC, B 38, f. 140v, 150v, 189v, to Beauharnais, June 23, July 14, Dec. 2, 1716; B 39, f. 9, to M. Buisson, Feb. 12, 1717; AM, B 1 9, f. 517v–19v, 579v–80, Lépinay, Oct. 31, Nov. 21, 1716; AC, C 13A 4, f. 871–74, Lépinay, Nov. 7, 1716. From the 1,800 quintals provided for by the council, purchases of flour were reduced to less than 1,400 quintals, and only part of this could be put aboard.

24. AC, C 13A 5, f. 29–29v, Lépinay and Hubert, May 30, 1717; f. 44–44v, Hubert, June 2, 1717; f. 46–46v, Hubert, Oct. 26, 1717; AM, B 1 9, f. 268–70v, Proceedings of the Council of the Navy, Aug. 29, 1716; f. 579v–80, Lépinay, Nov. 21, 1716; f. 620v–21, La Gallissonnière, Dec. 12, 1716.

Dauphine, the country's supplies were replenished in 1716 only by Crozat's brigantine the *Paix*, which, because of its small capacity (ninety tons burden) did not provide very effective "relief." The colony expected more substantial deliveries to arrive on the king's own frigates, after it had been left in isolation for nearly a year. Unfortunately, neither the imports supplied at the Crown's expense nor the "effects" sent by Crozat to serve his commercial activity represented what was needed to maintain the material life of the inhabitants and the garrison.

By this date, however, there was some indication that improvement was on the way. Crozat seemed to be wanting to make an effort to ensure better supplies for the colony. He had just sent out his brigantine with a larger cargo than in the previous years, and it contained, among other things, "goods suitable for trade with the savages." For fear of pirates, the vessel set out from Cap Français, in St. Domingue, under the protection of the royal frigates. Separated by "a storm of wind" from its escort, the brigantine arrived soon afterward at Dauphin Island. And so, in the spring of 1717, for the first time since the beginning of the French occupation, three ships were present together on the island's shore. And Crozat, when preparing for the brigantine's second voyage, announced his intention of sending back the *Dauphine*, on its return from Louisiana, with a "quantity" of goods that he said he had already obtained.[25]

There was another pointer that seemed to give the population cause for encouragement, namely, Crozat's promise to modify his price policy, the news of which reached Louisiana in March, 1717. There was, to be sure, no reason to expect from this any immediate change in the regime that the colony had lived under since the financier took charge of it. The price reduction was not to apply to foodstuffs: flour, wine, and brandy, which made up the bulk of the cargoes, were still to be subject to a 200 percent markup. For other goods, Crozat agreed in principle to a more advantageous tariff, since the markup of at least 100 percent above "the price in France," which had always been imposed on them, was now not to exceed 60 percent—50 percent for sol-

---

25. AC, B 38, f. 181, to Beauharnais, Oct. 13, 1716; AM, B 1 9, f. 556v–57, Proceedings of the Council of the Navy, Nov. 18, 1716; AE, Mem. & Doc., America, I, f. 293v–94v, List presented by Sr Crozat to the commissioners of the council appointed . . . for the liquidation . . . ; f. 183v, Crozat, Mémoire sur la Louisiane, 1717; AC, C 13A 4, f. 415, Proceedings of the Council of the Navy, Oct. 10, 1716; f. 916–17, Mémoire de Crozat, 1716; C 13A 5, f. 36–37, Lépinay, May 10, 1717.

diers. Actually, the reduction was not so great as it appears from these figures, because Crozat invoiced, in addition to the 60 percent markup, port charges and insurance costs. The *ordonnateur* Hubert considered this a crying iniquity at the expense of the population.[26]

The financier said he was ready to grant further concessions. He had just set up in Louisiana a "Council of Trade" to which he gave authority to reduce the "agreed prices, if they are too high" and to lay down the conditions under which the colony's products would be bought. Promising to increase his purchasing prices, he offered to pay 25 sols apiece for buckskins, instead of the previous 20 sols. Since the inhabitants and the Indians wanted 30 sols, he left it to the council to decide on a further increase if it considered this feasible.[27] In other words, the new regulation was not to come into force immediately upon the arrival of the ships. An inquiry and perhaps some discussion with the inhabitants would be needed before a price regime could be established in the colony that would ensure for the population the advantages that the Council of the Navy wished to secure for it, without encroaching on the financier's interests.

If Crozat's monopoly had continued, it was not out of the question that the country's economic life might have quickened somewhat. The financier might have increased the amount of merchandise he imported, and by increasing, as he said he intended, his supply of articles suitable for trade with the Indians, and above all by modifying his price policy, he might have mitigated one of the chief causes of the colony's distress.

But his resignation annulled, for the moment at least, these prospects of betterment. This event had already occurred when the *Ludlow* and the *Paon* reached Dauphin Island. A charge of 6,600,000 livres imposed upon him by the Chambre de Justice clinched his decision. Crozat expressed to the king his "mortification" at being put on the same footing as "all the rogues" in France. He claimed to have rendered "essential services" to the Crown—since 1712 his operations had enriched the realm to the

26. AC, C 13A 4, f. 980, 986–87, Draft of memorandum from the king to Lépinay and Hubert, October, 1716; C 13A 5, f. 28v, 31, Lépinay and Hubert, May 30, 1717; f. 34, Invoice for the goods put aboard by order of M. Crozat, La Rochelle, July 18, 1717; AE, Mem. & Doc., America, I, f. 290–91, Mémoire servant à l'intelligence. . . .

27. On the Council of Trade, see p. 86 below. For the previous purchase prices, see Giraud, *History,* I, 295–96. AC, C 13A 4, f. 523, La Mothe, Jan. 2, 1716; f. 987–89, Draft of memorandum from the king to Lépinay and Hubert; AM, B 1 9, f. 424v–25, Duclos, June 3, 1716.

tune of 300 millions in specie. "How did he deserve to be ill used a hundred times worse than others?"[28] Declaring himself incapable of resuming henceforth the supply of funds required for Louisiana, he proposed to give up his monopoly, requesting the Regent to set against the charge imposed by the Chambre de Justice the amount of capital he had invested in the Mississippi enterprise up to January, 1717.[29] This meant, of course, the ruin of his plan to use the resources of his fortune without restriction in order to develop the trade of Louisiana, in return for an extension of his monopoly and more generous participation by the Crown in the task of colonization, which was, in his view, the only way to obtain a result that could not be won "without much time and patience and through immense expenditure." But his fiscal burden would at least be alleviated.[30]

From that moment, Crozat, who soon afterward ceased to be a director of the Company of Saint-Domingue, lost interest in Louisiana.[31] The *Dauphine*, which returned to France at the beginning of 1717, remained at La Rochelle, and the Council of the Navy had to put off still longer the dispatch of those provisions and reinforcements that it had been unable to send the previous year. The financier's agents ceased to supply the money needed for "the expenses of the King's state" in the year 1717. Crozat stopped paying the salaries of the officers who had not managed to set out in 1716 and were awaiting, on the Ile d'Oléron, the fitting out of the next ship bound for the Mississippi. Six months after the expiration of the contract period laid down for successful bidders, Crozat's correspondent at Lá Rochelle declared that he had neither order nor funds for "full payment" for the "munitions and merchandise" sent out the previous year. In 1718 the Sieur Desplaces had still not obtained full payment for the clothes he had supplied.[32] Crozat even failed to attend to the

28. AE, Mem. & Doc., France, 1228, f. 70–72, Mémoire de Crozat, 1717; Buvat, *Gazette de la Régence*, 122–23.
29. AE, Mem. & Doc., America, I, f. 183v, 239v–40, Mémoire de Crozat, 1717; AC, Fortifications records, Louisiana, 5–6, Mémoire de Crozat, January, 1717.
30. AC, Fortifications records, Louisiana, 6; Giraud, *History*, I, 252–53.
31. AC, B 39, f. 144–44v, Decision confirming the agreement made with the directors of the Company of Saint-Domingue, June 21, 1717.
32. AC, C 13A 5, f. 46v, 47, Hubert, Oct. 26, 1717; f. 83–83v, 88v, Mémoire sur la Louisiane, 1717; AC, B 39, f. 1v, to Beauharnais, Jan. 2, 1717; f. 28, to M. de Montholon, April 12, 1717; f. 34, to Beauharnais, May 1, 1717; f. 64–64v, to Crozat, July 3, 1717; f. 104, to Crozat, Jan. 2, 1717; B 40, f. 91v, to Beauharnais, Sept. 22, 1717; AM, B 1 19, f. 302–302v, M. de Montholon, Rochefort, March 16, 1717; f. 493–493v, Beauharnais, April 17, 1717; B 1 20, f. 386v, Proceedings of the

needs of the families of the workmen whom the council had engaged for service in Louisiana in 1716. Two longboat masters and an edged-toolmaker had left Rochefort for the colony at that time, on the understanding that their families would be looked after. Crozat stopped his payments to them, and the families were reduced to appealing in vain to the port authorities for the material help they had the right to expect.[33]

It is clear that, from the day he announced his intention to give up his monopoly, Crozat considered himself released from any and every obligation toward the colony. His view—logical enough—was that, having returned his privilege to the king, together with the capital he had invested in the Mississippi "affair" either in the form of advances of money or in "ships, goods, and effects," he could not be expected to contemplate further expenditure, which "would be a mere loss for him." He asked merely that this capital be set against the tax being imposed on him.[34] Eventually the Regent yielded to Crozat's arguments and agreed that he would not be "required to pay [the suppliers] out of his own pocket."[35] When the king accepted Crozat's resignation in a "conditional decision" of August 23, 1717 (the definitive decision had to wait for the judicial liquidation of the "value of the effects" handed over by the financier), he officially released him from all responsibility. The Crown would itself guarantee "full payment" for the previous year's supplies, would settle in state bank notes the debts owed to the Sieur de La Combe, and would pass on to the company that took over from Crozat the obligation to pay the salaries of the officers who had not yet left France.[36]

It was Crozat who first suggested this idea of entrusting Louisiana once more to a trading company. When he terminated his privilege, he addressed several *mémoires* to the Council of the Navy, in which he emphasized, with more complacency than

---

Council of the Navy, July 14, 1717; B 1 21, f. 88v, Beauharnais, Sept. 23, 1717; B 1 30, f. 23, Representations by Sr Gendron, Council of June 1, 1718; B 1 20, f. 339–39v, Bonnille, June 16, 1717; AC, C 11A 37, f. 92v–93, 344–45, Vaudreuil, Nov. 2, April 20, 1717.

33. AM, B 1 29, f. 336–36v, M. de Montholon, Rochefort, March 19, 1718.
34. AM, B 1 20, f. 410v–11, Crozat, July 12, 1717.
35. *Ibid.*, f. 413–13v.
36. AC, A 22, f. 69v–71v, Aug. 26, 1718; AC, B 39, f. 86v, to Beauharnais, Sept. 1, 1717; f. 158v–59, to M. Amelot, Aug. 18, 1717; B 40, f. 112–12v, Certificate given to M. de la Combe, March 23, 1718; AM, B 1 20, f. 524, 525v, Beauharnais, Aug. 19, 1717; B 1 21, f. 88v, Beauharnais, Sept. 23, 1717.

was justified, the benefits his management of the colony had produced. Since the end of 1712, he claimed, Louisiana had made great progress. Reduced at that time to a population of fifty to sixty persons, with a garrison consisting of "fifty beggars," the colony had been "ready for occupation by the first comer." Now it was ripe for a "great establishment." Crozat had revealed the colony's potential, and if he had been able to complete his work, he would have exploited its mineral wealth and, by bringing in settlers and workmen, would have created tobacco plantations that would have freed the French tobacco monopoly from its dependence on England. More than ever, then, Louisiana constituted a possession of capital importance for the realm. Its strategic value was growing with the growth in British power on the American continent, and its economic future was henceforth assured. The Crown's imperative duty was to "support" it, and the most effective means of bringing the colony the help it needed was to seek the cooperation of a trading company, which would add its capital to the credits that the king assigned to Louisiana.[37]

It was from this suggestion of Crozat's that the Company of the West was to emerge. The Council of the Navy accepted his idea unhesitatingly. Marshal d'Estrées reported it to them on January 11, 1717, and, approving the financier's views, the council resolved "that steps would be taken . . . to form" a company "to pursue the enterprise of Louisiana." The Crown, being unable "to enter into all the commercial details inseparable therefrom," could not itself assume charge of the colony.[38]

It does not seem that Crozat's monopoly resulted in the adverse balance commonly attributed to it. His operations in Louisiana were undoubtedly always subject to a narrow conception. He sent out too few goods, and at too high prices, to expand his trade with the natives, and the somewhat more substantial shipments that arrived in 1717 did not noticeably improve the situation. His attempts at trade with the Spaniards resulted in no more than a slight traffic with the garrison of Pensacola. Altogether, Crozat got little out of the colony. According to his agent Le Bart, his business in Louisiana consisted essentially in sales

37. AC, 13A 5, f. 233–36, Crozat, Mémoire pour faire connaître . . . , Jan. 11, 1717; AE, Mem. & Doc., America I, f. 238–40, Mémoire de Crozat, May, 1717; f. 289–89v, Mémoire servant à l'intelligence . . . ; f. 185, Crozat, Mémoire sur la Louisiane, 1717.

38. AM, B 1 19, f. 46v–47, Council of the Navy, Jan. 13, 1717, proceedings on Louisiana; BN, FF 23664, f. 93, Regency Council, session of Jan. 11, 1717.

of produce and goods—not very large, given the smallness of the population—to the inhabitants and the garrison.[39]

And yet, when the years of his monopoly were at an end, and after having frequently claimed that Louisiana had brought him no return, Crozat twice declared himself satisfied with his gains and able to say that despite the loss of the ship the *Justice* he was "in profit."[40] Perhaps he wanted to exaggerate his gains in the hope of obtaining from the commission charged with liquidating his accounts a substantial indemnity compensating him for the ten years that remained of his privilege in 1717. But the spirit in which he carried on his operations and the conditions he imposed on the population certainly sufficed to ensure him profits that the low figure of his imports into Louisiana seemed to rule out.[41] Even if the ships he fitted out for the colony found there only an insignificant return cargo, they made up for this by putting in at Havana or St. Domingue, where they took on raw materials and even managed, when circumstances allowed, to dispose of goods from France or at least of timber from Louisiana. Although the first ships did return empty, the voyages of the *Dauphine* and the *Paix* were certainly not profitless for the financier.[42] When the commission offered Crozat a compensation payment of 748,547 livres, the members undoubtedly knew what they were doing and founded their calculations on evidence produced by him. Their estimate, worked out on the basis of an annual profit of nearly 75,000 livres, met with complete approval from the directors of the Company of the West.[43]

Besides, Crozat did not suffer any actual loss in tying up a considerable capital in his advances of money and purchases of the provisions, ships, and goods indispensable for his commercial activity. No doubt he did deprive himself in this way of the

---

39. AC, C 13A 5, f. 27v–28, Lépinay and Hubert, May 30, 1717; f. 65, Bienville, May 10, 1717; AE, Mem. & Doc., America, I, f. 167v, Mémoire du Sr Le Bartz, June, 1717.

40. AC, A 22, f. 65, Decision liquidating the expenditure of M. Crozat on Louisiana, June 20, 1718; AM, B 1 9, f. 362–63, Proceedings of the Council of the Navy, Sept. 8, 1716; AC, C 13A 5, f. 297, Crozat, Mémoire à S.A.S. Mgr. l'Amiral [1715 ?]; AE, Mem. & Doc., America, I, f. 289v, Mémoire servant à l'intelligence. . . . On the wreck of the *Justice*, see Giraud, *History,* I, 269, 297–99.

41. Giraud, *History,* I, 297–299.

42. AM, B 1 19, f. 247–47v, Magnin, at Cap Français, Nov. 15, 1716; AC, C 13A 5, f. 46, Hubert, Oct. 26, 1717; C 13A 4, f. 914–15, Mémoire de Crozat, 1716. *Cf.* Chap. X below.

43. AC, A 22, f. 65v, 68, Decision liquidating the expenditure of M. Crozat on Louisiana, June 20, 1718.

chance to invest his capital in more lucrative enterprises, and on several occasions he reminded the Crown that he could have done better with it, since "a trader," he wrote, "would be lacking in skill if he did not double his capital when he chose to risk it . . . boldly."[44] However, whatever he might say, neither principal nor interest was lost to him. Contrary to the figures he compiled, which gave a total of 1,298,000 livres advanced to the Crown, the king's commissioners, after examining the evidence, arrived at a total of 1,251,562 livres. The directors of the Company of the West came to the same conclusion, which Crozat accepted unreservedly. It even emerges from the evidence that the advances he had made for the colony's service, both in France and in Louisiana itself, came not to 300,000 livres, as he claimed, but 175,088 livres, and this, when diminished by the duc de Noailles's partial repayment and the price of supplies Crozat had received for his personal use from the king's storehouse at Rochefort, was further reduced to no more than 139,833 livres.[45] These figures relate to Crozat's capital together with accrued interest, which the financier, after conferring with his partners, proposed to fix at 10 percent, in conformity with what the king "has almost always paid . . . in rather difficult times."[46] As for the goods belonging to him in the colony, Crozat transferred these to the Crown, for subsequent conveyance to the Company of the West, at the prices prevailing in France plus between 70 and 80 percent, depending on the date they arrived in Louisiana.[47] The capital he had invested in the Mississippi business was thus wholly reconstituted.

The only point on which, at most, one might agree that there was a deficit was that relating to losses and damage suffered during voyages to and from the colony. When they calculated

---

44. AE, Mem. & Doc., France, 1228, f. 71, Payments made by Sr Crozat to Sr Olivier in fulfilment of his tax obligation, 1717; America, I, f. 290–90v, Mémoire servant à l'intelligence. . . .

45. AC, Fortifications records, Louisiana, 6, Mémoire du Sr Crozat (1717); AE, Mem. & Doc., America, I, f. 293–95v, List which Sr. Crozat presents to the commissioners of the council nominated by decision . . . for liquidation, estimating the remittance he has made to the king . . . ; f. 296–98v, List of what is owed to Sr. Crozat to reimburse him for moneys advanced by him in France . . . ; AC, A 22, f. 66–68, Decision liquidating the expenditure of M. Crozat. . . . , June 20, 1718; AE, Mem. & Doc., France, 1228, f. 71, Payments made by Sr Crozat to Sr Olivier . . . , 1717.

46. AE, Mem. & Doc., America, I, f. 291, Mémoire servant à l'intelligence. . . .

47. Ibid., AC, A 22, f. 71v, Letters patent on the decision of June 20, 1718.

the amounts that Crozat was to be allowed, the commissioners did not take account either of the wreck of the *Justice* or of the deterioration to which foodstuffs were always exposed. In reality, however, the figure representing these losses, according to Crozat himself, was not much above 150,000 livres—200,000 at most—and he was amply compensated for them in the indemnity he received.[48]

When he acknowledged a debt of two million livres to Crozat, the king did justice to all the claims that the financier could reasonably put forward. These two million livres were credited to Crozat, and on June 20, 1718, when the commission had completed the general liquidation of the merchant's accounts, the king ordered that the tax imposed on him by the Chambre de Justice be reduced by this amount.

Crozat's monopoly ended, for Louisiana, in conditions that were deeply disappointing, at a moment when the financier seemed disposed to modify his economic policy and when he had just secured the nomination of the governor and the *ordonnateur* he wanted. Nothing remained of the promises that these initiatives had seemed to offer the population. Not only did his plan for reforming the price regime result in mere half measures of no serious consequences, but the arrival of a new set of personages failed to restore that spirit of collaboration needed for the good government of the colony.

48. Crozat evaluated his investment at 1,254,000 livres (AC, Fortifications records, Louisiana, 6). Elsewhere he gave the figure as 1,298,876 livres (AE, Mem. & Doc., America, I, f. 299–300). But if losses and damage were to be taken into account, he made it 1,447,577 livres (AE, Mem. & Doc., America, I, f. 299–300).

VII The Government and Its Personalities

1. The Renewal of the Leading Personnel

THE INITIATIVE in entrusting the government of Louisiana to a new group of men, like so many other initiatives concerning the colony, was taken by Crozat. Already at the end of 1715, in the first *mémoires* he sent to the comte de Toulouse, Crozat was urging the recall of the acting governor, La Mothe, and Duclos, the *ordonnateur*. He accused them of concurring only to do harm to his interests, of encouraging infractions of his monopoly, and of authorizing St. Domingue merchants freely to purchase in the colony goods that they then sold abroad from their ships.[1] Duclos, Crozat said, had left France "determined to act against the company," and the two men had no other aim than to grab all they could from the country.[2]

In proposing that these men be dismissed, Crozat was inspired primarily by his own interests. His purpose was to replace them with persons devoted to him who would ensure that his monopoly was respected. Nevertheless, in 1716 the situation in the colony was such that there was justification for the financier's initiative. Internal dissension had become much worse since the arrival on the *Dauphine*, in September, 1715, of Crozat's new representative, a man named Raujon, who as a director of the Company of Louisiana took over from Derigoin but was armed with greater powers than his predecessor, since—and this was something quite new in Louisiana—he was also a comptroller of the navy.[3] The Council of the Navy had conferred this additional title upon him at Crozat's request, but without

---

1. Doubtless an allusion to the stay at Dauphin Island of the merchant Baron, who actually came from Martinique, and whose ship proceeded subsequently to Holland, but without having taken anything on board in Louisiana. *Cf.* Giraud, *History*, I, 308–309.

2. AC, C 13A 4, f. 1031–32, Mémoire de Crozat à Son Altesse Sérénissime, 1715; C 13A 5, f. 297, Mémoire à S.A.S. Mgr l'Amiral [1715 ?].

3. AE, Mem. & Doc., America, I, f. 293, List presented by Sr Crozat to the council's commissioners appointed . . . to liquidate . . . .

attaching any salary to it. As comptroller, Raujon had a difficult task to perform, and he soon became aware of the responsibilities it entailed and of its self-contradictory character. Being a director of the company, and consequently obligated to pay the troops, he could indeed hardly "supervise himself." He therefore advised Crozat, less than a year after his arrival, to assign the functions of comptroller of the navy to Sieur Le Bart, who would find it easier to perform them along with those of comptroller of the company, which post he held already.[4] Meanwhile, though, Raujon's authority was markedly strengthened by the additional title, and inevitably this increased the occasions for conflict between him and La Mothe.

The latter soon accused Raujon of arrogating to himself excessive power over the population, to a degree that actually voided the governor's power, especially since Crozat had granted his representative complete freedom of action in the colony. As La Mothe saw it, the situation constituted a formal breach of the agreements on which the Company of Louisiana was based, a usurpation of the right that Crozat had approved for his associates, La Mothe and Le Bart, to "give orders" to the director and to his "other agents."[5] Thereafter La Mothe, while denying that he wished to exercise his rights to the full and claiming to be acting only "in the name of peace," became Raujon's sworn enemy. He condemned whatever Raujon proposed and accused him of falsifying the "muster rolls" and of neglecting the fundamental task of feeding the troops, failure in which was a constant cause of desertions. Above all he criticized the new director for incompetence. Raujon, who had previously been an intendant's secretary, was not qualified, La Mothe said, to direct a commercial undertaking.[6]

In his continual indictments, La Mothe not only called into question the director's policy, notably the meanness of his purchasing prices, which harmed both the inhabitants and the Indians and compromised the interests of Crozat's associates. La Mothe also attacked the policy of the financier himself, so becoming a disparager of the monopoly he had been sent out to

---

4. AC, C 13A 4, f. 186, La Mothe to the Council of the Navy, Jan. 2, 1716; f. 692, Duclos, June 7, 1716; AM B 1 9, f. 416–16v, Chastelain, Dauphin Island, July 22, 1716; AC, D 2C 51, f. 17v, Extract from the musters of the detached naval companies maintained in Louisiana, January, 1716.

5. AC, C 13A 4, f. 514, 580–81, La Mothe, Jan. 2, Feb. 7, 1716.

6. AM, B 1 9, f. 265, Proceedings of the Council of the Navy, Aug. 29, 1716; AC, C 13A 4, f. 568–69, 583–84, La Mothe, Jan. 31, Feb. 7, 1716.

defend. According to him, Crozat had brought his business into jeopardy by not giving him, La Mothe, supreme authority over the colony's trade and by not acting as he advised.[7] This being so, La Mothe considered it pointless to continue his partnership with Crozat and Le Bart. It was "against nature," he wrote, "to watch one's property going to ruin . . . without protest." Since his interests were being deliberately sacrificed to an ever greater extent, and since Raujon was no longer paying him the 3.5 percent commission on the colony's trade that Crozat had promised him, at the beginning of 1716 La Mothe informed the Minister of the Navy, whom he supposed to be still in office, that he intended to withdraw from an association into which he claimed to have entered against his will.[8]

Needless to say, Crozat, for his part, was free with his own complaints against La Mothe. He ascribed to La Mothe responsibility for the "frightful disorder" in the colony and even accused him of concealing the truth about the mineral wealth of Louisiana, allegedly in the hope of forming, under his own direction, a new company that would divert to itself the profits to be gained from this wealth.[9]

It seems, though, that La Mothe's indictments were not entirely unfounded. When he criticized the inadequacy of the prices offered by Raujon and advised that, for one buckskin, 30 sols should be paid to Indians "who were allied to the British" and 25 sols to the *voyageurs* from the Illinois country, rather than the 25 and 20 sols, respectively, laid down by the director, he was giving sound advice.[10] In any case, he was providing the Council of the Navy with insight that the comte de Toulouse would need in order to make the financier modify his commercial policy. The missionary Le Maire agreed with La Mothe in deploring Raujon's arbitrary power, and his tendency to fix the company's price lists as he saw fit and even to determine selling prices that exceeded Crozat's instructions.[11] As for Raujon's incompetence, this was attested at the same time by Duclos, who—without questioning the man's personal honesty, as La

---

7. AC, C 13A 4, f. 523, 525, La Mothe, Jan. 2, 1716; f. 568–69, La Mothe, Jan. 31, 1716; f. 573, La Mothe, Feb. 2, 1716; f. 595–97, La Mothe, June 22, 1716.

8. AC, C 13A 4, f. 513, 525, La Mothe, Jan. 2, 1716; AM, B 1 29, f. 434v–35, Proceedings of the Council of the Navy, May, 1718.

9. AE, Mem. & Doc., America, I, f. 279–79v, Crozat (to the Duc de Noailles), Sept. 28, 1716.

10. AC, C 13A 4, f. 523, La Mothe, Jan. 2, 1716.

11. AC, C 13A 4, f. 573, La Mothe, Feb. 2, 1716; BN, FF 12105, f. 19, Le Maire, Mémoire sur la Louisiane, March 1, 1717.

Mothe did, and without having any preconceived hostility toward him—blamed him for "knowing nothing about trade."[12]

Whatever excuses La Mothe might have had, however, his break with the director had the effect of bringing a fresh factor of division into the colony. Personal rivalries assumed a scale unprecedented in Derigoin's time. In those days, when La Mothe was still upholding Crozat's monopoly, he had managed to maintain reasonably trustful relations with its director. By antagonizing Raujon, La Mothe now furnished a new ally to his own long-standing enemies, Bienville and Duclos. Between them and the governor, relations were as strained and ill will as lively as in previous years.[13] But La Mothe also complained of the formation of a "cabal" that united in opposition to him Bienville, Duclos, and the new director of the company, and he accused them of joining forces to block the fulfillment of his orders, engage in commercial operations that violated Crozat's monopoly, and deceive the Crown with impunity.[14]

In reality, the situation was much more confused than that. Bienville and Duclos, who had always opposed Crozat's monopoly and his policy, persisted in their hostility, in spite of everything, and agreement between them and the financier's men could therefore never be either complete or lasting. On several occasions they clashed with Raujon and Le Bart, who ascribed to Duclos' bad keeping of accounts the difficulties experienced by Crozat in obtaining reimbursement of his advances of funds. Bienville complained of Raujon's lack of foresight and the difficulties this caused him during the Natchez campaign. It would seem that they agreed only in opposing La Mothe. The latter did not hesitate to take up the financier's cause when he could thereby harm the director and blame the stagnation of trade mainly upon his management.[15]

12. AM, B 1 9, f. 416–16v, Chastelain, July 22, 1716; f. 424, Duclos, June 3, 1716.

13. AC, F 3 24, f. 79, Mémoire de ce que Richebourg a ordre de Bienville de représenter à Lamothe-Cadillac (comments by La Mothe); AC, C 13A 4, f. 581–82, La Mothe, Feb. 7, 1716; f. 601–602, Observations by La Mothe-Cadillac to the Council of the Navy, June 22, 1716; f. 656–57, Duclos, Jan. 25, 1716.

14. AC, C 13A 4, f. 515–16, 533, La Mothe, Jan. 2, 1716; f. 545–49, 577, La Mothe, Jan. 23, Feb. 7, 1716; AC, F 3 24, f. 74, Mémoire de ce que Richebourg a ordre de Bienville . . . ; BN, FF 12105, f. 20, Le Maire, Mémoire sur la Louisiane, March 1, 1717.

15. AC, C 13A 4, f. 551, La Mothe, Jan. 23, 1716; AM, B 1 9, f. 463–63v, Council of the Navy, Mémoire de Crozat, Oct. 11, 1716; AC, F 3 24, f. 79, Mémoire de ce que Richebourg a ordre de Bienville . . . .

Just as in the past, quarrels among the leaders were reflected in the coteries that formed around La Mothe and Bienville. The *lieutenant de roy* had on his side, generally speaking, the residents of Canadian origin whose "cabal" La Mothe never tired of denouncing, including Captain Chavagne de Richebourg and Lieutenant de La Tour Vitral, who was related to Bienville through his marriage to one of Le Sueur's daughters.[16] Faced with a coalition as powerful as this, containing a number of officers of high rank, the governor, whose unpopularity grew steadily, had but few partisans—Ensign Terrisse de Ternan and Captain François Mandeville, who, according to La Tour, were held "in execration" in the colony on this account.[17] Both men were, in any case, La Mothe's men, and when a dispute, leading to acts of violence, broke out between a protégé of Crozat's who had recently arrived in Louisiana, Benoist de Saint-Clair, and La Mothe's son, Terrisse de Ternan at once joined the fight on the latter's side. The governor used this incident as his excuse to forbid the wearing of weapons "to all commoners, to all of M. Crozat's agents, and to newcomers," gentlemen alone being excepted from the ban. As this ordinance was obviously directed against La Mothe's personal enemies, Crozat brought the matter before the Council of the Navy, calling for justice against those who had wounded his protégé, the nephew of a "comptroller in ordinary of the king's dining table," and for the recall of Terrisse de Ternan, whom he described as an undesirable.[18]

In this deeply divided society, the least personal incident sufficed to provide the opposing factions with an occasion for conflict. Whatever group one looks at, one finds the same animosities, the same petty and futile quarrels. Such quarrels occurred among Crozat's agents and between these agents and the military officers, who were offended by the haughty attitude of the financier's representatives. These disputes were complicated by arguments about precedence that arose in every sphere of collective life—in processions, in sessions of the Conseil Supérieur—and which assumed disproportionate importance in a colony where from the outset the civil and military population had been stubbornly devoted to honoring social distinctions.[19] The

16. Giraud, *History*, I, 275.
17. AC, C 13A 4, f. 520, 533, La Mothe, Jan. 2, 1716; f. 571, 590, La Mothe, Feb. 2, Feb. 7, 1716; AM, B 1 9, f. 324v–25v, La Mothe, Feb. 9, 1716.
18. AM, B 1 9, f. 415–16, Chastelain, July 22, 1716; AC, C 13A 4, f. 384, 417–18, Proceedings of the Council of the Navy, Oct. 9, 10, 1716.
19. AC, C 13A 4, f. 384, Proceedings of the Council of the Navy, Oct. 9, 1716; f. 611–12, Observations of La Mothe-Cadillac to the Council of the Navy, June 22,

missionaries' interference in the private lives of the inhabitants; the agitation this gave rise to when the director, Raujon, who was personally affected, sought to band the settlers together against the curé of Dauphin Island; and the continuing disagreement between the latter and the members of the Conseil Supérieur—all were reminiscent of the worst period of the War of the Spanish Succession.[20]

The situation was perhaps even more serious in 1716, for these dreary quarrels had become so intense that they blocked any possibility of achieving solidarity when danger threatened the colony. Far from dying down, they grew worse at such a time, reducing still further the population's already feeble means of defense. The first Natchez war, an early preface to the tragic events of 1729, actually emphasized the depth and tenacity of the colony's internal antagonisms. La Mothe refused any sort of loyal cooperation with Bienville and showered him with recriminations in the hope of proving his incompetence to the Council of the Navy, while Raujon, who seemed unaware of the danger, provided him with insufficient material aid.

When La Mothe, reversing the policy he had advised at first, called on Bienville at the end of 1715 to proceed, by setting up Fort Rosalie, to subject the Natchez territory to military occupation, he encountered doubts on the part of the *lieutenant de roy*. As we know already, the latter considered it unwise to enter upon a campaign that he knew would be difficult, since he had no more than the forty soldiers, still unfamiliar with the country and its peoples, whom the governor had assigned to him. The force at his disposal included neither a surgeon nor a blacksmith—specialists indispensable for any long-distance expedition—and although La Mothe gave him an interpreter, because Bienville did not know "the languages of the Mississippi country," the governor declined to pay the man any wages.[21] In the face of such obvious ill will, Bienville, to whom La Mothe had in any case given orders that could not be carried out, wondered—

1716; AM, B 1 9, f. 325–25v, La Mothe, Feb. 9, 1716; f. 416–16v, Chastelain, July 22, 1716; f. 417–18, La Mothe, July 23, 1716; AC, B 38, f. 341, to Lépinay, Oct. 28, 1716.

20. AC, C 13A 4, f. 527–29, La Mothe, Jan. 2, 1716; f. 578–80, La Mothe, Feb. 2, 1716; BN, FF 12105, f. 12, Le Maire, Mémoire sur la Louisiane, March 1, 1717.

21. Giraud, *History*, I, 354–55; AC, C 13A 4, f. 567–68, La Mothe, Jan. 31, 1716; f. 764–68, Bienville to Pontchartrain, Jan. 2, 1716; AC, F 3 24, f. 73, Addition to instructions in the king's *mémoire* of Dec. 17, 1714, given by La Mothe to Bienville, Jan. 5, 1716.

and appearances suggest that he was right—if the governor's aim was not to cause him to suffer a defeat that would discredit him with the Court and with the population.[22] Bienville's mistrust of the Natchez, the uncertain attitude toward France which he attributed to them, and above all his fear that La Mothe might have offended the Indians during his recent tour through their villages by failing to perform the ceremony of the peace pipe, all made it necessary, in his view, to take very special security measures.[23]

Bienville's apprehensions were confirmed at the beginning of January, 1716, by news of the murder of four Canadian *voyageurs* whom the Natchez had ambushed on the Mississippi on their way to the Illinois country. The killing had been followed by plundering of the goods the *voyageurs* were carrying. Large-scale thefts had taken place at the same time from Crozat's storehouse in Natchez, and the agent in charge of it, the Sieur de La Loire des Ursins, had fled.[24] Bienville thus found that he had to undertake before anything else a punitive expedition made necessary in the first place by La Mothe's clumsy behavior. And the governor decided, at this very moment, to leave him for the accomplishment of so perilous a task no more than the thirty-four men of Richebourg's company, who would have to face eight hundred Natchez warriors.[25] Yet La Mothe took advantage of Bienville's hesitation to accuse him of wanting, with Raujon's complicity, to evade obeying his order for immediate departure, although preparations for the expedition made some delay inevitable. A considerable number of pirogues had to be assembled, and men found who knew how to maneuver these craft—men other than the young, newly arrived soldiers of Richebourg's company. Bienville had to recruit some Canadians, at substantial expense, and he was in a position to leave Dauphin Island, with most of his force, only on February 15, 1716. Ensign François du Tisné and the agent François Derbanne had

22. AC, C 13A 4, f. 767–68, Bienville to Pontchartrain, Jan. 2, 1716.

23. AC, C 13A 4, f. 765, 775–76, Bienville to Pontchartrain, Jan. 2, Jan. 20, 1716.

24. AC, C 13A 4, f. 775–78, Bienville to Pontchartrain, Jan. 20, 1716; f. 787, 793, Mémoire en forme de journal de ce qui s'est passé dans la première expédition que M. de Bienville fit aux Natchez en 1716 . . . ; AC, F 3 24, f. 74v, Mémoire de ce que Richebourg a ordre de Bienville . . . ; Giraud, *History*, I, 305–306.

25. AC, C 13A 4, f. 676–77, Duclos, June 7, 1716; f. 787, Mémoire en forme de journal . . . ; AC, F 3 24, f. 77v, Mémoire de ce que Richebourg a ordre de Bienville . . . .

preceded him fifteen days earlier, accompanied by a few men and a convoy of provisions.[26]

The operation, which needed to have general goodwill behind it, thus began in an atmosphere of disagreement, and the tension grew worse and worse as the campaign progressed. La Mothe, who before Bienville set out had taken several ill-intentioned measures against him—even putting him under arrest and threatening to "suspend" him on account of his alleged delays—now called him to account with increasingly hate-laden bitterness. Every step Bienville took, every request he addressed to the governor, led to a reprimand from the latter. La Mothe declined to acknowledge that the expedition was in any way successful and reduced the reasons for all its difficulties to the lateness of its departure, for which he held Bienville alone responsible. He even represented Bienville's intention to force the Natchez to make amends for what they had done as being due to a desire to frustrate the realization of any peaceful agreement with these Indians and to start a war that would compel the French to leave their territory. In fact, what he principally blamed Bienville for was acting independently and drawing up his plan of campaign without seeking the governor's opinion. Since La Mothe could not admit that an action carried out independently of him had achieved a result that the absurd flimsiness of Bienville's resources had made it impossible to hope for, he systematically denounced Bienville's entire policy in a series of unbridled commentaries that implicitly asked that the *lieutenant de roy* be recalled.[27]

However, by the time these commentaries became known in France, the dismissal of La Mothe himself had already been decided since the beginning of the year, and they only served to convince the Council of the Navy of the need to take the government of the colony out of this man's hands. His continual recrim-

26. The date of departure is given by Bienville. See AC, F 3 24, f. 74, Mémoire de ce que Richebourg a ordre de Bienville. . . . Bienville says elsewhere that he left on March 15 and arrived among the Tunicas on April 23, but this is disproved by the letter he wrote from the Tunicas' country as early as April 15 (AC, F 3 24, f. 73v, Mémoire de Bienville à Richebourg au fort Saint-Joseph des Tonicas, April 15, 1716). AC, C 13A 4, f. 515–16, 533, La Mothe, Jan. 2, 1716; f. 575–76, La Mothe, Feb. 7, 1716; f. 788, Mémoire en forme de journal . . . ; AM, B 1 9, f. 462v, Mémoire de Crozat, Oct. 11, 1716; AC, F 3 24, f. 74, 74v, 75v, Mémoire de ce que Richebourg a ordre de Bienville . . . .

27. AC, C 13A 4, f. 771, 778–79, Bienville to Pontchartrain, Jan. 2, 20, 1716; AC, F 3 24, f. 73v–79v, Order by Bienville to Richebourg, and Mémoire de ce que Richebourg a ordre de Bienville . . . .

inations had exhausted the patience of the comte de Toulouse. In his correspondence, the governor increasingly scattered blame and criticism over everyone else who held any position of authority in the colony.[28] The Council of the Navy, without rejecting out of hand all of La Mothe's denunciations, and without putting aside the useful suggestions he made from time to time about the need to strengthen the discipline of the garrison, to fortify Dauphin Island, and to increase the colony's stock of munitions in proportion to its defense needs, yet concluded from his endless complaints and passionate invectives that he was no longer able to cope with the responsibility of governing Louisiana. It was not practicable to direct the affairs of a colony when one was surrounded by general enmity. The Natchez events completed the discrediting of La Mothe: the council did not accept his version of what had happened (according to which the massacre of the French resulted from an accidental fire in the Indians' temple), and ignoring his comments, it expressed unreserved approval of Bienville's conduct.[29] The execution of the Natchez who had committed the murders, which Bienville ordered, might have got him into trouble with Pontchartrain, since La Mothe had taken care to emphasize the cruelty of the proceeding, which, he wrote, was contrary to "good faith" and to "the law of nations." But the Council of the Navy did not share the scruples of the secretary of state. The punishment seemed to the council to be appropriate to the offense, and it had no hesitation in taking its stand with Bienville.[30]

The council had too many reasons to be dissatisfied with the governor to refuse to grant Crozat the sanctions he was requesting for his own interested reasons. In recalling La Mothe and Duclos, who, it said, lacked "all the intelligence needed for the exercise of their functions" and who "act in all matters contrary to the Company's views,"[31] the council obeyed both its desire

---

28. AC, C 13A 4, f. 578–82, 589–90, 575–76, La Mothe, Dauphin Island, Feb. 7, 1716; f. 611, Observations of La Mothe-Cadillac to the Council of the Navy, June 22, 1716.

29. AC, C 13A 4, f. 785–86, Mémoire en forme de journal . . . ; C 13A 5, f. 59–59v, Bienville, at Fort Louis, May 10, 1717; AM, B 1 9, f. 278–78v, 279–79v, Proceedings of the Council of the Navy, Aug. 29, 1716; AC, B 38, f. 326v–327, to Bienville, Oct. 28, 1716.

30. AC, F 3 24, f. 76v–77, 79v, Mémoire de ce que Richebourg a ordre de Bienville . . . ; AM, B 1 9, f. 279–79v, Proceedings of the Council of the Navy, Aug. 29, 1716.

31. AC, C 13A 4, f. 75–76, Mémoire sur la colonie de Louisiane conveyed to the Regency Council, Feb. 11, 1716.

to satisfy the financier and a concern to get rid of men whose protracted hostility had spread agitation and confusion in the colony.

Crozat could not contemplate proposing Bienville to succeed La Mothe, because he had too openly denounced the financier's policy and was still somewhat distrusted at Court. The name he put up to the Council of the Navy was that the Sieur de Lépinay (Jean Michiele, Seigneur de Lépinay et de La Longueville), a lieutenant commander who had served in the navy since 1683 and had acquired in Canada some experience of colonial service. The council was all the readier to agree to the proposal because this candidate enjoyed the particular protection of the comte de Toulouse. On March 12, 1716, Lépinay was appointed governor of Louisiana. The comte's favor brought him, a few months later, the Cross of St. Louis.[32] For the post of *ordonnateur*, the Council of the Navy thought first of Martin d'Artaguiette (Jean-Baptiste Martin d'Artaguiette d'Iron), who, after proving himself in Louisiana as a ordinary commissioner during the difficult years of the war, had resumed in France his previous functions as commissioner in charge of the impressment service.[33] However, the post of *ordonnateur* was eventually given, in circumstances unknown to us, to Marc-Antoine Hubert, "commissioner of the navy by His Majesty's commission."[34]

The measure taken against him did not mean absolute disgrace for Duclos, the former *ordonnateur*, who had been on the point of asking to be recalled. Even though Duclos did not receive the home posting he wanted, he was given in 1718 "the place of *commissaire-ordonnateur*" at Cap Français in St. Domingue.[35]

32. AC, C 13A 4, f. 81–82, Proceedings of the Council of the Navy, March 3, 1716; f. 441–42, Council of the Navy, Oct. 20, 1716; f. 809–810, Lépinay, March 10, 1716; f. 867, Lépinay, Nov. 3, 1716; f. 1032, Mémoire sur la colonie de la Louisiane; C 13A 5, f. 269–70, Lépinay, June 13, 1719; AC, B 38, f. 88, to Lépinay, March 3, 1716; AC, F 1A 20, f. 59, Order for payment . . . to La Mothe-Cadillac . . . , May 6, 1718; AE, Mem. & Doc., America, I, f. 280v, Reflections on everything that might best contribute to the establishment of the Mississippi colony.

33. AC, F 1A 19, f. 71–71v, General Staff of Louisiana, 1716; AM, C 2 55, f. 12, gives the stages in Martin d'Artaguiette's career. *Cf.* Giraud, *History*, I, 126ff. AC, A 22, f. 63, List of the directors of the Company of the West, Aug. 4, 1718.

34. The clue to this title is the reduction of the *offices* of commissioners of the navy to mere *commissions* at the beginning of the Regency. AC, C 13A 4, f. 711–12, Duclos, June 26, 1716; AC, F 1A 19, f. 78v, List of the expenditure that the king . . . orders . . . for Louisiana, Oct. 1, 1716; F 1A 20, f. 51, Order for payment to Duclos, Feb. 3, 1718.

35. AC, C 13A 4, f. 719–21, Duclos, June 26, 1716; AC, B 40, f. 419v, 422v, to Chateaumorant and Mithon, July–August, 1718.

For La Mothe, however, the disgrace was absolute. Crozat's brigantine brought the news of his dismissal to the colony in May or June, 1716. La Mothe lost no time in conveying his resentment to the Council of the Navy and begging it to take account of his long service, his family responsibilities, and his poverty.[36] But the assignment to Bienville in October, 1716, of provisional command over the colony, the arrival of Lépinay, and the king's order to return to France with all his family left La Mothe no choice. The disgraced governor had to hand over his powers to his successor forthwith. To add to La Mothe's humiliation, Lépinay ordered that all his property in the colony be confiscated. He arrived at La Rochelle on the *Paon* at the end of August, 1717, ending ingloriously, at the age of sixty, a long colonial career in which blunders and inconsistencies overshadowed his few concrete achievements.[37]

Even worse disappointments awaited La Mothe when he set foot on the soil of France. Punished with five months' imprisonment in the Bastille for hostile remarks he made about Louisiana and the Company of the West, he found himself on leaving prison in March, 1718, in a difficult situation, without "employment" or "pension." This was his excuse for not paying the wages and gratuities that were owed to his secretary, Olivier, who had served him for more than four years in Louisiana. Substantial arrears of his salary as governor were due to La Mothe himself. His son, who had been condemned to the same period of imprisonment in the Bastille, had just been stripped of his lieutenancy in the colony's forces, although he had not yet received his salary as ensign in the infantry for the years 1712 and 1713.[38]

However, La Mothe's disgrace did not last long. It may be that the views expressed by the *ordonnateur* Hubert, essentially a eulogy of La Mothe's "goodwill" and courage that Hubert sent back to the Council of the Navy soon after his arrival in Louisi-

36. AM, B 1 9, f. 418v–19, La Mothe, July 24, 1716.
37. AM, B 1 21, f. 15–15v, La Mothe, Aug. 29, 1717; B 1 29, f. 248v, Requests by La Mothe to the Council of the Navy, March 11, 1718; AC, C 13C 2, f. 150v, Du Sault, on board the *Paon*, Aug. 29, 1717; AC, B 38, f. 326v–27, to La Mothe, to Bienville, Oct. 28, 1716; AC, F 1A 20, f. 49, Order for payment to La Mothe-Cadillac, May 6, 1718.
38. AC, C 13A 5, f. 113–13v, 116, Petitions from La Mothe and his son to the Council of the Navy, March 11, 1718; C 13A 4, f. 567, La Mothe, Jan. 31, 1716; AM, B 1 21, f. 15–15v, La Mothe, La Rochelle, Aug. 29, 1717; f. 286v–87, Petition from Sr Olivier, Council of the Navy, Nov. 29, 1717; BN, FF 22709, f. 264v, Annals, Dangeau collection, Oct. 2, 1717.

ana, together with continuing curiosity concerning the mineral riches of the colony and the belief that La Mothe might be able to provide useful information on this subject drawn from his own experience, contributed to soften the attitude of the comte de Toulouse.[39] The *ordonnateur*'s testimony, which was corroborated by the Canadian Bourdon,[40] showed that La Mothe had been more active during his stay in the Illinois country than had been supposed. His prospecting, though superficial, had revealed the existence not far from the Saline River of a lead deposit that was given, and kept, the name of "Monsieur de La Mothe's mine."[41]

La Mothe's requests were, in any case, given favorable attention, and the Regent accorded him all the satisfaction he could have wished. His back pay, which dated from 1710, was paid to him in full, and a gratuity even assigned to him, "in consideration of his services" and to make up for the gap in his income between the date of the nomination of his successor and that of his return to France. Furthermore, when La Mothe pointed out that governors were always housed at the king's expense, the Regent reimbursed him the rent of the house he had leased in Louisiana from the Sieur de Chateaugué.[42] More generously still, the Regent agreed to continue payment of La Mothe's salary as governor beyond the day of his arrival at La Rochelle, without stating, moreover, when this payment should cease: we know that it was still being paid in 1718.[43]

Emboldened by this return to favor, La Mothe strove now to recover for himself the colony of Detroit, the basis for which he had personally laid. He declared that he had owned there considerable property of which he had been despoiled by the ill will of his successors, and he called on the Regent to right the wrongs he had suffered.

Once more the duc d'Orléans granted La Mothe's petition. After obtaining information from the governor of New France, the Regent decided in 1719 to recognize La Mothe as owner of

39. AC, C 13A 5, f. 134, Hubert, Mémoire sur la colonie de la Louisiane, October, 1717; C 13C 2, f. 159, Bienville, June 12, 1718; AC, B 40, f. 98, to M. de la Motte, Feb. 13, 1718; f. 119v., to M. de La Motte, April 22, 1718.
40. See Ch. IV, p. 40, above.
41. AC, G 1 465, Des Ursins, Détail du voyage des mines, July 10, 1719; Mémoire sur le mines, sent by M. de La Chaise, May 20, 1724.
42. AC, F 1A 20, f. 46–48, 49, Orders for payment to La Mothe-Cadillac, April 9, May 6, 1718; AM, B 1 29, f. 248v, 272v–73v, 397–97v, 434, 437, Petitions from La Mothe-Cadillac, March 11, April 5, May, 1718.
43. AC, B 40, f. 181v, to M. Le Couturier, Sept. 30, 1718.

the lands in Detroit that he had caused to be cleared and to authorize him to levy from the plots he had leased out the dues that Pontchartrain had allowed him to claim. The Regent also ordered that La Mothe be given back the cattle and goods of every kind that had been in his possession when he left for Louisiana. But La Mothe then, pushing his claims still further, asked to be given full concession of Detroit, which would be transformed into a countship or marquisate, with power of high, middle, and low justice, fishing and hunting rights, and a monopoly of trading activity. These benefits, he said, Pontchartrain had meant to grant him, and they would compensate him for the years he had been dispossessed. Naturally, his son would take command of the new *seigneurie*.[44]

To these demands, however (which La Mothe maintained until his death in 1730), the Regent refused to agree. On the recommendation of Governor Vaudreuil, a decision of the Council of State (May, 1722) settled all La Mothe's claims, more or less, on the same basis as in 1719. He was confirmed in the benefits provided for in the Regent's ruling, with this difference alone—that he was granted, to cover the expenses he had incurred and the losses he had suffered, a final and total indemnity of 2,000 livres. The council also rejected his son's claim to the command of Detroit.[45] Although the sum granted fell far short of the expenditure that La Mothe had undertaken in the colony,[46] the Crown held thereafter to the decision made in 1722. And La Mothe actually gained nothing from that decision, since he was never able to return to Detroit or to get himself represented there.[47] After his death his sons sought vainly to assert their father's rights, but their resources were modest: the governorship of Castelsarrasin, which La Mothe had purchased with his "savings," had been abolished, and all that was left to his family was a small life annuity, itself reduced to one-third of its value.[48] The

---

44. AC, C 11E 15, f. 86–87, 92–93, 97–98, 107–108, 152, 154v–55, 156–56v, La Mothe to the comte de Toulouse and the Council of the Navy, 1718, 1719, 1720; f. 156–56v, Warrant of concession to Sr de La Mothe of the lands . . . , July 23, 1720; f. 204–206, Petition from La Mothe's son to Mgr de Rouillé, April 17, 1752; AC, F 3 10, f. 169v–70v, to Vaudreuil and Bégon, July 24, 1720.

45. AC, C 11E 15, f. 125–28v, Vaudreuil and Bégon, Quebec, Nov. 14, 1719; f. 190–91v, Refutation of La Mothe-Cadillac's claims upon Detroit, January, 1727; f. 198–200, Comte de Maurepas to Joseph de La Mothe-Cadillac, February, 1732.

46. AC, C 11E 15, f. 125–28v, Vaudreuil and Bégon, Quebec, Nov. 14, 1719; AC, F 1A 21, f. 280, Decision of the Council of the Navy, June 14, 1720.

47. AC, C 11E 15, f. 196–97, Joseph de La Mothe-Cadillac to the comte de Maurepas, February, 1732.

48. *Ibid.*

sons asked permission to go to Detroit "to settle there," or else to be granted a pension sufficient for them "to subsist for the rest of their lives," in return for which they offered to renounce all their father's claims. They succeeded only in obtaining confirmation of the decision of 1722; thirty years later their heirs were still vainly appealing for this to be put into effect.[49]

2. The New Personalities

With a view to ensuring that the men whom the Council of the Navy had placed in charge of the colony would follow a policy more in accord with his interests, Crozat indirectly gave them membership in his company by offering them participation in the profits of his trading activity. He assigned to Lépinay, as governor, the most advantageous conditions: a fixed commission of 2,000 livres a year for two years, a charge of 2 percent on produce exported from the colony, and permission to bring from France, free of charge, six casks of personal effects, and to buy "at current prices" a substantial quantity of flour and brandy for the needs of his household.[50]

Less highly favored, the *ordonnateur* Hubert was to have a charge of 2 percent on "merchandise produced in the country," and the Crown would allow him to bring in five casks of provisions on the *Ludlow*. Possibly, as Bienville alleged, Crozat also permitted Hubert to bring in a certain quantity of goods on his own ships, but this is not certain.[51] We have no exact information regarding the benefits allocated to the captain in command of the garrison, Sieur Artus. According to Bienville, they were more than his own share, which was a mere 1 percent of the value of such local merchandise "as shall go out by the St. Louis [*i.e.*, Mississippi] River."[52] Altogether, with the exception of Lépinay's benefits, the concessions granted by Crozat were modest and are of no interest except insofar as they show that he was now slightly more generous than previously, and a little less resistant to any idea of compromise.

But the most original measure was linking the functions of the *ordonnateur* with a power to inspect the financier's affairs.

---

49. *Ibid.*; f. 198–200, Maurepas to Joseph de la Mothe-Cadillac, February, 1732; f. 202–203, Joseph de La Mothe-Cadillac to Maurepas, June, 1745; f. 206–206v, Joseph de La Mothe-Cadillac to Mgr de Rouillé, April 17, 1752.

50. AC, F 3 241, f. 125–26, Lépinay and Crozat, agreement of April 4, 1716.

51. AC, C 13A 5, f. 57, Hubert, Dauphin Island, Oct. 26, 1717; f. 64v–65, Bienville, May 10, 1717; AC, B 38, f. 175, to Beauharnais, Sept. 14, 1716.

52. AC, C 13A 5, f. 57, Hubert, Dauphin Island, Oct. 26, 1717; f. 64v–65, Bienville, May 10, 1717.

Crozat hoped in this way to prevent any reappearance of the opposition he had encountered from Duclos, to ensure full enjoyment of his monopoly, and to rebut the allegation that he entrusted his interests to incompetents. Henceforth, "just as is the case with all nations in the Indies," Crozat's affairs would be managed by a council made up of his principal agents and presided over by the *ordonnateur* Hubert. This Council of Trade would work out the new price policy.[53] The financier's staff still included a director and a comptroller, Raujon and Le Bart, and an attorney, Louis Guérin, but it was increased in 1716 by the addition of a storekeeper and "keeper of the books," a man named Roger, and a clerk, Chastelain, who had formerly been employed as a royal scrivener in the Rochefort workshops. The latter, having tried without success to step into Duclos' shoes, was now trying to make a career under the financier's aegis. Like Benoist de Saint-Clair, he was a nephew of Sieur Benoist, the "comptroller of the king's dining table," and he aimed at quick promotion; being disappointed in the job he was given, he did not wait long before he went back to France.[54] After this, François Derbanne combined the functions of "clerk of the king's and the financier's storehouses." Above him, Sieur Poirier was still, as before, the king's storekeeper on Dauphin Island.[55]

While Crozat expected that this new way of managing his affairs, together with the change in the leading personnel, would mean that he could now enforce his monopoly without any hindrance, the Council of the Navy hoped that these innovations would put an end to the regrettable disputes of previous years. The council asked Lépinay to settle the current conflicts, to wind up the incident between La Mothe's son and Benoist de Saint-Clair, to look into the truth of the complaints laid against La Mothe by Lieutenant de La Tour, and to decide in a spirit of equity the various quarrels about precedence. The new governor

53. AM, B 1 9, f. 424, Duclos, June 3, 1716 (observations of the Council of the Navy); f. 338, Duclos, Jan. 27, 1716.
54. AM, B 1 8, f. 164, Council of the Navy, March 7, 1716, request by Sr Chastelain; B 1 9, f. 416–16v, Chastelain, Dauphin Island, July 22, 1716; f. 417–18, La Mothe, July 23, 1716; AC, C 13A 4, f. 417–18, Representations by Crozat to the Council of the Navy, Oct. 10, 1716; C 13A 5, f. 34, Invoice of goods loaded by order of M. Crozat, July 18, 1716; f. 44, Hubert, June 2, 1717; AC, F 3 241, f. 128, Raguet, October, 1717; Parish register of Mobile, Ala., Dec. 20, 1717.
55. AC, F 3 24, f. 79v–80, Copy of the articles of the letter from Sr Derbanne, clerk of the king's and the company's storehouses . . . , April 27, 1716; AC, C 13A 5, f. 44, Hubert, June 2, 1717. The king's storekeeper on Dauphin Island was doubtless Christophe Poirier (AC, F 3 241, f. 139).

was to follow a policy of conciliation that might result in calming internal dissensions, the underlying causes of which should have been eliminated by the recall of La Mothe and Duclos and the direct association of the new *ordonnateur* with Crozat's commercial activity.[56]

It seemed to the Council of the Navy no longer possible to continue the provisional judicial regime under which the colony had lived until then. Convinced that Louisiana would henceforth receive regular contingents of immigrants and was destined soon to become "established," the council considered it necessary to give a stable foundation to the Conseil Supérieur of the colony, which had originally been regarded as something provisional.[57] Consequently, an edict of September 10, 1716, made the Conseil Supérieur "perpetual and irrevocable, as in the other colonies." The task of deciding where it should sit was left to the governor and the *ordonnateur*, who had the choice between Dauphin Island and Fort Louis at Mobile. The Conseil's composition and functions remained as they had been defined in the Letters Patent of 1712. At its head were the governor and the intendant of New France, who "shall preside *ex officio*." In their absence, however, the Conseil would actually consist of the seven members who ranked after them: the "special governor" of Louisiana, a first councillor (in the person of the *commissaire-ordonnateur*), the *lieutenant de roy*, two councillors, an attorney general, and a registrar. Only the last-mentioned two would lack the right to take the chair, which would be exercised *ex officio* by the members preceding them. The first councillor, or in his absence the more senior of the two others, would, like the "first presidents" of the courts in France, conduct the voting and promulgate the decisions taken.[58]

The Conseil Supérieur remained primarily a civil and criminal tribunal with responsibility to give judgment free of charge and without appeal, according to the terms of the Custom of Paris (which the Crown ordered should be strictly applied in the over-

56. AC, C 13A 4, f. 417–18, Proceedings of the Council of the Navy, Oct. 10, 1716; f. 901, Hubert, Nov. 23, 1716; f. 963, 966, Draft of *mémoire* from the king to Lépinay and Hubert, October, 1716; B 1 9, f. 324v–25, La Mothe, Feb. 9, 1716; f. 415–16, Chastelain, July 22, 1716; AC, B 38, f. 314–17v, Mémoire du Roy . . . au Sr de Lépinay, Oct. 20, 1716; f. 327–28, to Lépinay and Hubert, Oct. 28, 1716.

57. AM, B 1 9, f. 350–50v, Proceedings of the Council of the Navy, Sept. 2, 1716; Giraud, *History*, I, 303–304.

58. AC, A 22, f. 19–20v, Edict for the establishment of a Conseil Supérieur in Louisiana, September, 1716.

seas provinces), in all cases that might arise in the colony.[59] The *ordonnateur* was still to be the judge of first instance, and as in previous years, he was forbidden to issue any definitive judgment, so that the population should not be subjected to "two degrees of jurisdiction." Following a principle that he sought to establish in all the colonies, the king intended, in fact, that "cases" be "dealt with summarily," and to prevent the introduction of "pettifogging" into Louisiana, he recommended that no lawyers be allowed to enter the colony, except such as desired "to settle there."[60]

From now on Louisiana was in line, so far as its main administrative machinery was concerned, with the Crown's other possessions. Its demographic backwardness and the sparseness of its settlements account for the still elementary character of its organization. All judicial activity was concentrated in this modest Conseil Supérieur, which had barely emerged from its trial period and whose "first president" did not even reside in the country. Unlike Cape Breton Island—although that colony had been opened for colonization only a few years earlier—Louisiana had no bailiff's jurisdiction nor any sort of administrative division, and it was still an exception to the rule providing for the establishment in the American colonies of offices and officers of the Admiralty.[61] With the coming of Lépinay, however, Louisiana emerged from this provisional situation, which reflected its uncertain origins, and began to participate more fully in the life of the French empire. The Conseil Supérieur henceforth received and registered all the royal ordinances and declarations that applied to the colonies as a whole. This was the first step toward the establishment of that principle of uniformity to which the Council of the Navy wished to subject the administration of all parts of the empire.

To what extent did these changes produce for the colony the

---

59. AC, B 39, f. 203–205, Decision to annul in deeds and concession contracts drawn up in Canada those clauses which are contrary to the Custom of Paris . . . , May, 1717; AC, F 3 82, f. 91v, Bénard, Mémoire concernant l'état présent des colonies du Vent de l'Amerique . . . , Sept. 13, 1723.

60. AC, A 22, f. 19–20v, Edict for the establishment of a Conseil Supérieur in Louisiana, September, 1716; AM, B 1 9, f. 140–40v, Draft of instruction to Sr de La Varenne, August, 1716; f. 351–52v, Draft of edict on the Conseil Supérieur of Louisiana; AC, B 38, f. 303–304, Mémoire du Roy . . . au Sr Hubert, Oct. 20, 1716; f. 315, Mémoire du Roy . . . au Sr de Lépinay, Oct. 20, 1716; f. 366, to the marquis de Chateaumorant, July 13, 1716.

61. AC, B 39, f. 136v, Council of the Navy to Attorney-General, Paris, June 21, 1717; BN, FF 11332, f. 78, Observation concerning the regulation about the admiralty's representation in the colonies.

effects that Crozat and the Council of the Navy hoped to achieve? On the commercial plane, there could be no immediate result, as has been said, and there was no time for a really new formula to come into force. We know nothing of the activity of the Council of Trade in the few months between Lépinay's arrival and the cession of Louisiana to the Company of the West, and we cannot say if it began a change that could have seriously altered the price regime. It does not appear, though, that this new cog in the system ensured the desired cooperation between the members of the government and the financier's representatives. To judge by remarks in the correspondence of Hubert and Lépinay, Crozat's agents did as they pleased, without troubling much about what the *ordonnateur* wanted.[62]

As for the calming effect that the Council expected would result from the installation of new leaders, this did not last long. In this sphere, everything depended on the personal attitudes of the governor and the *ordonnateur*. The division of powers remained more or less what it had been under their predecessors. Following the established practice in Canada, St. Domingue, and the Windward Islands, "everything that relates to the dignity of command and military matters" fell to the governor, while the administration of justice, together with "money, provisions, munitions, and merchandise," were the *ordonnateur*'s business, since there was no intendant.[63] But since both officers had to allot concessions of land and to exercise the police function, and since expenditure ordered by Hubert had to be paid out with the governor's "consent," the two were often obliged to act jointly—more often than La Mothe and Duclos had had to, because the Council of the Navy increased Lépinay's prerogatives, giving him power to undertake "extraordinary expenditures" and conferring on him the right to oversee the management of the hospital and royal storehouses and the feeding of the troops, responsibilities that consequently allowed him to intervene in spheres that, in principle, were the *ordonnateur*'s affair.[64] The council also gave Lépinay the right to dispose abso-

---

62. AC, C 13A 5, f. 27v, Lépinay and Hubert, Dauphin Island, May 30, 1717.
63. AC, C 13A 4, f. 964–65, Draft of *mémoire* to Lépinay and Hubert, October, 1716; AC, B 38, f. 378ff., to Chateaumorant and Mithon, Aug. 25, 1716; f. 455–55v, Instructions to Sr de Ricouart, Aug. 25, 1716; AC, F 3 9, f. 374v–75, Mémoire pour servir d'instruction aux Srs de Vaudreuil et Bégon, June 15, 1716; Giraud, *History*, I, 303.
64. AC, C 13A 4, f. 964–65, Draft of *mémoire* to Lépinay and Hubert, October, 1716; AC, B 38, f. 341, to Lépinay, Oct. 28, 1716; AM, B 1 9, f. 466, Proceedings of the Council of the Navy, Oct. 11, 1716.

lutely of the funds provided "for gifts to the savages," a right that his predecessor had always shared with Bienville. Accordingly, the council invited Lépinay to reside at Mobile, which was nearer the territory occupied by the Indians, whereas Hubert was to set up his headquarters on Dauphin Island.[65]

This strengthening of the governor's authority and the latitude allowed him to encroach on the role of the *ordonnateur* blurred the frontiers of their respective powers and risked giving rise to fresh occasions of conflict between them. Inevitably, the prerogatives granted to Lépinay (which were due perhaps to the favor of the comte de Toulouse) evoked among those around him a discontent that was all the sharper because these prerogatives were accompanied by privileged material conditions. Lépinay received considerable benefits from Crozat, and the Council of the Navy, in agreeing to pay him almost all of his arrears of salary in silver, had done him a favor that few others enjoyed. Hubert was paid in state notes only, and he found himself in a worse position relative to the governor than his predecessor had been, because the gap between his salary of 1,500 livres and Lépinay's of 4,000 livres—which, increased by Crozat's commission, amounted to an annual income of 6,000 livres—was greater than that between the salaries of Duclos and La Mothe.[66]

Bienville especially felt injured by the governor's many privileges. Added to the humiliation of still not having obtained the Cross of St. Louis, like Lépinay—which, it seemed to Bienville, unjustly increased the new governor's prestige among the Indians and the Spaniards—was the disappointment of being admitted to only an insignificant share of Crozat's trade.[67] Bienville was also deeply upset by the decision of the Council of the Navy to reduce the area of command that had been given him in 1715. He was no longer to have command of the Mississippi and of the valleys of its tributaries "from the Wabash to the sea," which had been assigned to him in the instructions that came by the *Dauphine*. The council reserved for him only the control of a territory as yet undefined—perhaps the zone of the Wabash (the lower

---

65. AC, C 13A 4, f. 967, 972, 982, Draft of *mémoire* from the king to Lépinay and Hubert, October, 1716.

66. AC, B 38, f. 53v–54, to M. Le Couturier, Sept. 20, 1716; f. 323, to Lépinay, Oct. 24, 1716; AC, C 13A 4, f. 825–27, Lépinay, Rochefort, July 11, 1716; AM, B 1 9, f. 3888v. Proceedings of the Council of the Navy, Sept. 21, 1716; AC, F 1A 19, f. 75, Order to the Treasurer of the Navy . . . , Sept. 22, 1716; f. 78v–79, List of expenditure that the king . . . orders . . . for . . . Louisiana, Oct. 1, 1716.

67. AC, C 13A 5, f. 61v–62, 64–65, Bienville, at Fort Louis, May 10, 1717.

Ohio Valley) with Tennessee, or the Yazoo country, or the Red River—and this gave Bienville a feeling of painful diminution, especially since his services to the Crown and his long experience of the country provided no justification for this loss of authority.[68]

In fact, Bienville was in no way the object of any hostility on the part of the Council of the Navy. In appointing him to an inland command, the council was acting on its conviction that he was the only man qualified to assume it, owing both to his influence among the natives and to his popularity with the Canadians, on whose cooperation any distant and difficult enterprise was dependent. This was also Crozat's view, and the fact that the financier had himself suggested, despite his grievances against Bienville, that he assume interim command of the colony until Lépinay arrived, together with the council's immediate agreement to this proposal, shows that there was no enmity toward him.[69] A few months later, Bienville received at last the promotion he had wanted for several years, but for the moment, comparing his position with the honors showered upon Lépinay, he was discontented at being relegated to a subordinate position that did not bring him the consideration he thought he deserved, or even the means of living, since his salary (1,200 livres) could not cover the costs entailed by the many moves that an inland command would make necessary.[70] His brother Chateaugué, whom the Council of the Navy had passed over when choosing a commander in chief of the troops (a position that he coveted as the most senior captain in the colony) in favor of an officer from France, shared Bienville's disappointment.[71] And it was certainly true that by increasing to an excessive degree the powers of the governor, the council gave his subordinates, especially those who had to their credit longer service in Louisiana, legitimate reasons for dissatisfaction.

To soothe the feelings of jealousy that surrounded him, Lépinay would have needed a great deal of tact and moderation. Unfortunately, because he knew he enjoyed high protection, he

---

68. *Ibid.*, f. 62v–64; AC, B 38, f. 288v–89, to Bienville, Feb. 15, 1716; f. 326v–27, to Bienville, Oct. 28, 1716. On the inland posts, see p. 152f. below.
69. AC, C 13A 4, f. 306, Proceedings of the Council of the Navy, Sept. 8, 1716; f. 502–506, Mémoire de Crozat, 1716; f. 806, Mémoire en forme de journal . . . ; AC, C 13C 4, f. 47, Mémoire sur les services de M. de Bienville [1724?]; AC, B 38, f. 288v–89, to Bienville, Feb. 15, 1716; f. 326v–27, to Bienville, Oct. 28, 1716.
70. AC, C 13A 5, f. 62–65, Bienville, May 10, 1717.
71. AM, B 1 9, f. 552–54, Chateaugué, July 17, 1716.

showed no consideration whatsoever. Increasing his prerogatives still further and exceeding the king's instructions, he took to himself the right to dispose absolutely of public funds and to direct alone the policing of the colony. On the pretext of eliminating "pettifogging" and preventing useless lawsuits, he also took charge of the judiciary, ignoring Hubert's remonstrances.[72]

Thus the traditional conflict between the governor and the *ordonnateur* reappeared—with this difference, that they revived the practice, which had been abandoned by La Mothe and Duclos, of reporting to the council on the general affairs of the country in a joint letter, and that the antagonism between them lacked the extreme character of the earlier period, because Hubert, being less headstrong than his predecessor, submitted and left the field free to Lépinay.[73] In his own reports to the Council of the Navy, however, Hubert gave free expression to his discontent and to his disapproval of the governor's conduct. He criticized Lépinay's "haughtiness" and arrogance, and the harshness he showed toward the population, and he accused him of adopting in relation to the Indians a policy of parsimony that earned their contempt and compromised the cause of France, while at the same time he tended to increase the colony's expenditures without troubling that he might be paying out more than was to be had.[74] Bienville was not slow to back up the *ordonnateur*'s charges. He too denounced Lépinay's haughty attitude, and he condemned unreservedly the mistakes and pettiness of his policy toward the natives, which revealed an elementary ignorance of the outlook of primitive peoples.[75]

If it had continued, Lépinay's reign would undoubtedly have revived the dissensions of the preceding years. This man was no more fitted by nature than La Mothe to make himself popular, and the inhabitants consequently accepted with difficulty the orders he tried to get them to obey.[76] A rapprochement was already beginning between Bienville and Hubert. The latter, who refrained from inquiring into the past record of the *lieutenant de roy* as he had been instructed to do, presented Bienville as the person most competent to run the colony, and he suggested to the Council of the Navy, in an obvious spirit of hostility to Lépi-

72. AC, C 13A 5, f. 50–50v, 51v, 54–54v, Hubert, Dauphin Island, Oct. 26, 1717.
73. *Ibid.*, f. 50, 51v, 54v–56.
74. *Ibid.*, f. 54v–56.
75. AC, C 13A 5, f. 66, Bienville to Hubert, Sept. 19, 1717.
76. AC, C 13A 5, f. 49v, 54v–55, Hubert, Dauphin Island, Oct. 26, 1717.

nay, that Louisiana be divided into two "special" governorates, one of which should be given to Bienville. So that the operation might not entail any extra expense, part of the salary of the governor then in office should be allotted to him.[77] Already, too, the population was beginning to split into opposing groups, which recalled the cliques of La Mothe's time. The soldiers, dissatisfied with their material conditions, blamed the *ordonnateur* for the inadequacy of their resources and openly declaimed against him, and Lépinay refrained from giving Hubert any support. At the same time, we observe in Hubert's correspondence a certain stiffening of attitude toward the governor's discretionary procedures. When Lépinay, committing funds that were not provided for in the budget, required that several houses be purchased with a view to establishing a hospital on Dauphin Island and enlarging his own residence and the royal storehouses, Hubert agreed in order to avoid conflict, but he informed the Council of the Navy that he took no responsibility for this expenditure. He also refused, risking the hostility of the officers whom Lépinay wished to favor, to make any change in the schedule for the distribution of provisions that had been laid down by the Crown. On this point he kept to the letter of the instructions he had been given, which specified that no "consumption" take place "except on his orders." Finally, the doubts he expressed regarding the governor's honesty and the allusions to his "scandalous" way of life that appear in his correspondence are significant of a development that seemed to promise a rapid reawakening of all the petty squabbling of previous years.[78]

That outcome was avoided only by the entry on the scene of the Company of the West and the recall of Lépinay. He had spent only a few months in Louisiana and had brought the colony none of the benefits that might have been hoped from the dismissal of La Mothe.

Hubert himself had little opportunity to show what he was worth during that short period. He seems to have displayed conscientiousness and exactitude in his work, but he was overshadowed by the governor. Moreover, the Council of the Navy had burdened him with a task beyond his powers—the liquidation of the innumerable notes and orders-to-pay that the commandant and the successive commissioners had issued during the war and the following years to meet expenses in excess of the

77. *Ibid.*, f. 56–56v.
78. *Ibid.*, f. 42v, 51v, 52–52v, 54–54v; AC, C 13A 4, f. 964, Draft of *mémoire* from the king to Lépinay and Hubert, October, 1716.

funds provided by the Crown to cover officers' salaries, the pay of sailors and soldiers, the wages of workmen in their employ, the cost of foodstuffs and other supplies obtained from the inhabitants, and even goods purchased in Vera Cruz.[79] This practice had resulted in an accumulation of claims to payment, some going back to 1706, the bearers of which now demanded settlement from the treasurers of the navy. Crozat, too, had issued notes of the same kind when he was without funds in the colony. However, the treasurers refused to honor these orders-to-pay because the funds for the earlier financial years were exhausted and because these documents, not having been drawn up in accordance with the proper legal forms, were valueless in their eyes. Consequently, Jean-Baptiste Baudreau Graveline failed to realize an order-to-pay of 2,500 livres that Bienville had given him in 1710 as payment for the ship the *Marguerite*, which was requisitioned for the colony's needs, and there were officers who had over a period of eight years received as salary only notes that they were now unable to validate.[80]

The task confronting the *ordonnateurs* was thus to "make an inventory" of all these notes, to "put them into proper form," and to determine, year by year, the exact amount of the debt they represented, so that the Council of Finance could arrange for the additional credits needed for its liquidation to be effected.[81] It was a complex and difficult operation. In Canada, liquidation of the card money issued during the war presented a similar problem, but there was less confusion there than in Louisiana, the accounts were not so disordered, and the Crown could, by calling on Law's bank for financial aid, look forward to a system of gradual resorption of the cards that were paralyzing the commerce of New France.[82] In Louisiana, Duclos was unable

79. Giraud, *History*, I, 291–92.
80. AC, C 13A 5, f. 158–59, Bienville, June 12, 1718; f. 257–58v, Proceedings of the Council of the Navy, March 25, 1719; f. 333v, Proceedings of the Council of Trade assembled at Dauphin Island, Sept. 6, 1719; AM, B 1 8, f. 446–46v, Proceedings of the Council of the Navy, April 28, 1716; B 1 9, f. 330–32, Duclos, Sept. 8, 1715. On the *Marguerite*, see Giraud, *History*, I, 173–74.
81. AM, B 1 9, f. 331–32v, Proceedings of the Council of the Navy, Sept. 1, 1716.
82. AC, B 38, f. 200v–201, to Vaudreuil and Bégon, June 16, 1716; B 39, f. 242–42v, Mémoire du roi à Vaudreuil et Bégon, July 6, 1717; B 40, f. 93v, to M. Law, Jan. 23, 1718; f. 198v, to M. Law, Nov. 6, 1718; f. 210v, to M. Law, Dec. 18, 1718; AM, B 1 19, f. 151–51v, Proceedings of the Council, Feb. 26, 1717; B 1 20, f. 355v–56, Draft of *mémoire* to Vaudreuil and Bégon, July, 1717; B 1 29, f. 80v–81, 176v–77, Proceedings of the Council, Jan. 18, Feb. 15, 1718; B 1 30, f. 172v–73, 382–82v, Proceedings of the Council, July 12–Nov. 1, 1718; AM, B 247, f. 10, duc de Noailles to comte de Toulouse, May 17, 1717.

to complete a task requiring the consultation of account books that had been kept only irregularly and of multifarious documents, many of which had been mislaid.[83]

The Crown therefore instructed Hubert to take over the task and to send to France all the claims to payment that were "in suspense," so that they might be converted into "state paper money," in the same way as the debts contracted in the home country before the death of Louis XIV.[84] Unfortunately, Hubert had no better success than his predecessor. The latter had asked in vain to be supplied with staff familiar with the accounting methods of the Ministry of Marine—one or two royal scriveners and especially a clerk from the treasurers of the navy capable of establishing the authenticity of the "receipts" and "putting all the expenditure in proper form." Hubert was treated hardly better than Duclos, since, although the Council of the Navy promised him the assistance of one of the treasurer's clerks, all he actually got was a royal scrivener, Sieur Couturier, who was of no use to him.[85]

Consequently, the *ordonnateur* was able to accomplish no more than some preliminary work, clearing up the muddle in a mass of "petty expenses" for which the years given did not correspond to the years of the funds to which they had been related. When Hubert applied himself to dispatching the "receipts," he could not find the vouchers that would have enabled him to put them in acceptable form, and fearing that they would be "disallowed" by the Chambre des Comptes, he suspended his activity until he should receive instructions from the Council of the Navy.[86] This was how matters stood when the Company of the West took over management of the colony. The persons who held notes and orders-to-pay were still loaded down with

83. AC, C 13A 4, f. 781, Bienville, Jan. 20, 1716; f. 899–900, Hubert, Nov. 23, 1716.

84. AC, B 38, f. 271v, to Costebelle and Soubras, May 5, 1716; f. 301–301v, to Lépinay and Hubert, Oct. 19, 1716; f. 519v–20, to d'Orvilliers and d'Albon, May 12, 1716.

85. AC, C 13A 4, f. 729–35, 753–57, Duclos, July 6, July 16, 1716; f. 781, Bienville, Jan. 20, 1716; C 13A 5, f. 290, Hubert, Oct. 4, 1719; AC, B 38, f. 181, to Beauharnais, Oct. 13, 1716; AM, B 1 9, f. 330–31, Duclos, Sept. 8, 1715; f. 413v–14, Proceedings of the Council, Oct. 9, 1716; AC, F 1A 19, f. 280–82, Draft of expenditure for Louisiana for 1717. There is an allusion to the presence of a treasurers' clerk in Louisiana (AM, B 1 23, f. 191v, Proceedings of the Council, Nov. 14, 1717), but Hubert does not mention such a person; he merely complains of the uselessness of Couturier (AC, C 13A 5, f. 29, Lépinay and Hubert, May 30, 1717; f. 52–53, Hubert, Oct. 26, 1717; f. 290, Hubert, Oct. 4, 1719).

86. AC, C 13A 5, f. 53, Hubert, Oct. 26, 1717; f. 158–59, Bienville, June 12, 1718; f. 192–92v, Hubert, June 10, 1718; f. 289–90, Hubert, Oct. 4, 1719.

paper that was effectively valueless and payment for which they were waiting in vain. Although Bienville and Chateaugué, who had a correspondent in Paris to look after their interests, obtained partial satisfaction, most of these people had grounds for fearing that the delay in settlement would end with repudiation of the Crown's debts.[87]

The stabilization of the Conseil Supérieur made practically no difference to the life of the colony. As in all the new and poorly inhabited possessions, the problem of recruitment was hard to solve. Even in St. Domingue the governor found himself obliged, for lack of competent persons, to improvise his "officers of justice," and the difficulty was even greater in Louisiana, where there were few educated people and the population had no means of obtaining education.[88] Hubert's views on the personnel of the Conseil Supérieur, though more measured in expression, were in fact just as unfavorable as La Mothe's. Like Le Maire, he regretted that it was necessary to retain as councillors the surgeon–medical officer Clairin Deslauriers and the former "miller's boy" La Fresnière, both of whom, being virtually illiterate, were not suited to "the dignity of a Conseil Supérieur." He was unable to fill the bench of judges.[89] Appointment of a registrar of the council, in the person of the scrivener Couturier, might have meant some slight progress if only the man had possessed the abilities required. However, though invested with the functions of registrar, notary for Louisiana, and storekeeper at Mobile, Couturier was without qualification for any of these jobs. Hitherto, La Mothe and Duclos, for lack of an officially appointed registrar, had employed in that post Jean-Baptiste Raguet, who also acted as notary and did his work to everyone's satisfaction.[90] Consequently, the arrival of Couturier in March,

---

87. AC, C 13A 5, f. 257–58, Proceedings of the Council of the Navy, March 25, 1719; AM, B 1 8, f. 446–46v, Petition from the wife of Clairin Deslauriers, Council of April 28, 1716; B1 23, f. 191v–92, Proceedings of the Council, Nov. 14, 1717; f. 205v–206, Proceedings of the Council, Nov. 28, 1717.

88. AC, B 38, f. 509v, Mémoire du Roy . . . à M. Dorvilliers, May 4, 1716; AC, C 9a 13, Chateaumorant and Mithon, March 19, 1717.

89. AC, C 13A 4, f. 611, Observations by La Mothe-Cadillac to the Council of the Navy, June 22, 1716; C 13A 5, f. 51, Hubert, Oct. 26, 1717; AM, B 1 9, f. 360–61, Request by Sr Lesterier, royal attorney for the jurisdiction of St. Laurent, council of Sept. 8, 1716; BN, FF 12105, f. 12, Le Maire, Mémoire sur la Louisiane, March 1, 1717. Nicolas Chauvin, Sr de La Fresnière, was a native of Montreal. AC, F 1A 11, f. 219v, List of all persons making up the garrison and others who are in Louisiana, Sept. 14, 1714; Parish register of Mobile, Ala., Jan. 17, 1718.

90. AC, C 13A 5, f. 51–52, Hubert, Oct. 26, 1717; f. 190v, Hubert, June 10, 1718; AC, F 3 241, f. 143–44, Raguet, Fort Louis, in Louisiana, Oct. 10, 1717; Parish register of Mobile, Ala., Nov. 12, 1716; Giraud, *History*, I, 304.

1717, would have meant taking a step backward from the previous arrangement if Lépinay, taking into consideration the scattered pattern of settlement, had not soon after this authorized Raguet to operate as before in the capacities of notary and registrar to the Conseil Supérieur. It appears that Raguet placed himself in Dauphin Island, leaving to Couturier, who retained the privilege of his commission, the built-up area of Mobile—visiting that place himself when there was a meeting there of the Conseil Supérieur, of which he was also the court usher. In August, 1717, Michel Rossard was sent by Lépinay to "perform the work of notary and registrar to the council" on Dauphin Island, jointly with Raguet.[91]

Only then did notarial records begin to be kept in Louisiana. That same year, the Council of the Navy, responding to a proposal by the attorney general of the Conseil Supérieur of New France, decided to introduce into the colonies the regulations that applied in France regarding the keeping of records of the deeds and contracts signed before a notary. A royal declaration, the text of which was sent to the governor of Louisiana, ordered that an inventory be made of existing deeds and that henceforth notarial records be deposited in the registry, whereas previously notaries or their heirs had been allowed to dispose of these records as they chose (August–September, 1717).[92]

We lack evidence of the precise role that the Conseil Supérieur played under Lépinay's rule, but it appears that it did less than under La Mothe. In those days it had been able to involve itself in the administration of the colony, participating in the settlement of the innumerable problems of detail that arose in the functioning of all the nascent groupings of population. In 1714 and 1715 the Conseil had issued ordinances concerning the standardization of weights and measures, the trade in alcoholic drink (the sale of which it prohibited "during divine service"), and the maintenance of streets, which it had made the responsibility of house owners, who were ordered to fill the ditches and "burn the brush" that hindered traffic in front of the

---

91. AC, F 3 241, f. 138–39, Deed drawn up by the notary Couturier, collated by Raguet in his capacity as notary in Dauphin Island, Oct. 28, 1717; f. 142, Commission given by Lépinay to Jean-Baptiste Raguet, June 21, 1717; f. 147, Ordinance by Lépinay, Aug. 22, 1717; f. 148, Extract from an inventory made in Louisiana by Sr Couturier, Aug. 22, 1717.

92. AC, C 11A 37, f. 217–22, Representations by Sr Collet, attorney-general of the Conseil Supérieur of Canada, Council of the Navy, June 5, 1717; AC, A 23, f. 10–12, Declaration on the keeping of notarial records in the French colonies, Aug. 2, 1717; AC, B 39, f. 134, to Joly de Fleury, attorney-general, June 9, 1717; AM, B 3 247, f. 409–15, Joly de Fleury to the Council of the Navy, July 12, 1717.

"grounds" around their residences. It had even drawn up a series of regulations concerning the control of slaves.[93] The Conseil Supérieur had thus operated alongside the governor and the *ordonnateur*, without prejudice to their right to promulgate such ordinances on the same subjects as they might consider necessary.[94] The inhabitants had been allowed to contribute their opinions, being convened by La Mothe and Duclos to assemble "in the priests' house" to be informed of the regulations affecting them and to make their own suggestions.[95]

Lépinay's arrival put an end to all that. In the contemporary documents we find no further trace of consultation with the public or of any administrative role for the Conseil Supérieur. The ordinances that have come down to us bear the signature of the governor alone. Lépinay ruled personally on the pay and feeding of the troops, on the policing of the colony, and on the sale of food stuffs,[96] so that the Conseil Supérieur now possessed only judicial functions. And there is no proof that it actually performed these. The governor required the Conseil to hold its meetings in his house, and according to Hubert, who as first magistrate should have presided, Lépinay himself gave judgment in cases both civil and criminal, instead of contenting himself with the "place of honor" normally assigned to "provincial governors" in the higher courts of the realm.[97] The silence of the documents, which show no sign of any activity by the Conseil Supérieur, seems to confirm the testimony of the *ordonnateur*.

After the many years of dissension through which it had passed, the colony might have known under this regime of discretionary authority the unity of direction it had hitherto lacked. For that to be so, however, a personality different from Lépinay's would have been needed, and also a system of government not based upon the principle of division of powers. By taking to himself, without possessing any experience of the colony's problems, an authority that exceeded his instructions, Lépinay could

---

93. AC, A 23, f. 5–6, Regulations made by the Conseil Supérieur of Louisiana concerning the slaves, Nov. 12, 1714; Ordinance and regulation by the Conseil Supérieur, April 1, 1715. *Cf.* pp. 130–31 below.
94. AC, A 23, f. 6–6v, Ordinance by La Mothe and Duclos, Aug. 23, 1716.
95. *Ibid.*
96. AC, F 3 241, f. 141–41v, Ordinances by Lépinay, April 30, May 24, 1717; f. 142, Commission given to Jean-Baptiste Raguet, June 21, 1717; f. 145–68, Decisions by Lépinay, July 27, Nov. 7, 1717.
97. AC, C 13A 5, f. 50–50v, Hubert, Oct. 26, 1717.

only revive the antagonisms of the past and condemn himself to suffer a defeat that became obvious at the end of the summer of 1717.

At least the military policy of the Council of the Navy and its efforts to increase the colony's means of defense did result during these years of transition in more solid achievements. Although not meeting all of Crozat's wishes, these measures freed the settlements on the Mississippi from the state of weakness that had left them at the mercy of the slightest act of aggression.

VIII   The Defense of the Colony

DESPITE THE REINFORCEMENTS that arrived in 1715, the colony's garrison was inadequate for its defense. There was as yet no militia in Louisiana, and the population was too small for any prospect of organizing one in the near future.[1] The only military forces in the country consisted of four companies, the actual size of which was gradually being reduced by deaths and especially by desertions. From 150 or 160 men at the end of August, 1715, their numbers fell to 137 at the beginning of 1716, and soon after that they were down to 126, of whom 8 or 10, "old or infirm," could no longer effectively serve.[2] The officers were, however, almost up to establishment. Although a few officers, such as *Major* de Boisbriant and Captain François Mandeville, returned to France in 1716, they soon came back to the colony—some after handing over to the Council of the Navy the mail they had brought, or after settling their personal affairs, others after obtaining the promotion they sought. Pailloux de Barbezan, a former Protestant from the Cevennes who had served since 1714, in the absence of Sieur Charles d'Auteuil de Monceaux, as *aide-major* of Louisiana (but who was in fact merely an ensign in the colonial troops), came back from France at the end of 1716 with the commission that until then he had not held.[3]

    1. AC, B 38, f. 314v, Mémoire du Roy pour servir d'instruction au Sr de Lépinay, Oct. 20, 1716.
    2. AC, D 2C 51, f. 9, Muster of the detached naval companies, end of August, 1715; f. 17–17v, Extract from the muster of the detached naval companies maintained in Louisiana, January, 1716; AC, B 38, f. 314v, Mémoire du Roy pour servir d'instruction au Sr de Lépinay, Oct. 20, 1716; AM, B 1 9, f. 419–19v, La Mothe and Duclos, July 15, 1716; Giraud, *History*, I, 269.
    3. AM, B 1 9, f. 388, Petition from Sr Pailloux, Council of the Navy, Sept, 21, 1716; f. 414, Petition from Captain Mandeville, Council of Oct. 9, 1716; AC, B 38, f. 341v, to M. de Lépinay, Oct. 28, 1716. *Cf.* Giraud, *History*, I, 274–76. D'Auteuil de Monceaux appears in the payrolls as assistant *major* from 1706 to 1713. Not having resumed his position, he was replaced by Pailloux de Barbezan from 1714 onward (AC, F 1A 13, f. 113–14, Roll of *majors* and petty-officers . . . showing salaries and pay due to them at the end of 1706; F 1A 14, f. 58–61, List of expenditure that the king orders . . . , 1707; F 1A 15, f. 63–64, List of expenditure for the

However, this stability of the complement of officers did not make up for the weakness of the garrison, and at the beginning of 1716 the Council of the Navy, having studied Crozat's proposals, decided to double the colony's defense forces by raising four additional companies. Instead of detaching these troops, as the financier suggested, from the companies of naval infantry maintained in France, or recruiting them, like the companies of 1715, from among the civilian population, the council ordered that they be formed from six companies of the land-service army, which were, to this end, transferred to the navy. To receive them, the council dispatched to the Ile d'Oléron Captains de Lause de Villemarets and Joachim de Gauvry, assisted by an *aide-major* and a naval commissioner.[4] This operation failed to produce the body of 200 men the Council of the Navy had aimed at, since many of the soldiers were incapable of serving in Louisiana, either because of their age or their state of health. To the 114 men obtained from the companies mentioned above, there had to be added a certain number of persons enrolled at Oléron, Paris, and Rochefort, recruits who had been destined for other colonies, and also deserters from various French regiments.[5]

The new companies made up in this way were not eager to go to Louisiana. Although some young men of good family had requested to join them, and although the council had recommended that men who showed "absolute repugnance to going" to the Mississippi should not be coerced, there were among them too many elements who were leaving France from necessity—deserters and persons who had enlisted out of poverty—for there not to be some malcontents in the companies.[6] And the

---

year 1708; F 1A 16, f. 106–110, List of expenditure for the year 1710; F 1A 18, f. 100–102, 136–37, List of payments ordered for Louisiana, 1713, 1714; on Pailloux, see AC, C 13A 7, f. 22, De La Chaise, New Orleans, Sept. 6, 1723).

4. AC, B 38, f. 92v, to Beauharnais, March 20, 1716; f. 109v, to Beauharnais, April 28, 1716; f. 289v–90v, Mémoire du Conseil de Marine aux Srs de Lause et Gauvry, March 20, 1716; AM, B 1 8, f. 374v, Beauharnais, Rochefort, April 21, 1716; B 1 9, f. 9, Proceedings of the Council of the Navy, July 7, 1716.

5. AC, B 38, f. 93, to Beauharnais, March 20, 1716; f. 117, to La Gallisonnière, May 16, 1716; f. 126v–27, to Beauharnais, May 28, 1716; f. 128v–29v, to La Gallisonnière, May 28, 1716; f. 174, 180–80v, to Beauharnais, Sept. 14, Oct. 10, 1716; AM, B 1 8, f. 528v–30, Beauharnais, April 30, 1716; f. 608, La Gallissonnière, June 2, 1716; f. 614v–15, Beauharnais, June 9, 1716; AC, C 13A 4, f. 307, Crozat to the Council of the Navy, Sept. 8, 1716; C 13A 5, f. 36, L'Epinay, May 10, 1717; AM, B 1 9, f. 358, Beauharnais, Sept. 1, 1716.

6. AC, B 38, f. 93–93v, 110, 119v, to Beauharnais, March 20, April 28, May 19, 1716; f. 122, to La Gallissonnière, May 19, 1716; AM, B 1 9, f. 129v, Lépinay, Aug. 6, 1716.

delay—which was Crozat's fault—in issuing their pay, given the pitiful state of most of the recruits set down on the Ile d'Oléron without "shoes or shirts," soon gave rise to irritation. Several desertions took place in the weeks before the ships were ready, and in order to prevent more, the intendant of Rochefort even put off issuing clothes to the men until the eve of embarkation. But for the intervention of the Council of the Navy, which, helped by the intendant Beauharnais, succeeded in providing some of the pay that was due, a mutiny would have broken out.[7]

However, the soldiers' departure took place without any incident. The men seemed to have "goodwill enough," and although Louisiana was not very popular with them, they approached it in a better state of mind than the recruits of 1715. They were in better material conditions, too, since their clothing had been renewed and they had received for the crossing the hammocks and blankets that the council prescribed should be issued to troops going to the colonies.[8]

The weak spot was recruiting the workmen whom the Council of the Navy, applying a rule that it meant to extend to all troops raised for colonial service, had ordered to be included in every company, as in the previous year.[9] The additional payments of 3 to 6 livres that the council granted these men were no more likely than in 1715 to attract skilled workers, especially since the first payment had to be devoted to purchasing the tools they would need. In general, moreover, good workmen did not join the army, and if many such arrived at Rochefort intending to go to Louisiana, they had in mind their private purposes, with no idea of enrolling in the army.[10] Consequently, the officers experienced the same difficulty as in 1715 in assembling the

---

7. AM, B 1 8, f. 528v–30, Beauharnais, April 30, 1716; f. 562–63, Complaints by Srs de Lause and Gauveret, Council of May 19, 1716; B 1 9, f. 155v–56, Beauharnais, Aug. 15, 1716; f. 257v, La Gallissonnière, Aug. 18, 1716; f. 324, La Gallissonnière, Aug. 25, 1716; f. 414v, De Lauze, Sept. 18, 1716; f. 481, La Gallissonnière, Oct. 10, 1716; f. 495–95v, Beauharnais, Oct. 20, 1716; f. 558–58v, Hubert, November, 1716.

8. AM, B 1 9, f. 558–58v, Hubert, November, 1716; f. 644, La Gallissonnière, Dec. 19, 1716; B 1 19, f. 4, M. de Montholon, Dec. 20, 1716.

9. AC, A 22, f. 17v–18, Ordinance for an additional four companies for Louisiana, Marly, March 1, 1716; AC, B 38, f. 80v–81, 106, 181, to Beauharnais, Jan. 26, April 22, Oct. 13, 1716; f. 297–97v, to Hubert, Oct. 13, 1716; f. 527, to Le Febvre d'Albon, May 12, 1716; B 39, f. 7, to La Gallissonnière, Jan. 25, 1717; f. 67, to Beauharnais, July 5, 1717; Giraud, *History*, I, 267–68.

10. AM, B 1 8, f. 560–60v, L'Epinay, May 9, 1716; B 1 9, f. 559, Hubert, November, 1716; AC, B 38, f. 80v–81, to Beauharnais, Jan. 26, 1716.

complement of eleven workmen per company, with the range of skills required by the Council of the Navy. Their efforts resulted only in forming a mediocre collection of men, less than half as many as the council ordered and far from including all the special skills required. There was no cartwright, no armorer, no stonecutter, and only four masons instead of twelve. Only joiners, carpenters, and edged-toolmakers were included in the group, and most of these were apprentices who would not be of much use.[11]

The medical personnel were no more satisfactory. The Council of the Navy was unable to recruit a surgeon for the inland posts. The best it could do was to attach to the new companies four "assistant surgeons" of dubious capacity, to contribute their mediocre help to the only surgeon employed in the colony.[12]

Officers, on the other hand, were easily found. The sentiment in favor of the Mississippi that had begun to appear at the end of Louis XIV's reign continued for the same reasons in subsequent years.[13] We again observe among young noblemen and increasingly among retired army officers (who made a case out of their many years of service or their family responsibilities) the desire to be given commissions in the Louisiana companies. These requests, often backed by influential persons, were all the more numerous because the Regent decided to allow the officers concerned to keep the ranks and rates of pay they had obtained in France, out of consideration of the hardships of colonial service, and to permit them, should their health or personal affairs recall them to the home country, to recover the benefits they had previously enjoyed there.[14] The commands of three of the new companies were thus obtained, through the "protection" of Crozat, Duché, and Rouillé du Coudray, by Sieur de Bonnille, a retired captain of the Blaisois regiment who had twenty years of

11. AM, B 1 8, f. 528–30, Beauharnais, April 30, 1716; B 1 9, f. 403, Beauharnais, Sept. 22, 1716; f. 545–45v, Lépinay, Nov. 10, 1716; f. 558–58v, Hubert, November, 1716; AE, Mem. & Doc., America, I, f. 208v, Bienville, June 10, 1718.

12. AE, Mem. & Doc., America, I, f. 208v, Bienville, June 10, 1718; AM, B 1 8, f. 636–36v, Proceedings of the Council of the Navy, June 16, 1716; B 1 9, f. 38–38v, Beauharnais, July 11, 1716; f. 268, Proceedings of the Council, Aug. 29, 1716; f. 479v, Lépinay, Oct. 9, 1716; AC, C 13A 5, f. 45v, Hubert, June 2, 1717.

13. Giraud, History, I, 274–76.

14. AM, B 1 8, f. 285–86, Requests for the Louisiana companies, Council of the Navy, March 3, 1716; f. 447v, 450v, 459v, Requests for the companies, Council of April 28 and May 17, 1716; AC, B 38, f. 41v–42, to the duc de Guiche, June 16, 1716; AC, D 2C 51, f. 11–11v, Requests from various officers for the Louisiana companies, March 3, 1716.

commissioned service and had won the Cross of St. Louis at the Siege of Barcelona; de Lause de Villemarets, a retired officer of the Poitou regiment; and Joachim de Gauvry, a former infantry lieutenant detached to serve as *major* of the Castle of Landskron. The fourth company was assigned, together with overall command of the troops, to Sieur Artus, engineer in ordinary to the king, who was to have in Louisiana the title of engineer-in-chief and director of fortifications.[15]

Crozat would have preferred for this latter post the Chevalier Jean-Charles de Follart, a former captain of infantry who was at that time commanding the citadel of Bourbourg and was regarded as one of the best of the royal engineers, equally qualified to direct a mining enterprise and to choose the location of new posts and decide on the fortifications appropriate to them. But Follart declined the offers of Crozat and the Regent, despite the privileged conditions promised to him, and his refusal entailed, apparently, that of his brother as well, to whom the Council of the Navy had wished to give command of a company. This was a matter of regret for the colony: Artus, who stepped into the job, did not have the same service behind him and was not so distinguished.[16]

As for the ensignships, which were even more in demand than the captaincies, the council decided to reserve these for midshipmen and to reject all "outsiders," whatever their record of service or nobility of birth.[17] The difficult circumstances of many of them and the assurance they were given of regular promotion up to "the highest positions in the colony" stimulated much rivalry among these young gentlemen, who often came from military or naval families, and some of whom had already won distinction in privateering activity. The Marquis de La Galissonnière was thus able to put forward, in the *département* of Rochefort alone, a list of ten candidates for three vacant ensign-

---

15. AM, B 1 8, f. 285–86, 580v–81, Positions vacant in the Louisiana companies, Proceedings of the Council, March 3, May 25, 1716; B 1 9, f. 426, Services of Srs De Bonnille, de Lause, and Gauvry, Council of Oct. 9, 1716; AC, D 2C 51, f. 11, Requests for the Louisiana companies, March 3, 1716; AC, B 38, f. 57, to Crozat, Oct. 26, 1716; AC, C 13 A 4, f. 467–68, Services of Sr de Bonnille, Council of Nov. 18, 1716; AC, F 3 241, f. 138, Deed drawn up by the notary Couturier, April 28, 1717.

16. AC, F 1A 19, f. 71–71v, General staff of Louisiana, 1716; AM, B 1 8, f. 580v–81, Positions vacant in Louisiana, Council of May 25, 1716; AC, C 13A 4, f. 502–504, Mémoire de Crozat, 1716; AC, D 2C 51, f. 11v–12, 13. Proposals for Louisiana, Council of March 3 and 9, 1716.

17. AM, B 1 8, f. 207v, La Gallissonnière, March 19, 1716; AM, B 2 245 (I), f. 108v, to La Gallissonnière, March 14, 1716.

ships; they were all under his own patronage or under that of the intendant Champigny, or Jérôme Bignon, the provost of the merchants, or the marquis de Rouvroy, or the comte d'Evreux. The Council of the Navy decided in favor of the Chevalier de Saint-Julien, who was related to Champigny; of François Descoublan de Gillan, who was recommended by La Galissonnière; and of the Chevalier de Tusseau and Du Mouchel de Villainville, who were nephews respectively of Commodore du Magnou and the *ordonnateur* Hubert. Finally, at the request of Sieur d'Ibaignette, the council appointed the Chevalier d'Artaguiette d'Itouralde, brother of Martin d'Artaguiette, and Vaucher de La Tardière, who enlisted as a cadet in the new companies, was promised an ensignship upon the first vacancy.[18]

In the allotment of lieutenancies, it was experience in colonial life, and especially direct experience in France's American possessions, that decided the choices made by the Council of the Navy. The council called forward two ensigns from the Canadian forces, Sieur Etienne Rocbert de La Morandière and Chevalier de La Longueville, both of whom were used to the demands of the primitive milieu, while the latter wished to join in Louisiana his uncle, Governor Lépinay.[19] Similarly, the council accepted the request of Bernard Diron d'Artaguiette, who could refer to his five years of activity in the colony, where, under the administration of his elder brother, the commissioner Martin d'Artaguiette d'Iron, he had, despite his youth, served as ensign in the local companies and had even taken part in expeditions "against the savages." The council added to his functions as lieutenant those of draftsman, so it evidently expected that he would contribute to the achievement of the fortification work that was needed in Louisiana.[20]

---

18. AC, B 38, f. 116–16v, 130v, to La Gallissonnière, May 16, June 9, 1716; f. 345, to L'Epinay, Nov. 21, 1716; AM, B 1 8, f. 289, 580v–81, 604, 649–50, Proceedings of the Council of the Navy, March 3, May 25, June 7, June 16, 1716; B 1 9, f. 81v, Proceedings of the Council, July 28, 1716; AC, D 2C 51, f. 13, 15v–16, Proposals for the Louisiana companies; Parish register of Mobile, Ala., Aug. 27, Sept. 18, 1717; AC, G 1 465, Declaration by Mme de Lignac regarding Abbé de Resseguier's concession, 1734.

19. AC, C 11A 36, f. 91, Vaudreuil, Nov. 2, 1716; C 11A 37, f. 346, Vaudreuil, April 20, 1717.

20. AC, B 38, f. 128, to La Gallissonnière, May 28, 1716; AC, F 1A 19, f. 78v, List of the expenditure that the king . . . orders . . . for Louisiana, Oct. 1, 1716; f. 280–82, Draft of expenditure for Louisiana in 1717; AC, D 2C 51, f. 11, Requests for the Louisiana companies, March 3, 1716; Giraud, *History*, I, 126,126n81, 214, 214n7. The service records of the three d'Artaguiettes are given in Laffilard's index, AM (C² 55) and AC.

The Council of the Navy was thus endeavoring to put together a competent body of men whose experience would bring support to the officers who had served in the colony for several years. Only Lieutenant Hersent, who was a son of the provost of the merchants at Crépy and had been accepted at the request of Crozat and Duché, was without any background of life in the colonies.[21] The presence among these new recruits of a number of gentlemen would strengthen the noble element already present in Louisiana society and would inevitably intensify those prejudices concerning rank and birth that had made themselves felt there from the outset.

The delay in payment of their salaries certainly caused much discontent among these officers during the months that passed before the ships were ready to set out for Louisiana.[22] However, none of them defected, and the companies left France with the complement of officers ordered by the Council of the Navy. Owing to the overloading of the ships, only three of the companies embarked in 1716 on the *Ludlow* and the *Paon*. Bonnille's company remained on the Ile d'Oléron awaiting the departure of the vessel that Crozat proposed to provide the following year.[23] For the moment, then, Louisiana had seven companies stationed at Dauphin Island, Mobile, and the inland posts. The forces at Dauphin Island were responsible for protecting the coast and for cooperating in action ordered by the Crown against the pirates of the islands and the Gulf of Mexico.[24]

At the same time as it increased the military forces in Louisiana, the Council of the Navy, following the general principles of its colonial policy, took care to provide the country with the fortifications needed for its defense. The fact that it chose the engineer Artus as commander in chief of the troops and attached to him as aides Bajot and Diron d'Artaguiette in the capacities of subengineer and draftsman, respectively, shows how important they considered this matter.[25] Nothing had so far been done

---

21. AC, C 13A 4, f. 167, Proceedings of the Council of the Navy, Aug. 17, 1716; AC, D 2C 51, f. 13, Proposals for Louisiana, March 9, 1716; f. 19–19v, the Company of the West to the Council of the Navy.

22. AM, B 1 9, f. 414v, De Lauze, Sept. 18, 1716; f. 544, Proceedings of the Council, Nov. 18, 1716.

23. AC, C 13A 4, f. 887–89, L'Epinay, Dec. 1, 1716; C 13A 5, f. 83, Mémoire sur la Louisiane, 1717.

24. AC, C 13A 4, f. 967, 972–73, Draft of *mémoire* from the king to Lépinay and Hubert, October, 1716; AC, B 38, f. 347v–48, to L'Epinay, July 15, 1716.

25. AC, C 13A 4, f. 968, Draft of *mémoire* . . . ; AC, F 1A 19, f. 280–82, Draft of expenditure for Louisiana in 1717.

about fortifications in the colony. At Mobile there was only a fort made of "cedar stakes," without any earthworks, and Dauphin Island had no defense system beyond a surrounding wall of the same kind, begun at the end of 1715, which passed irregularly around its little built-up area.[26] Consequently, the Council of the Navy agreed with La Mothe and Crozat that these elementary structures must be abandoned and stone substituted for wood, starting with Dauphin Island, where there was nothing to guard the approach to the colony.[27] Instructions to this effect had already been given to the engineer Bajot, and he, before leaving France in 1715, had proposed that a fort with a pentagonal wall be built on the island to contain the storehouses belonging to the Crown and the company, together with the hospital, the chapel, and the lodgings of the officers and workmen. This plan was not carried out, so the council returned in 1716 to the classical concept of a fort with four bastions, the modest dimensions of which—100 or 150 fathoms round—would be appropriate to the small size of the built-up area. It also prescribed that the entrance to this fort be protected by a trench and a battery.[28] The stone needed to build the fort, which had to be brought, with the soldiers' help, from a place six leagues distance, would be transported in vessels crewed by the men who operated the colony's ferryboat, under the orders of two longboat masters whom the intendant Beauharnais had just hired at Rochefort. The first works would be paid for at piece rates, this being the principle that the council, despite the contrary view of Crozat and Duclos, recommended for application in Louisiana as in the other colonies.[29]

26. Giraud, *History*, I, 285–86; AC, C 13A 4, f. 389–91, Observations by Crozat, Council of the Navy, Oct. 9, 1716; f. 597–99, Observations by La Mothe-Cadillac to the Council of the Navy, June 22, 1716.

27. AC, C 13A 4, f. 597–99, 609–610, Observations by La Mothe-Cadillac to the Council of the Navy, June 22, 1716; AC, B 38, f. 324–24v, Mémoire du Conseil de marine au Sr Artus, Oct. 26, 1716.

28. AC, F 3 241, f. 113–13v, Mémoire du Roy au Srs de La Mothe-Cadillac et Duclos, Dec. 27, 1715; AC, Fortifications records Louisiana, 131, Distribution of lodgings in the fort on Dauphin Island, the plan of which has been sent from France, 1715.

29. AC, C 13A 4, f. 597–99, Observations from La Mothe-Cadillac to the Council of the Navy, June 22, 1716; f. 663, Draft of the expenditure which Duclos considers essential for maintaining the colony, June 5, 1716; AC, B 38, f. 174v, to Beauharnais; f. 305, Mémoire . . . au Sr Hubert, Oct. 20, 1716; f. 324–25, Mémoire du Conseil de marine au Sr Artus, Oct. 26, 1716; f. 346v, to L'Epinay, Nov. 30, 1716; AM, B 1 9, f. 465, Mémoire de Crozat au Conseil de marine, Oct. 11, 1716; AC, F 3 241, f. 114v–16, Mémoire du Roy à La Mothe-Cadillac et Duclos,

Since building a stone fort presupposed a more exact knowledge of the topography of Dauphin Island, Artus was under orders to produce surveys of this territory that would enable the Council of the Navy to decide on a final plan. Meanwhile, it would be enough for Artus to select the location and surround it with a trench, and he was to confine himself, in the case of such buildings as were necessary, to using the technique customary in the country.[30] It would in any case have been impossible for him to act otherwise, given the small number and poor quality of the companies' workmen and the inadequacy of the funds available for fortification work. These funds had not only not been calculated to provide for masonry but were also partly absorbed by the cost of maintaining the colony's boats and by purchases of cannon, ammunition, and other articles.[31] The council does not seem, above all, to have appreciated the complexity of the task, the obstacle created by the sandy nature of the soil, and the difficulty that would be encountered in cutting the stone on the spot. Le Maire suggested that the stones be prepared in France and that they be used only for the angles of the fort, the spaces between to be filled with mortar and bricks made in the colony—Crozat having sent out in 1715 the materials needed for constructing a "furnace for baking brick."[32] Nor did the Council of the Navy have a precise notion of the instability of the harbor of Dauphin Island. When the harbor became blocked in 1717 the *ordonnateur* decided that it was pointless to pursue the plan to build a masonry fort. It seemed to him that it would now be sufficient to ensure by means of a "fort of stakes" an elementary degree of security for Dauphin Island, which occupied a strategic position at the entry to the Mobile River. This idea eventually prevailed. A timber fort was erected, "surrounded by pinewood stakes," probably in the last months of 1717 or at the beginning of 1718. It appears in the "list of buildings erected on land on

---

Dec. 27, 1715; AC, C 13A 4, f. 985, Draft of *mémoire* from the king to Lépinay and Hubert, October, 1716.

30. AC, B 38, f. 325–25v, Mémoire du Conseil au Sr Artus, Oct. 26, 1716; f. 346v, to L'Epinay, Nov. 30, 1716; AM, B 1 9, f. 545v, Lépinay, Nov. 10, 1716.

31. AC, C 13A 5, f. 30–30v, L'Epinay and Hubert, May 30, 1717. Duclos estimated at 250,000 livres the cost of a masonry fort (C 13A 4, f. 699–703, Duclos, June 24, 1716).

32. AC, C 13A 4, f. 1021, Mémoire de Crozat [December, 1715 ?]; BN, FF 12105, f. 21.

Dauphin Island" that was handed over on March 1, 1718, to the Company of the West.³³

When Crozat's regime came to its end, what had been achieved in practice did not amount to much. According to Hubert, Artus was completely taken up with his responsibilities as commander and neglected his duties as engineer. The flat-bottomed lighters that were available for transporting stone confronted only with difficulty the waters of Mobile Bay, which the violence of hurricanes made "as dangerous as the sea." And, although the subengineer Bajot had drawn a plan of Dauphin Island, the only defensive measure undertaken there had been the "entrenching" of a battery around the harbor. The Mobile settlement had no protection but its old fort of four bastions, which now enclosed a guardhouse, a storehouse, a powder magazine, and a small prison. Thanks to what Crozat and the Council of the Navy had sent out, the artillery of Fort Louis and Dauphin Island consisted of about fifty pieces of various calibers, served by two gunners. At the end of 1717, however, many of these weapons were unserviceable, and the battery on Dauphin Island, badly maintained, soon ceased to be of any use. When Charles Legac arrived in 1718, it was "in ruins."³⁴

In the sphere of fortifications as in many others, these years of transition are of mainly theoretical interest. Ideas were put forward that were to show the way for Crozat's successors, but the financier's resignation and the prolonged period of uncer-

33. See p. 137–39 below. AC, C 13A 4, f. 597–99, Observations by La Mothe-Cadillac to the Council of the Navy, June 22, 1716; C 13A 5, f. 46, Hubert, Oct. 26, 1716; f. 182, General inventory of all the effects . . . which have been handed over . . . to the Company of the West, March 1, 1718; C 13C 2, f. 155–56, Le Maire, Mémoire sur la Louisiane, 1718; C 13C 1, f. 82v–83, Hubert, n.d.; Giraud, *History*, I, 63–65, 285–86.

34. AC, C 13C 1, f. 82–82v, 83 bis, Hubert, n.d.; C 13A 4, f. 986, Draft of *mémoire* from the king to Lépinay and Hubert, October 1716; C 13A 5, f. 54, Hubert, Oct. 26, 1717; f. 139, Hubert, Mémoire sur la colonie de la Louisiane, October, 1717; f. 180–80v, 182v, General inventory of all the effects . . . , March 1, 1718; f. 205, List of the guns in the province of Louisiana, July 6, 1718; AM, B 1 8, f. 634–34v, List of consignments for despatch to Louisiana, Council of the Navy, June 16, 1716; B 1 9, f. 478v, Beauharnais, Oct. 10, 1716; f. 517v–19, Lépinay, Oct. 31, 1716; AC, B 38, f. 140, 177, to Beauharnais, June 23, Sept. 30, 1716; f. 311, Mémoire au Roy pour servir d'instruction au Sr de L'Epinay, Oct. 20, 1716; AE, Mem. & Doc., America, I, f. 82, Charles Legac, Etat dans lequel a été trouvée la colonie de la Louisiane le 25 août 1718; BN, FF 12105, f. 12, Le Maire, Mémoire sur la Louisiane, March 1, 1717.

tainty that this initiated in January, 1717, prevented their application for the time being.

The reinforcement of the garrison provided only an imperfect solution to the problem of defense. This measure would have been fully effective only if it had been accompanied by a number of steps calculated to improve the soldiers' living conditions. Actually, the accommodation problem was made worse by the increase in the numbers of the troops. The barracks on Dauphin Island and at Mobile were in a poor state and too small to contain the new recruits, and the few houses that Lépinay ordered to be purchased were not big enough to meet their needs. The inhabitants, who themselves mostly lived in crowded conditions, could offer no solution. The opening of a hospital on Dauphin Island henceforth saved the sick from the long journey to Fort Louis, which often lasted four days. In both places, however, the hospital was only a primitive structure of "stakes in mud," where for lack of funds the soldiers found neither the expensive food nor the medicines that they needed.[35]

The problem of the men's pay was no less serious. Officially, salaries remained as small as in the past—9 livres a month, which after deductions for food and clothing left the soldier with a monthly "balance" of 25 to 30 sols. Pay was issued at that rate to the new companies when the ships were ready to embark.[36] But in fact, in a colony where the cost of living was so high, this rule could not be respected. On the one hand, the men were still being fed at a cost that was higher than the deduction of pay they suffered, and they managed to increase their income by selling part of their ration of flour. On the other hand, contrary to the Crown's instructions, they were actually paid 12 livres 5 sols a month. Lépinay tried to enforce the official regulations, but faced with a threat of mutiny, he was obliged to confirm by ordinance the prevailing system—with which the soldiers were still not satisfied, since they received their "balance" in the form of goods. The Council of the Navy had merely obtained from

---

35. AC, F 3 241, f. 138–38v, Deed drawn up by the notary Couturier, April 28, 1717; AM, B 1 9, f. 461v, Mémoire de Crozat, 1716; AC, C 13A 5, f. 47v–48, Hubert, Oct. 26, 1717; f. 182v–83, General inventory of all the effects . . . handed over . . . to the Company of the West, March 1, 1718; C 13C 1, f. 83 bis, Hubert, n.d.

36. AC, A 22, f. 17v–18, Ordinance for an additional four companies for Louisiana, March 1, 1716; AC, C 13A 4, f. 589, La Mothe, Feb. 7, 1716; f. 638–39, Duclos, Jan. 25, 1716; f. 895–96, Hubert, Nov. 23, 1716; AM, B 1 8, f. 635v, Proceedings of the Council of the Navy, June 1, 1716; Giraud, *History*, I, 223, 314.

Crozat a promise that payment would be made in silver when some was available "on the spot"; since the financier's "coffer" was empty of silver, this commitment remained quite illusory, like Lépinay's subsequent decision (April, 1717) to pay in silver part of what was due to the soldiers.[37] As in previous years, the soldiers received as their "balance" notes "to be taken in goods" at the company's storehouse—a means of payment that was unreliable because of the inadequacy of the available stocks of goods.[38]

The last months of Crozat's regime were especially difficult. The financier withdrew from all responsibility and the Company of the West had not yet taken the colony in hand, so the *ordonnateur* Hubert, in October, 1717, after drawing on his personal resources to give the soldiers their pay, no longer knew how to meet expenses. He was worried about the reactions of the men, who, dissatisfied with their pay, which always fell short of the prices of the goods they needed, blamed him unjustly for the hardships they suffered.[39] The sailors and the workmen enrolled in the companies had no better grounds for satisfaction with their wages. Only the few workmen whom the Crown maintained in the colony, with their pay of 30 livres a month, to which the Council of the Navy added the privilege of a free issue of food, were a little better off. Like the others, though, they were paid only in goods, and those among them who had families to support found it hard to survive.[40]

37. AC, C 13A 4, f. 447–50, Lépinay, Oct. 31, 1716; f. 637–39, Duclos, Jan. 25, 1716; f. 988, Draft of *mémoire* from the king to Lépinay and Hubert, October, 1716; AM, B 1 9, f. 283–85, Duclos, Dec. 27, 1715; AE, Mem. & Doc., America, I, f. 144v, Mémoire au sujet de l'éstablissement de la colonie de la Louisiane, 1717; f. 207v, Bienville, June 10, 1718; AC, C 13A 5, f. 49, Hubert, Oct. 26, 1717; f. 209v, Bienville and Larcebault, April 15, 1719; f. 343, Proceedings of the Council of Trade, Dauphin Island, Oct. 26, 1719; AC, F 3 241, f. 141–41v, Ordinance by M. de Lépinay, April 30, 1717.

38. AC, C 13A 5, f. 47–47v, Hubert, Oct. 26, 1717; f. 209v, Bienville and Larcebault, April 15, 1719.

39. AC, C 13A 5, f. 47–47v, 49, 51, Hubert, Oct. 26, 1717.

40. AM B 1 9, f. 264v, 266v, Proceedings of the Council of the Navy, Aug. 29, 1716; f. 517–17v, Proceedings of the Council, Nov. 16, 1716; f. 559v, Hubert, November, 1716; f. 642, Beauharnais, Dec. 17, 1716; AC, C 13A 4, f. 578, La Mothe, Feb. 17, 1716; C 13A 5, f. 47v, Hubert, Oct. 26, 1717; f. 203–204, Roy, master-gunner of the province of Louisiana, to the Council of the Navy, July 6, 1718; AC, 38, f. 54v, 55v, to Lusançay, Oct. 6 and 19, 1716. To the four workmen already maintained in Louisiana the Council of the Navy in 1716 added an edged-tool maker (AC, F 1A 19, f. 70, List of expenditure for the colony of Louisiana during the year 1716). AM, B 1 8, f. 560–60v, L'Epinay, May 9, 1716; B 1 9, f. 403v,

The food supply for the troops was subject to the same risks as in the past. It still depended on what came from France. The soldiers, convinced that "the king ought to feed them," expected distributions of flour, bacon, and dry vegetables, if they could not have fresh meat. The supplies that arrived in 1717 did not, as we know, correspond in quantity to the increased size of the garrison, and the Council of the Navy seemed unaware of the needs created by the presence of three additional companies. It imagined solutions which, being based on the alleged resources of the colony, were actually unrealizable. To make up for the smallness in the amount of flour sent out, the council advised that maize flour be mixed with the wheat flour. It prescribed also that fish be substituted for meat, to a limited extent, and so that the local sources of fish might be exploited, it sent to Dauphin Island two seines that it had had made by the skilled workers of Mornac. But a mixture of the two kinds of flour, made impracticable by the virtual absence of "flour of Indian corn" in a colony that as yet had no mill, would not have been suitable for bread making, and the amount of red fish (which the Louisiana colonists called *sarde*) caught fell short of the council's expectations.[41]

If he was to rescue the troops from the ever-latent threat of hunger, Hubert quite logically saw no alternative but to renounce the parsimonious policy that had been followed up to then based on an extremely precise calculation of the amount of flour to be sent to Louisiana. Hubert advised that a quantity be provided in excess of the garrison's immediate needs to make up for shortfall due to deterioration suffered on the voyage, and also that the colony be allowed a margin that would make it possible, when services or goods had to be obtained from the inhabitants, for them to be paid in kind.[42] As for the problem of meat supplies, if the amount of bacon or salt beef sent out was not to

---

Beauharnais, Sept. 26, 1716; AC, B 38, f. 168v, to Beauharnais, Sept. 5, 1716; AC, C 13A 5, f. 40v, Lépinay, May 10, 1717.

41. AM, B 1 9, f. 328, Duclos, Dec. 25, 1715; f. 402v, Beauharnais, Sept. 22, 1716; f. 466, Lépinay, Oct. 3, 1716; B 1 19, f. 302–302v, Montholon, March 16, 1717; AC, C 13A 4, f. 635–37, Duclos, Jan. 25, 1716; f. 664, Draft of the expenditure which Duclos considers essential for maintaining the colony, June 5, 1716; f. 979, Draft of *mémoire* from the king to Lépinay and Hubert, October, 1716; C 13A 5, f. 209v, Bienville and Larcebault, April 15, 1719; AC, B 38, f. 178v, to Beauharnais, Oct. 6, 1716; f. 304–305, Mémoire . . . pour servir d'instruction au Sr Hubert, Oct. 20, 1716.

42. AC, C 13A 5, f. 29v, L'Epinay and Hubert, May 30, 1717; f. 44–47, Hubert, June 2, Oct. 26, 1717; f. 52v, Hubert, Oct. 26, 1717.

be increased, the only solution must be the introduction of more cattle into the colony. However, no fresh steps were taken to this effect, so the soldiers were obliged for many years to make up for the shortage of meat by acquiring provisions from the inhabitants in exchange for the "subsistence vouchers" they were given "on account for their pay." Nowhere was the feeding of the garrisons so precarious as in Louisiana.[43]

The progress made in clothing the troops was far from correcting all the deficiencies in a situation that had been neglected for so long. The new companies alone received the "major issue of clothing" provided for by the Council of the Navy. The council said it was unable to supply the arrears due to the companies that had gone out earlier and allowed merely the "minor issue of clothing." In fact, however, nothing at all was sent out for the soldiers, so that in 1717, when Crozat's regime ended, half of the garrison had "had no new clothes for four years."[44]

Discontent was inevitable under such conditions. The officers complained of the ruthlessness of the inhabitants, who charged them usurious prices for the goods they needed. They complained above all about the smallness and irregularity of the salaries they received; in 1717 the only payment they got took the form of some "trade goods" that enabled them at least to obtain some food.[45] But they did not express their discontent so openly as the soldiers did. From the latter, Hubert feared "sedition." Their exasperation was such that he dared not "carry out a mustering of the troops," and he was afraid that their state of mind might lead to desertions, which had already been frequent during 1716. Nevertheless, the number of deserters seems to have been smaller in 1717, as a result, no doubt, of the increase in the number of officers and the reduction in opportunities for escape that this entailed.[46] The absence of Sieur La Morandière, whom

---

43. AC, C 13A 4, f. 447–50, L'Epinay, Oct. 31, 1716; C 13A 5, f. 209v, Bienville and Larcebault, April 15, 1719; f. 277, Bienville, Oct. 20, 1719; C 13B 1, f. 24, Mémoire de la Compagnie des Indes servant d'instruction pour Mr Périer, Sept. 30, 1726.

44. AC, B 38, f. 141, to Beauharnais, June 23, 1716; AM, B 1 9, f. 326v–27, Duclos, Dec. 25, 1715; AE, Mem. & Doc., America, I, f. 144v–45. Mémoire au sujet de l'établissement de la colonie de la Louisiane [October, 1717?]; f. 208, Bienville, June 10, 1718; f. 296–96v, List of what is owed to Sr Crozat.

45. AC, C 13A 5, f. 47–47v, 52, Hubert, Oct. 26, 1717.

46. AC, C 13A 4, f. 553, La Mothe, Jan. 23, 1716; f. 578, La Mothe, Feb. 2, 1716; f. 631–32, Duclos, Jan. 25, 1716; f. 771–72, 775–76, Bienville, Jan. 2, 20, 1716; C 13A 5, f. 51–51v, Oct. 26, 1717; AE, Mem. & Doc., America, I, f. 144v, Mémoire au sujet de l'établissement de la colonie de la Louisiane.

Governor Vaudreuil kept in Canada because of the services he could render there, and the delay in Chevalier de La Longueville's return to his post still left some gaps in the ranks of the officers, and in October, 1717, the premature death of Sieur de Lause removed a particularly useful individual. But there were officers enough now to ensure that discipline was better observed.[47] However, the soldiers who had left France "with goodwill enough" no longer served willingly in Louisiana. Their living conditions induced in them an outlook that endangered the defense of the colony. Despite the increase in the military forces, an element of uncertainty prevailed that Louisiana would be unable to shake off until the day when those material difficulties that kept the garrison in a state of permanent unease could be overcome.

47. AC, C 13A 5, f. 51, 57v, Hubert, Oct. 26, 1717. La Longueville did not leave Montreal for Louisiana until October, 1717. The delay was due to the dangers created by the war with the Fox Indians along the route he had to travel. He made his way to the Jesuit mission in the Kaskaskia country with, as guide, a *voyageur* named Nicolas Rose, who agreed to provide at his own expense the equipment needed for the expedition. Vaudreuil had allowed him to leave with "three dinghies to go and trade with the Indians" (AC, C 11A 36, f. 91, Vaudreuil, Nov. 2, 1716; C 11A 37, f. 92–93, 344v–46, Vaudreuil, Nov. 2, 1716, April 20, 1717; C 11A 38, f. 105–107, 117–18, Vaudreuil, Oct. 12, 1717; AC, B 40, f. 491, to Vaudreuil, July 6, 1718; AM, B 1 29, f. 202v–203, Vaudreuil, Oct. 12, 1717; Agreement made between the Chevalier Sr de La Longueville . . . and Sr Nicholas Rose, *voyageur*, Sept. 2, 1717, before the royal notary, at Villemarie, in Schmidt Collections, Vol. I, 195, Manuscript Department, University of Illinois, Urbana).

Emigration and Colonial Society   IX

EAGER TO PROMOTE the peopling of Louisiana, the Council of the Navy had agreed without hesitation to the idea of an annual emigration of illegal saltmakers and girls taken from the poorhouse.[1] This plan would have been carried out, starting in 1716, had there been room for passengers on the *Ludlow* and the *Paon*. For lack of space, however, the departure of the illegal saltmakers had to be postponed, and Crozat's resignation, which meant suspension of the voyage that the *Dauphine* was to have made in March, 1717, again put off their departure.[2]

But the principle had been accepted. The council announced its intention to send to Louisiana every year a certain number of "illegal saltmakers sentenced to the galleys," and while waiting for a ship to be made ready to set out for the Mississippi it prepared the first contingent of these men.[3] Taking account of Crozat's proposals, the council selected a large number of men from prisoners who came from the agricultural provinces of the West and who were provisionally held in the Tour Grenetière at Saumur. Violations of the salt monopoly were so frequent in that part of France that the prison was not large enough to contain all the persons convicted of this offense. Instead of sending them to Provence, the Crown would henceforth reserve them for the Mississippi colony. To the thirty-nine men it took from the tower at Saumur the Council of the Navy added more from the prisons of Bourges, Moulins, Tours, and Paris—a group that included plowmen, day laborers, and craftsmen, all in the prime of life.[4]

1. See p. 47 above.
2. AC, C 13A 5, f. 83–83v, Mémoire sur La Louisiane, 1717; AC, B 38, f. 56v, to marshal de Villeroy, Oct. 24, 1716.
3. AC, C 13A 5, f. 101–101v, Proceedings of the Council of the Navy, July 5, 1717.
4. AC, B 39, f. 10v–11v, to marshal de Villars, Feb. 15, 1717; f. 35–35v, to M. de Creil, May 1, 1717; f. 116v, to M. Berthelot de St.-Laurent, March 6, 1717; f.

In mid-April, 1717, the convoy, led by the "chain gang conductor," reached Rochefort, The sixty-four illegal saltmakers of which it consisted were at once divided between Fort Chapus and the Tour de Fouras, where they spent some months in custody under extremely harsh conditions. The group in the Chapus prison were the worse off because of their isolation from the mainland. The causeway linking the fort to the village was usable only at low tide, so that it was more difficult to bring in supplies, and the bread ration could be renewed only twice a month. Actually, neither group of prisoners received the amount of food usually allowed to convicts, which consisted of two pounds of bread per day together with a "bowlful of beans seasoned with salt and olive oil." Since they were fed exclusively on bread and water, the prisoners were given as compensation, and only after several weeks had passed, "the king's pay" of two sols per day. The council decided on this measure in view of the intendant Beauharnais' observation that it would be less expensive to pay the men than to give them a daily ration of beans.[5]

So this was how the saltmakers spent the months preceding embarkation—underfed, some sleeping on straw but most on "rushes or reeds," chained together, "almost naked," having to cover themselves only the shirts and smocks given them when they were locked up. Two men were "employed to bring them water and wash them."[6] Many of the prisoners, unable to endure this regime and suffering from scurvy, dysentery, or "continuous fever," had to be admitted to the hospitals of Brouage and the Ile d'Aix. Inevitably there were attempts to escape, and despite the precautions taken to "keep them secure," several managed to cut their chains and get out of the Tour de Fouras—only to be caught soon after.[7]

---

116 bis, Mémoire du Conseil de marine au Sr Moneau, May 8, 1717; AM, B 1 19, f. 485, La Gallissonnière, April 15, 1717; AM, B 3 248, f. 134–34v, 139, M. de Creil, Jan. 26, Feb. 22, 1717; AN, G 7 1849 (6th register), f. 68, Proceedings of the Council of Finance, Dec. 1, 1716.

5. AC, B 39, f. 40, 46, to Beauharnais, May 23, June 9, 1717; AM, B 1 19, f. 496–96v, M. de Creil, April 17, 1717; B 1 20, f. 136v–37, Beauharnais, May 30, June 1, 1717; AM, B 3 248, f. 141–41v, M. de Creil, April 17, 1717; f. 143–44, Record of the allocation of the bread contract for Fouras and Chapus.

6. AC, B 39, f. 43–43v, to M. de Creil, June 5, 1717; AM, B 1 20, f. 48v, 136v, Beauharnais, May 2, 30, 1717; AM, B 3 248, f. 148, M. de Creil, May 23, 1717; AC, F 1A 19, f. 279, Council of the Navy to Champigny, June 25, 1717.

7. AM, B 3 247, f. 118, marshal de Villars to the comte de Toulouse, May 22, 1717; B 3 248, f. 147v–48, M. de Creil, May 23, 1717; AM, B 1 20, f. 48v, 137v, Beauharnais, May 2, June 1, 1717; f. 308, 340, Beauharnais, June 10, June 26, 1717.

The decision to add every year a certain number of illegal saltmakers to the population of Louisiana in a sense took the place of the compulsory shipments of indentured servants that the Crown had for so long arranged where the Caribbean colonies were concerned. If the Council of the Navy were to carry out Crozat's proposals, the Mississippi colony would after a few years have the benefit of a group of people who, when their terms of service were up, would become absorbed into the colony's free society.[8] But the project was not without its risks. The council itself felt some apprehension, knowing as it did that in the island dependencies freed convicts had not always proved to be satisfactory additions to the population.[9] Besides, the rigorous conditions of detention experienced by the convicts in Chapus and Fouras might well evoke an aversion to Louisiana that would prevent the men from playing a useful role there. Although they had been told their destination, they were as yet unaware of the circumstances in which they were to serve in the Mississippi colony. For the moment, they were "in custody" in the prisons and still subject to the "penalties" inflicted on illegal saltmakers. The council did not intend to give them their "letters of commutation" until they arrived in Louisiana—failing to consider the consequences that might result from the demoralization to which this uncertainty exposed these men. The permission accorded by the Crown to the married ones among them to take along their families made up, for some, for the harshness of exile, but this measure affected only a minority of the convicts, who were mostly bachelors.[10]

All the same, in Louisiana, where there was still a shortage of labor, people looked forward to the arrival of this group of illegal saltmakers, who would at any rate contribute some plowmen and workmen. Awaited with particular impatience were the "hospital girls" whom the council had agreed to attach to the convoy. Unfortunately, owing to its usual caution where expense was involved, the council, which had originally thought, like Crozat, in terms of a hundred girls, actually sent no more than thirty to the colony, and just as with the illegal saltmakers,

---

8. See p. 43 above.
9. AM, B 1 9, f. 465, Proceedings of the Council of the Navy, Oct. 11, 1716; B 1 19, f. 103, M. Mesnier, at Martinique, Oct. 10, 1716. Mithon says, on the contrary, that the "freed convicts sent to Martinique are fine recruits to the population" (AC, F 2C 1, f. 4–4v).
10. AC, B 39, f. 58, to Beauharnais, June 23, 1717; f. 113v–14, to M. de Creil, Feb. 15, 1717; AM, B 1 20, f. 308v, M. de Creil, June 12, 1717; AM, B 3 247, f. 118, marshal de Villars, May 22, 1717.

their departure had to be put off to a later date because of the overcrowding of the ships.[11]

Consequently, until the entry on the scene of the Company of the West Louisiana obtained no real benefit from the official emigration projects. Nor could the clause that provided for the discharge every year of the two "oldest soldiers in each company" and their establishment in the country as settlers promote an increase in the population. For that to happen, more numerous discharges would have been needed, as in New France, where the governor was authorized to discharge all married soldiers who wished to settle. The Council of the Navy did not contemplate repeating in Louisiana the experience of Carignan's regiment, which Rémonville said had been "the starting point" for the peopling of Canada.[12]

The emigrants who went to the Mississippi in these years of transition acted in a purely personal capacity, with the government doing no more than encouraging departures by granting requests for free passages. In this way it did indeed show "favor and protection" to Louisiana. Rarely was such a request refused, and to free passage was usually added free sustenance during the voyage. Similar requests with respect to St. Domingue, Martinique, and Guadeloupe often failed to receive approval.[13] These encouragements, along with the fact that Louisiana was now being talked about more in France and people's knowledge of it was less vague than in the past, may have had something to do with the desire to emigrate thither that became apparent at this time.

Poverty and unemployment constantly gave rise to requests from among the common people to leave the country. In May, 1716, Lépinay noted that "workmen of all sorts" presented themselves every day at Rochefort, ready to go to Louisiana.[14]

---

11. AC, C 13A 4, f. 977–78, Draft of *mémoire* from the king to Lépinay and Hubert, October, 1716; AC, F 1A 19, f. 283, Draft of expenditure for Louisiana in 1717.

12. AC, A 22, f. 18v, Ordinance for an increase of four companies for Louisiana, March 1, 1716; AM, B 1 19, f. 65, Vaudreuil and Bégon, Oct. 14, 1716; B 1 20, f. 171–71v, Draft of *mémoire* from the king to Vaudreuil and Bégon, June, 1717; AC B 40, f. 475, Mémoire du Roy à Vaudreuil et Bégon, July 5, 1718; AC, F 3 24, f. 88, Rémonville, Description du fleuve St-Louis, 1715.

13. AM, B 1 9, f. 28v, 33v–34, 46v, 110v, 175v, 230v–31v, Proceedings of the Council of the Navy, July 14, July 27, Aug. 11, Aug. 22, Aug. 27, 1716; B 1 19, f. 322v–23v, Proceedings of the Council, April 9, 1717.

14. AM B 1 8, f. 560–60v, L'Epinay, May 9, 1716; B 1 9, f. 34, 382v, Proceedings of the Council of the Navy, July 14, Sept. 21, 1716; AM, B3 243, f. 308–308v,

Increasingly, however, the practice grew of officers and administrators taking their relatives and servants with them to the colony. Raujon left accompanied by his son; Lieutenant Hersent with his two brothers; Couturier arrived at Dauphin Island with his wife and child, his nephew, a clerk, and a servant; and Artus and Lépinay each took several servants with them to Louisiana.[15] A certain number of women also went out to join their husbands, sons, or more distant relatives. Thus there took place the reassembly, in a society on the way to stabilization, of several families that had been obliged to split up when the country was still at the initial stage of colonization.[16]

At the same time the scheme for "indentured servants," which had seemed to be dropped after the first years of the occupation, was the basis for the departure of some young men recruited by Elie Jappie, captain of the *Paix*, possibly at the request of settlers who wished to procure in this way a work force they could not find on the spot. Six indentured servants aged between eighteen and twenty-two, including a farrier, a mason, two plowmen, and a butcher—all natives of Poitou, Saintonge, Aunis, or Angoumois—set out on Crozat's brigantine. They were all bound, according to practice, by a contract to work for three years, while the master they served undertook to provide for all their material needs and at the end of their period of engagement to pay them a wage equivalent to "the value of three hundred pounds of raw sugar."[17]

But the most original development—and the one most indicative, also, of the way French public opinion was beginning to change where Louisiana was concerned—was the appearance of a group of persons who wished to install themselves in the colony in order to exploit its natural resources. Some of these went there without a precise notion of what they were going to do. Desirous of "establishing" themselves in Louisiana, their in-

---

Mémoire des négociants de Nantes, July 19, 1717; AC, B 38, f. 157, 178, to Beauharnais, July 28, Sept. 30, 1716.

15. AC, C 13A 4, f. 169, Proceedings of the Council of the Navy, Aug. 22, 1716; f. 533, La Mothe, Jan. 2, 1716; AC, B 38, f. 166v, 177v, 339, to Beauharnais, Aug. 29, Sept. 20, Oct. 28, 1716.

16. AM, B 1 9, f. 11v, Sr Voutron, Rochefort, June 30, 1716; f. 111, comte de Béthune, Aug. 1, 1716; f. 175v, Jeanne Piron, Rochefort, Aug. 6, 1716; B 1 8, f. 634, Proceedings of the Council of the Navy, June 16, 1716; AC, B 38, f. 148v, 165, to Beauharnais, July 7, Aug. 25, 1716.

17. La Rochelle, Rivière and Soullard, 1716, f. 120v–22; Giraud, *History*, I, 48–50, 163–64.

tention was to take advantage, once arrived, of whatever possibilities might present themselves. This was the case with the son of a Paris merchant; with the sieurs Louis Maret de Lugé and François Maret de La Loge, the nephews of the secretary who executed the orders of Monsieur le Duc (Louis-Henri de Bourbon-Condé), who set out with a "train" of ten persons; and with other emigrants whose identity is unknown.[18] Others had better-defined aims. One royal attorney, Sieur Lesterier, wanted to resume his employment under the Conseil Supérieur of Louisiana and at the same time to develop a habitation.[19] A particularly interesting case is that of a group of merchants—Vincent Dubreuil, Jean-Baptiste Massy, and Pierre and Philippe Guénot de Tréfontaine—who joined forces to undertake commercial operations in the colony with their combined resources. They obtained from Crozat an "agreement" that allowed them "to carry on throughout the country such trade as they [should think] appropriate," and to "go and trade both with the savages and with the Spaniards." The Council of the Navy approved their initiative and to facilitate the fulfillment of their plan granted them and their four menservants free passage and sustenance on the king's ships. It also authorized them to take out a hundred *fusils* for the requirements of their trade and to stock up with provisions of flour and brandy for their personal consumption.[20] The merchants' decision could have opened a new future for Louisiana. Had Crozat honored his commitments, these entrepreneurs could have brought into the colony a first influx of capital, laying the foundations for commercial life. Their plan seemed to refute the belief held by the Council of the Navy that Louisiana could not yet be a target of spontaneous emigration.

Moreover, the interest that the colony seemed gradually to be arousing was not confined to the home country. A certain number of *voyageurs* from Canada were still attracted to it, several of them settling in the inland areas. Chateaugué was especially de-

18. AM, B 1 8, f. 663v, 681, Requests from M. Maret to the Council of the Navy, June 28, 30, 1716; B 1 9, f. 34v, 47, Proceedings of the Council of the Navy, July 14, 27, 1716; AC, B 38, f. 147–47v, 152v–53, 153, 154v, to Beauharnais, June 30, July 18, 21, 1716.
19. AM, B 1 9, f. 360v–61, Request from Sr Lesterier to the Council of the Navy, Sept. 8, 1716.
20. AM, B 1 9, f. 11, Voutron, Rochefort, June 30, 1716; f. 100–100v, Massy, Dubreuil, and Guénot to the Council of the Navy, Aug. 4, 1716; AC, B 38, f. 152, 159v, to Beauharnais, July 14, Aug. 8, 1716; AC, C 13A 5, f. 119, Extract from a request and ordinance presented to M. de Lépinay, at Fort Louis, Oct. 8, 1717; AC, F 3 241, f. 127, 127v–28, Raguet, October, 1717.

sirous that Canadian settlers arrive in large numbers. This would be the surest way of peopling the country, and as he saw it, his brother Bienville, who enjoyed the Canadians' confidence, would be able, were he entrusted with the government of the colony, to do a great deal to bring about immigration from that quarter.[21] From St. Domingue, where Louisiana ships usually put in, "humble inhabitants" petitioned Crozat to be allowed to settle in the colony. True, the Council of the Navy, inspired perhaps by representations from the administrators that "St. Domingue is short of people," resisted these proposals. Although it was pointed out to them how beneficial it would be to Louisiana to have settlers who knew how to grow rice and tobacco, the comte de Toulouse and Marshal d'Estrées rejected the suggestion, giving no other reason than that "we ought not to withdraw inhabitants from St. Domingue." Only a few isolated individuals who were not strictly speaking part of the population of St. Domingue left Cap Français for Louisiana at this time.[22] Nevertheless, the initiative that had been shown proved that the Mississippi was beginning to interest people in the neighboring colonies, and the idea that it might offer them outlets prepared the way for a new source of recruitment to its population.

Eighty persons altogether assembled at Rochefort with the intention of embarking on the *Ludlow* and the *Paon*, which were due to set out at the end of 1716. With the addition of the two hundred men of the newly raised companies, the crews, and the governor's household, this meant a total passenger list of over four hundred people, which was far beyond the capacities of the king's ships. A sacrifice was called for, and the Council of the Navy, persuaded that defense of the colony should have priority, favored removing some of the civilians. However, the council listened to Crozat when he said these persons should not be obliged, after incurring so much expense in expectation of their departure, to suffer a delay that might put them off any inclination to leave France. Hence the council's decision to leave Bonnille's company behind on the Ile d'Oléron. The emigrants were divided between the *Ludlow* and the *Paon*, while the indentured

21. AM, B 1 9, f. 552v–54, Chateaugué, July 17, 1716; B 1 19, f. 65, Vaudreuil and Bégon, Oct. 14, 1716.
22. AC, C13A 5, f. 37, L'Epinay, May 10, 1717; f. 102v, Proceedings of the Council of the Navy, July 5, 1717; AC, 9A 13, Chateaumorant and Mithon, May 30, 1717; AE, Mem. & Doc., America, I, f. 230v, Mémoire de Crozat (?), May 14, 1717.

servants and the agents went aboard the *Paix*, which was itself too overloaded to carry the soldiers.[23]

It is not possible, unfortunately, to give a precise figure for the proportion of useful emigrants among this group of eighty persons—skilled workers and other elements who would create solid "establishments" rather than swell the number of the "maintained" population. To all appearances, they were only a minority. The arrivals of March, 1717, did not solve the problem of peopling the colony, as the missionary Le Maire stated in the *mémoire* he addressed to the Court at this time. The colony was still without women who would make possible the creation of new households, and it lacked, above all, "hard-working" peasants. Louisiana needed an annual immigration of hundreds of families "capable of all kinds of work," and the presence of two plowmen among Captain Jappie's indentured servants did not amount to appreciable progress in that direction.[24] Despite its wish to innovate and its recognition of the importance of the colonial problem, the Council of the Navy continued to fall short of the vigorous achievements of the British that Hubert and Crozat urged them to take as their inspiration.[25] Any emigration on a serious scale presupposed financial means that the council did not have. The *ordonnateur*'s idea of drawing emigrants from among "families of plowmen and craftsmen . . . who are living on alms and are a burden on their parishes" would entail considerable costs of installation and the dispatch of foodstuffs to the colony at great expense, over a long period. Yet the council had not even solved the problem of providing subsistence for the passengers going out on the *Ludlow* and the *Paon*. It had merely arranged to send an extra supply of foodstuffs to meet the initial needs of the new arrivals and also decided that the ships should pick up some cattle at Havana, a scheme that was to come to nothing.[26]

23. AC, C 13A 4, f. 452, Crozat, Nov. 13, 1716; f. 863–64, L'Epinay, Nov. 3, 1716; f. 887–89, L'Epinay, Dec. 1, 1716; AM, B 1 9, f. 260, Beauharnais, Aug. 22, 1716; f. 521v–23, Beauharnais, Nov. 3, 1716; f. 555–56v, Proceedings of the Council of the Navy, Nov. 18, 1716.

24. AC, C 13C 1, f. 88, Hubert, n.d.; C 13A 5, f. 142–42v, Hubert, Mémoire sur la colonie de la Louisiane, October, 1717; AN, AHM 3 JJ 200 4, F. Le Maire, Mémoire sur la Louisiane, May 13, 1718; BN, FF 12105, f. 12, 17, Le Maire, Mémoire sur la Louisiane, March 1, 1717.

25. AC, C 13A 5, f. 142–42v, Hubert, Mémoire sur la colonie de la Louisiane, October, 1717.

26. *Ibid.;* AM, B 1 9, f. 522v–23, Beauharnais, Nov. 3, 1716; f. 554v–55, Lépinay, Rochefort, Nov. 7, 1716. See p. 133 below.

Faced with this poverty of resources, Crozat's only hope was that the Council of the Navy would devote the capital he was surrendering to it by giving up his monopoly to subsidizing the transport and settling-in of 1,200 to 1,500 new inhabitants.[27] In the absence of any program of subsidized emigration, Crozat saw the arrival of the eighty passengers in 1717 as an interesting pointer to future possibilities. That same year he provided for another hundred departures and pointed out that two ships would be needed to cope with the large demand for passages, many of those applying being relatively well-to-do persons who wished to convey their "few belongings" to Louisiana.[28] For the moment, however, the immigrants who landed at Dauphin Island were incapable, in either quality or quantity, of satisfying the colony's basic needs.

It is hard to say exactly how large Louisiana's population was at that time. Although we know it increased with the coming of 230 or 240 civilians and soldiers, the vagueness of our data on the number of people living in Louisiana at the beginning of 1717 forbids us to pronounce on the total, especially since no census was carried out when the royal frigates arrived. We can only suppose that, even allowing for desertions from the troops in the colony, Louisiana contained at least 300 people at the beginning of the year. If this was so, then the population would have grown in March, 1717, to nearly 550—which, given what the colonization process actually required, was a poor increase.[29]

Yet in this small society, a certain hierarchical structure began to appear, gradually emerging from the simplicity of the colony's first years. At the bottom were a majority of humble folk, mostly

27. AE, Mem. & Doc., America, I, f. 184, Mémoire concernant l'établissement de la Louisiane (1717).
28. AM, B 1 9, f. 557, Proceedings of the Council of the Navy, Nov. 18, 1716.
29. There can be no disguising the unreliability of these estimates. The figure of 300 is calculated on the basis of a military force of 120 men, which implies that the "maintained" people numbered about 180 (and not 215 [Giraud, *History*, I, 277–78]). To these are to be added some 40 families (confirmed by Le Maire [BN, FF 12105, f. 12]), or at least 120 persons, not counting the unmarried. It is therefore possible that there may have been more than 300 before the arrival of the *Ludlow*. On the other hand a *mémoire*—we cannot be sure if what it states is well-founded—gives as no more than 400 the size of the population when Crozat handed Louisiana over to the Company of the West (AC, C 13C 1, f. 329, Mémoire de l'état actuel où est la colonie de Louisiane pour juger ce que l'on peut en espérer).

without any definite occupation, who lived by doing a little farming and stockbreeding, together with trade with the Indians and small-scale business. Among these people were still a fairly large number of those Canadians who had been present at the start. Their names have come down to us through the parish register of Mobile: Jean Saussier, Claude Trépanier, Antoine Huché, Gilbert Dardenne, and the children of Charles Le Sueur, who came to the colony after their father's death.[30] Jacques Chauvin and Joseph Chauvin, known as de Léry, were also representatives of the first immigration. Several of these men married women who came out in the 1704 convoy—Geneviève Burel, Gabrielle Savary, Catherine Christophe. Among the troops as well, we find elements that went back to the colony's beginnings, but the military personnel were renewed as the garrison was reinforced and came increasingly to consist of newcomers who had arrived between 1713 and 1717. At a slightly higher level, but still to a large extent belonging to the first phase of the peopling of the colony, were the "craftsmen"—carpenters, brickmakers, gunners—men like Jacques Le Compte, Jean Fabvre, André-Joseph Pénigaut, Jean Alexandre, Jean Roy, and the shipbuilder Jacques Le Roux, who owed to their personal usefulness a degree of consideration that was increased, in the case of those who could claim it, by the title of "master" in their respective specialities. All of them had by now spent many years in the colony. Despite the hardships they suffered when they possessed no resources other than their wages, several had established themselves firmly, along with the families they had created. The case of the master gunner Jean Roy is significant. After vainly petitioning the Council of the Navy to grant him a wage increase in view of the "wretched state" to which the burden of his family had reduced him, he returned to the Mississippi intending to finish his career there.[31]

Needless to say, this lower stratum of the population consisted mostly of illiterates. The education of children was markedly neglected. No religious order had as yet undertaken educational work in the colony, and there is no evidence that the missionaries engaged in this activity. Only Marie-Françoise de Boisrenaud de Roisneau, who had led the girl emigrants of 1704, gave elementary instruction to the "daughters of inhabitants"

---

30. Giraud, *History*, I, 154–55, 223–24.
31. AM, B 1 9, f. 517–517v, Proceedings of the Council of the Navy, Nov. 16, 1716.

and also prepared Indian girls for baptism. But she was elderly, "burdened with infirmities," and—having belonged for a long time to the Abbey of Fontevrault as a member of the Community of the Annunciation and lived in Madame de Montespan's circle—was too proud of her antecedents to put up for long with residence in the colony. In 1718 she requested permission to return to France.[32]

Above this stratum we observe a group who were better educated and who for that reason and because of their role in the country's internal life held a relatively honored position. These were Crozat's subordinate agents; La Mothe's secretary, Olivier, who gave his profession as attorney; the keepers of the storehouses belonging to the Crown and to the company; and the notaries and registrars of the Conseil Supérieur. Along with them stand the few settlers who, like the Canadian Graveline, had attained a certain degree of affluence, and the small group of merchants who arrived in the frigates in 1717 intending to get commercial activity going in the colony.

Finally, at the top, we find the members of the government, the director and comptroller of Crozat's company, the officers, and the missionaries. The authority enjoyed by these men depended not so much on their functions as on the popularity they had been able to win for themselves. Neither La Mothe nor Lépinay was consequently surrounded with the respect that the dignity of governor should have commanded. Social rank and birth constituted a special factor of consideration, the importance of which increased as gentlefolk became more numerous in the colony. An officer who was a nobleman occupied a place of honor in this community where the least of the inhabitants strove to make his surname seem less plebeian.[33] But this officer was not isolated from the rest of the population. He did not hesitate to figure as godfather at the humblest of baptisms, and if necessary he would marry a woman of common origin, born in the colony.[34] The way of life of these officers, whose salaries barely kept them alive, was extremely modest. To judge by the inventory of property left by Captain de Lause de Villemarets,

---

32. AM, B 1 30, f, 429–29v, Mémoire de Marie-Françoise de Boisrenaud, Proceedings of the Council, Dec. 10, 1718; Giraud, *History*, I, 155–56, 179–80.

33. Thus, in the parish register of Mobile, Joseph Chauvin, known as de Léry, becomes "Chauvin de Léry," and Nicolas Bodin, known as Miragouin or Miragouenne, becomes "Sieur de Miragouenne" (Parish register of Mobile, Ala., Dec. 15, 1715, May 21, 1719).

34. Parish register of Mobile, Ala., Oct. 3, Aug. 24, 1717.

the furniture in the dwellings they leased for the period of their stay in Louisiana amounted to very little: a few trunks, a wooden chest, a curtainless bed with a flock mattress. Their clothes were their only wealth, together with the "trade goods"—fabrics from Mazamet and Cholet, knives, mirrors, glassware, shirts—which they usually bartered for furs or for food.[35]

In this society in process of formation, confined still to the two built-up areas of Mobile and Dauphin Island, a simple structure was thus beginning to take shape in which occupation and birth were the principal determining factors. The level of material wealth was too low to constitute a factor of differentiation. Although classes were beginning to appear, they lost all rigidity in contact with the living conditions, the material difficulties that these created for everyone, and the basically independent spirit that animated the population.

The missionaries exerted only a feeble moral authority over the people. Religious life made no progress in the colony. The clergy's ranks had not been renewed: after the departure of the chaplains of the *Dauphine*, the Irishman Anthony Fay and Abbé Capsole, the only priests left at Fort Louis and Dauphin Island were Alexandre Huvé and François Le Maire. They functioned as parish priests for these two places, respectively, though the former was in principle only the chaplain of the fort.[36] Antoine Davion, busy with his mission to the Tunicas, gave his colleagues only intermittent help. Yet neither man was capable of combating the indifference of the inhabitants to religion. Huvé's state of health made it hard for him to endure the climate and his living conditions, while Le Maire, who was too headstrong in his judgments and permanently at odds with the colony's leaders, proved unable to win the confidence of the popula-

---

35. AM, B 1 9, f. 420. Proceedings of the Council of the Navy, Oct. 9, 1716; AC, C 13A 5, f. 47v, Hubert, Oct. 26, 1717. The inventory of Sr de Lause's belongings, compiled in October, 1717, mentions a blue coat, made of camlet, with silver buttons, a gray coat, made of cloth, with silver frogs and red facings, a scarlet coat with gold buttonholes, some hats edged with gold and silver, a pair of silk stockings, four ells of red Mazamet, eight ells of Cholet linen, towels, nightshirts, cravats made of muslin trimmed with lace, and fine shirts also with lace trimmings (LSHM Archives, New Orleans).

36. AC, F 1A 19, f. 79, List of the expenditure that the king . . . orders . . . for Louisiana, Oct. 1, 1716; Sem. Missions, no. 45, M. de Brisacier, Paris, Oct. 31, 1716. On Anthony Fay, or Fahy, see Roll of crew of the *Dauphine*, in Archives Départementales, Nantes.

tion.³⁷ Dissatisfied with the inhabitants and disappointed in the Indians who had not responded to his apostolate, he did not hide his intention to give up a task in which he was provided with no backing and the remuneration for which was subject to long delays that aggravated its inadequacy.³⁸

The material conditions for worship completed Le Maire's discouragement. Lépinay had been urged by the Council of the Navy to see to the building of "commodious and proper churches," but his exhortations to the population to this effect proved vain. At Mobile the inhabitants remained satisfied with the room in which the missionaries had improvised a chapel.³⁹ On Dauphin Island the church that had been begun thanks to Rémonville's gift was not yet finished: the inhabitants, believing that the site was soon to be abandoned, lost interest in the work they had started. The "help" furnished by Rémonville was in any case partly exhausted, and neither the Crown nor the company assigned funds for completing this work.⁴⁰ As a result, services were held in the missionaries' house; and since the credits allocated for this residence amounted to very little, the upkeep of the place fell largely to the charge of the priests of the Seminary of Foreign Missions. They assembled here a few silver articles, some "chasubles of taffeta," a copper censer, a "picture in a gilded frame," and a "picture to be used as a banner," and they set up an altar decorated with a "frontal of taffeta." This was not enough, the *ordonnateur* considered, for "divine service" to be held with "dignity."⁴¹ But the religious ceremonies attracted

---

37. Sem., Missions, no. 47, Le Maire, Dauphin Island, May 28, 1717; no. 73, Petition from the Quebec seminary to the commissioners of the East India Company, 1723; AC, C 13A 4, f. 187–88, 527–29, La Mothe, Jan. 2, 1716; f. 578, La Mothe, Feb. 7, 1716; C 13A 5, f. 49v–50, Hubert, Oct. 26, 1717.

38. AC, C 13C 2, f. 134–35, 136v, 137v, Le Maire, Jan. 15, 1714; f. 158v, Mémoire de Le Maire, 1718; BN, FF 12105, f. 17, Le Maire, Mémoire sur la Louisiane, March 1, 1717; AM, B 1 9, f. 446–46v, Draft of instruction to Sr de Lépinay, governor . . . ; B 1 20, f. 141–42, Proceedings of the Council of the Navy, June 7, 1717; f. 433–33v, Proceedings of the Council, Aug. 3, 1717; B 1 33, f. 35, Proceedings of the Council, Jan. 9, 1718.

39. Giraud, *History*, I, 319–21.

40. AC, B 38, f. 302v, 313, Mémoires du Roy pour servir d'instructions à Hubert et Lépinay, October, 1716; BN, FF 12105, Le Maire, Mémoire sur la Louisiane, March 1, 1717.

41. AC, F 1A 19, f. 77–80, List of expenditure for Louisiana, 1715, 1716; AC, C 13A 5, f. 49–49v, Hubert, Oct. 26, 1717; f. 181–81v, General inventory of all the effects . . . found in the royal storehouse, March 1, 1718.

only a small congregation. Although the inhabitants assembled in the presbytery to discuss matters of common concern, and although on Sundays, when mass was ended, they went along to learn of the "acts of justice and other acts" that were read out at the door of the house used as the church, many declined, either from indifference or from hostility toward the *curé* of Dauphin Island, to attend the services.[42]

From the correspondence of François Le Maire, which expressed growing demoralization, we obtain the impression that the Seminary's mission was coming to its close. And yet, though he declared his desire to return to France, Le Maire did not contemplate immediate departure because he feared to leave the field free once more to the Jesuits. Two of the latter, Fathers Jean Le Boullenger and Guillaume Loyard, had in fact arrived in the colony on the ships that came in 1717. In principle, they were to remain on Dauphin Island or at Fort Louis only while waiting till they could get to the inland posts to which they had been assigned. But their presence worried Le Maire. He was afraid that they would supplant the representatives of the Seminary in the hearts of the population and the "principal persons of the colony" in order to take over a mission to which they had no rightful claim. He complained about the special attention paid them by the colony's leaders and about the intention shown by the governor, the *ordonnateur,* and the members of the general staff to entrust them with the chaplaincy of the garrison. While Hubert did reprove the attitude of one of the religious for his indiscreet interference in disputes between the authorities and the soldiers, it may be that his lack of enthusiasm for Le Maire's apostolate led him to favor the Jesuits, and also that the "principal persons in the colony" may have openly admitted "that they had no confidence" in the seminary priests.[43] The return of the Jesuits and the threat that this implied for the priests of the Seminary of Foreign Missions gave the latter, in any case, espe-

---

42. AC, A 23, f. 5v, Regulations made by the Conseil Supérieur of Louisiana concerning the slaves, Nov. 12, 1714; f. 6v, Ordinance of Mrs de la Mothe-Cadillac and Duclos, Aug. 23, 1716; f. 9–10, Declaration by the king, Aug. 2, 1717.

43. AC, C 13A 5, f. 51v, Hubert, Oct. 26, 1717; AC, B 38, f. 177v, to Beauharnais, Sept. 30, 1716; AN, K 1232 4, Le Maire to Messeigneurs of the king's council; Sem., Missions, no. 47, Le Maire, Dauphin Island, May 28, 1717; Jean Delanglez, *The French Jesuits in Lower Louisiana* (New Orleans, 1935), 77–80. Three Jesuits were appointed to go to Louisiana, but only two arrived at Dauphin Island in March, 1717.

cially François Le Maire, an additional reason for discontent and anxiety, and a new cause of fear for the future of the Louisiana mission.

Although he criticized rather harshly Le Maire's conduct and personality, the *ordonnateur* agreed that the state of mind of the population was partly responsible for the poor results the priest had obtained. Hubert spoke just as the missionary did of the "licentious life" of the inhabitants, of their ignorance of any "principle of honor," and of the "dissoluteness" and "impurity" of Louisiana society.[44] The "drink shops" and "public gaming houses," which were increasing in number and which, from 1716, were authorized to keep open on festival days, except during the hours of "divine service," were a standing cause of disorder. The trade in alcohol tended to become widespread, and Lépinay, whose view of the consequences was as severe as Le Maire's, had to reaffirm the ban on selling brandy to the slaves in the colony.[45]

The practice of slavery contributed greatly to this "licentious way of life" that the *ordonnateur* remarked on, for despite the missionaries, it had become established usage among the French at all levels, from Governor Lépinay to a company officer, and from one of Crozat's agents to a private soldier, to recruit their domestic servants from among the Indian women.[46] Together with the transient elements who stayed for brief periods in Fort Louis at Mobile, such as the Apalachees from the nearby mission who came in to have their children baptized, the slaves formed a permanent body in the colony that gave it the local color characteristic of a primitive country.[47] Children—such as Sieur Le Bart's son—were inevitably born of the relations established between masters and slaves. Le Maire denounced, as before, the trade in "savage female slaves" who provided concubines for those who bought them to perform domestic service. While most of these women were, as before, from the Chitima-

---

44. AC, C 13A 5, f. 49v, Hubert, Oct. 26, 1717; AE, Mem. & Doc., America, I, f. 146, Hubert, Mémoire au sujet de l'établissement de la colonie de la Louisiane, 1717.

45. AC, A 23, f. 6, Ordinance and regulation by the Conseil Supérieur, April 1, 1715; AC, F 3 241, f. 141, Ordinance by Lépinay, May 24, 1717; AN, G 7 1849 (6th register), f. 64, Proceedings of the Council of Finance, Nov. 27, 1716; AC, B 39, f. 291, Mémoire du Roy aux Srs de Costebelle et de Soubras, n.d.; BN, FF 12105, f. 12, Le Maire, Mémoire sur la Louisiane, March 1, 1717.

46. Parish register of Mobile, Ala., Sept. 12, 18, 29, 1717.

47. *Ibid.*, May 16–17, June 8, 22, Aug. 21, 24, Sept. 5, 1717.

cha tribe, there were also some from the Missouri tribes and from the Mobile people, with whom the French were not at war. It appears that Bienville's orders were no longer heeded, and Le Maire feared the possible consequences of this trade, which he thought might give rise among the Indians to ill feeling such as had caused them to revolt against the British traders.[48] Hubert frankly deplored the effects on public morality of cohabitation between white men and "female savages." However, the Crown's refusal to authorize marriages between Frenchmen and natives increasingly promoted these free unions. The director of the Seminary of Foreign Missions recognized that fact without hesitation, and Le Maire himself, despite the disapproval he expressed in his correspondence, showed in practice a great deal of indulgence in the matter.[49]

Nevertheless, the population, aware of the limited services that the Indian slaves could perform, demanded more and more insistently that a black work force be brought into Louisiana. The few blacks established at Mobile or on Dauphin Island, who belonged to a small number of privileged persons such as Bienville, were incapable of playing any appreciable role in the country's economic life.[50] Moreover, their small numbers apparently confined them to household tasks and gardening.

The blacks were subject like the Indians to the ordinary law concerning slaves. The status of both groups was defined in a series of administrative regulations that remained in force until the introduction of the *Code Noir*, and which were so severe because this was thought to be the way to parry the danger arising from the increase in the numbers of the natives. There is certainly no lack of examples of trust and devotion between masters and their servants of either sex, and nothing to show that these domestic relations ever created difficulty for the settlers at Mobile and on Dauphin Island.[51] But with elements who were accustomed to conceptions and disciplines different from those of the whites and who were being kept by force in a society that

---

48. *Ibid.*, April 11, Nov. 1, 1716, June 22, 1717; BN FF 12105, f. 17–18, Le Maire, Mémoire sur la Louisiane, March 1, 1717; Giraud, *History*, I, 179–81.

49. AC, C 13A 4, f. 977–78, Draft of *mémoire* from the king to Lépinay and Hubert, October, 1716; C 13A 5, f. 49v, Hubert, Oct. 26, 1717; Sem., Missions, no. 45, M. de Brisacier to Varlet, Oct. 31, 1716.

50. Parish register of Mobile, Ala., Jan. 6, 1716, June 14, 1717.

51. PRO, CO 5, 359, 15–16, Couturier to M. de Chammorel, French *chargé d'affaires* at the British Court.

was alien to them, the Conseil Supérieur considered these precautions essential.

Accordingly, it laid down rigorous penalties for offenses committed by slaves. Theft and "desertion"—that "marooning" of which the administrators in the islands complained continually—were punished by whipping, imprisonment, or even, if a theft involved a large amount, by death inflicted through strangling or hanging. Assaults on masters also entailed capital punishment, while threats of assault—the slave "merely raising his hand to strike"—were punished by thirty strokes of the whip. In order to prevent any possibility of concerted action or any plot against the inhabitants' lives, the council forbade slaves to bear arms and to assemble "in the woods" or "after sundown" in "any place at all." And it forbade the whites to sell to or "barter anything" with them, with special emphasis on alcoholic drink, the usual effect of which was to increase the incidence of thefts and escapes.[52]

From the provisions of this first slave code, it is clear that the black slave, even though he had not yet had the opportunity to prove himself and though he was subject to the same regime as the native, was already better appreciated than the latter in the colony. His official commercial value, three hundred livres, was double that of the Indian.[53] The *ordonnateur* Hubert agreed with his predecessors that black slaves, when available in sufficient numbers, would alone ensure the development of the country. White labor seemed to him of more dubious value because of the difficulty such workers had in putting up with the climate. Upon the blacks would depend not only the cultivation of the land but also all the numberless chores inseparable from the task of building a colony. For them to fulfill this role, it would suffice that they be taught the trades hitherto known only to workmen from France. Without this contribution by workers used to living in a hot country, Louisiana would remain, as Hubert saw it, doomed to an existence without prospect of progress.

52. AC, A 23, f. 4v, Ordinance by Mrs de La Mothe-Cadillac and Duclos, May 20, 1714; f. 5–5v, Regulations made by the Conseil Supérieur of Louisiana concerning the slaves, Nov. 12, 1714.

53. AC, A 23, f. 5, Regulations . . . concerning the slaves, Nov. 12, 1714.

X Economic Stagnation

THE COLONY'S ECONOMIC life confirmed the opinion expressed by the *ordonnateur*. During the years of transition, it reproduced much the same scene as in previous years. With some exceptions, the population took no interest in agriculture. When he arrived, Hubert noted that settlers lived essentially by trade with the Indians.[1] The poverty of the soil near the coast, from which assiduous labor and a large number of black slaves could produce scarcely anything, induced them to confine themselves in that unadventurous commerce. Confronted with the increasingly unfavorable reports that reached it, the Council of the Navy gave up the illusions it had at first entertained regarding the agricultural possibilities of those sandy tracts. The area around Fort Louis offered at most some poor harvests of maize and tobacco. As for Dauphin Island, it could offer no prospect of any crop that would "reward" the inhabitants for "their labors." Indian corn would not grow there, and the council eventually conceded that the island could produce nothing but grass and vegetables. There were so few trees that the council decided it would be prudent to bring these under a controlled regime of "periodical cutting," so as to protect a resource that the inhabitants and the garrison would soon destroy if they were allowed to exploit it freely.[2] Given these conditions, how could it be hoped that the population would devote itself to working the land? People might do so if richer soils were made available to them, but even then they would need the help of a black work force. Hubert doubted whether the availability of better soil would be enough to overcome the habits of heedlessness the inhabitants had acquired.[3]

 1. AC, C 13A 5, f. 53, Hubert, Oct. 26, 1717; C 13C 1, f. 87v, Hubert, n.d.
 2. C 13A 5, f. 53, Hubert, Oct. 26, 1717; C 13A 4, f. 595–97, Observations by La Mothe-Cadillac to the Council of the Navy, June 22, 1716; f. 969–71, Draft of *mémoire* by the king to Lépinay and Hubert, October, 1716.
 3. AC, C 13A 5, f. 53, Hubert, Oct. 26, 1717; C 13C 1, f. 87v, Hubert, n.d.; 13C 2, f. 158, Mémoire de Le Maire, 1718.

The food supply consequently continued to be as uncertain as in earlier years. The small amount of maize produced was insufficient for the inhabitants' needs. It provided them with only a raw material for their food, since for lack of a mill the colonists still had to pound the grain, and it was much less substantial than wheat, which Le Maire considered could be grown in Louisiana only if French wheat were replaced by the variety grown in New Spain.[4] Nor were there enough cattle to meet the needs of the population. All observers remarked on the small number of cattle in the colony, and this shortage was to continue long after the coming of the Company of the Indies.[5] Left to graze freely in the woods, the animals required little care, and the herds gradually increased. Nevertheless, the four hundred head of cattle that Charles Legac recorded as being in Louisiana in August, 1718, were not enough to provide a regular source of meat, especially in a climate that made it hard to preserve the product. The meat trade was not organized: there were no butchers' shops, and slaughtering was not regulated. The inhabitants sold whatever animals they casually killed in the woods, without bothering much who owned the animals, to such an extent that La Mothe and Duclos, with a view to reducing occasions for lawsuits, had to rule that "each individual" should slaughter "only his own animals."[6]

Although the Council of the Navy did not fully appreciate the difficulties of the situation, it sought to revive the project for importing cattle from Havana, but with no better success than Pontchartrain had, since the two attempts made in 1717 failed through the ill will of the Spanish authorities. The *Ludlow* was able to take on board no more than a score of cows, and that clandestinely, with the complicity of a "private person." Crozat's brigantine seems to have brought nothing back to the colony. Because of that vessel's small capacity, the trip it made to Havana in October, 1717, could not have been of much use, especially

---

4. AC, C 13A 4, f. 639–40, Duclos, Jan. 25, 1716; C 13C 2 f. 110v, Le Maire, Jan. 15, 1714; AE, Mem. & Doc., America, I, f. 210, Bienville, June 10, 1718; Giraud, *History*, I, 282.

5. AC, C 13A 4, f. 736–37, Duclos, July 6, 1716; C 13B 1, f. 24, Mémoire de la Compagnie des Indes servant d'instruction pour M. Périer, Sept. 30, 1726; C 13C 1, f. 347–47v (Véniard de Bourgmont), Exacte description de la Louisiane; AN, AHM 3 JJ 387 30, Alexandre, from the Chouachas, Sept. 10, 1722; AE, Mem. & Doc., America, I, f. 209v, Bienville, June 10, 1718.

6. AC, A 23, f. 6–6v, Ordinance by MM. de La Mothe-Cadillac and Duclos, Aug. 23, 1716; AC, C 13A 5, f. 277, Bienville, Dauphin Island, Oct. 20, 1719; AE, Mem. & Doc., America, I, f. 82v, Legac, Etat dans lequel a été trouvée la colonie de la Louisiane le 25 août 1718; Giraud, *History*, I, 283n27.

since Raujon said he lacked the funds needed to effect the purchases ordered by the Council of the Navy.[7] Consequently, the matter was still in suspense when Crozat's regime ended.

On Dauphin Island, farmyard animals—pigs and especially poultry—were all there was to make up for the shortage of "butcher's meat." At Mobile the population was a little better off, since it obtained venison during the winter, but this was a resource both too uncertain and too scanty to provide a permanent supply of provisions. Fishing does not seem to have played an appreciable part in feeding the colony. For lack of sufficient materials and expertise, the fisheries were exploited only by individuals and to a limited degree. After Lépinay had been in Louisiana for a few weeks, he said he was convinced that hunting and fishing, "being no more than a myth," could not replace the supply of foodstuffs from France.[8] The civilian population was even worse provided for than the soldiers, because Crozat's storehouse was poorly stocked. The wheat flour available did not meet the demand, and the inhabitants continued to be dependent, as always, "on the Indians' discretion." Since they had to obtain the additional maize they needed from the natives, they were subject, in the last analysis, to all the uncertainties characteristic of the farming methods of these Indians.[9]

During the last years of Crozat's monopoly, however, some new elements appeared in the colony's agriculture that countered to a slight extent the general mediocrity. In 1716 the first rice seeds arrived. Chateaugué brought from St. Domingue, where he had gone to procure food, "two casks of rice for sowing." There is no proof that the population then proceeded to cultivate rice, but this moment marked the beginning of an experiment that was later to expand the country's food production.[10]

   7. AM, B 1 9, f. 463, Crozat, Mémoire au Conseil de marine du 11 Oct. 1716; f. 554v–55, Lépinay, Rochefort, Nov. 7, 1716; AC, B 38, f. 307–308v, Mémoire du Roy . . . au Sr Hubert, Oct. 20, 1716; AC, C 13A 4, f. 736–37, Duclos, July 6, 1716; C 13A 5, f. 46, 53v–54, Duclos, Oct. 26, 1717; C 13C 1, f. 84–86, Hubert, n.d.
   8. AC, C 13A 5, f. 66, Bienville to Hubert, Sept. 19, 1717; AE, Mem. & Doc., America, I, f. 117, Charles Legac, Etat de la Situation de la province de la Louisiane, March 5, 1721; AC, F 3 241, f. 141–41v, Ordinance by Lépinay, April 30, 1717; AN, AHM 3 JJ 201, 4, Baron, Mémoire des Observations sur la colonie française du Misisipy, 1714.
   9. AC, C 13A 4, f. 639–40, Duclos, Jan. 25, 1716; C 13A 5, f. 53v, Hubert, Oct. 26, 1717.
   10. AC, C 13A 4, f. 445, Proceedings of the Council of the Navy, Oct. 20, 1716; AM, B 1 9, f. 492.

The Canadian Jean-Baptiste Baudreau, also known as Graveline, who had always been known for his activity, opened on the "black soil" of the Pascagoula River a "habitation" where he began to raise cattle. Between Nicolas Bodin-Miragouenne's establishment near the mouth of Mobile Bay, which occupied a piece of grazing land on similar soil, and Biloxi Bay, where isolated inhabitants may have resumed possession, there was now a new landmark adding another fragment to the settled zone of the shore. In the lower Mississippi Valley the situation was unchanged. The clearings made along the upper course of Bayou St. John, still in the possession of the original concession holders, remained the only agricultural establishments created by the French.[11]

At this time the Council of the Navy resolved to determine once and for all the system of land tenure, so as to prevent any recurrence of the irregularities that had appeared when Pontchartrain was in charge. Faithful to Pontchartrain's policy, the council opposed excessively large concessions acquired with a view to speculation rather than for development. For the same reason, and independently of the theory that "the king must be the only *seigneur*," it condemned the principle of seignorial concessions. Accordingly, it refused to concede Horn Island to Bienville on other than a nonfeudal basis.[12] And when, at the request of Marshal d'Estrées, the Regency Council undertook in October, 1716, to reorganize the system of "concessions of land granted in Louisiana," it acted in the conviction that the inhabitants had asked for excessively large tracts of land with the sole aim of "selling part of it" or of exploiting the timber.[13] The council's new decision consequently ordered that areas which had not been cleared should be reunited with the royal domain, leaving to the concession holders no more than the land already "built on and cultivated," together with such adjoining land as the governor and the *ordonnateur* should consider necessary "to

---

11. AC, C 13C 1, f. 400v, Bienville, Mémoire sur la Louisiane, n.d.; AE, Mem. & Doc., America, I, f. 82v, Legac, Etat dans lequel a été trouvée la colonie de la Louisiane, 1718; AN, AHM 3 JJ 201, Account of the Mobile River [1720?].

12. AC, A 22, f. 22, Decision regarding the lands of Louisiana, Paris, Oct. 12, 1716; AC, C 13A 4, f. 987, Draft of *mémoire* from the king to Lépinay and Hubert, October, 1716; AC, F 3 9, f. 312v, Mémoire du Roy au Sr de Ramezay, gouverneur de Montréal, July 10, 1715; AC, B 40, f. 524v, to M. de Mézy, Cape Breton Island, June 19, 1718; AM, B 1 30, f. 50v, Draft of instruction for Sr de Mézy; Giraud, *History*, I, 287–88.

13. BN, FF 23664, f. 73, Proceedings of the Regency Council, Oct. 12, 1716.

form a habitation." Subsequently it reiterated the provisions already formulated: the clause about obligatory validation by the Crown within two years; the provision that land must be reunited with the royal domain if it had not been "developed and was bringing a return" in the two-year period following grant of the concession; and the ban on any alienation until two-thirds of the surface had been cleared. As in the past, the Crown reserved the right to take from the concessions whatever timber and land might be needed for public works.[14]

However, the decision of 1716 was applied only to a limited extent. The clause providing for reduction of the concessions was actually implemented in very few cases; its enforcement would have displeased many, since La Mothe had distributed the land to everyone's liking. Consequently, the new regulation evoked no opposition, being interpreted essentially as conferring on the inhabitants a regular right of ownership to land that was for the moment exempt from any taxation.[15] For the first time, on the other hand, the council stipulated that the concessions be cultivated in accordance with the same pattern of long, narrow fields that prevailed in the country along the St. Lawrence River and which the Crown was at the same time insisting upon on Cape Breton Island. This principle, which was already applied in the clearings along Bayou St. John,[16] would henceforth be the rule for all lands in the colony. Everywhere, the inhabitants would be given plots of land "two or four arpents wide and forty or sixty deep," except on Dauphin Island where, while the form of the concessions remained the same, settlers would be given tracts of land only large enough "to build on and for gardens to be created," the rest of the island being left open as "common pastures" for the cattle belonging to the inhabitants and the garrison.[17]

Despite these innovations, the population did not succeed in

---

14. AC, A 22, f. 22–23v, Decision regarding the lands of Louisiana, Paris, Oct. 12, 1716; AM, B 1 9, f. 474v, Proceedings of the Council of the Navy, Oct. 12, 1716; Giraud, *History,* I, 288–89.

15. AC, A 23, f. 8, Decision by the Council of State to reduce the concessions of land granted in Louisiana, Oct. 12, 1716 (marginal note). On the opposition aroused in the colony by these clauses, see Giraud, *History,* I, 288–89.

16. Giraud, *History,* I, 356.

17. AC, A 22, f. 22v, Decision regarding the lands of Louisiana, Paris, Oct. 12, 1716; AC, C 13A 4, f. 969–70, 973, Draft of *mémoire* from the king to Lépinay and Hubert, October, 1716.

shaking off the feeling of uncertainty from which it had always suffered. Reality had proved too disappointing for people to feel able to hope they could do anything useful while staying near the coast. Hubert seems to have supported them in this view. His correspondence sounds the same note of discouragement as that of the merchant Baron or of Sieur Louis Bécard de Grandville.[18] Hubert believed it was futile to persist in an area that was the only barren part of Louisiana, when inland the soil was amazingly fertile. As he saw it, the entire plan for occupying Louisiana had to be looked at afresh, so as to bring the colony back to its original purpose, which was to ensure for France the domination of the Mississippi. Yet the French had turned their backs on "that great river . . . in order to go to the Mobile River" and take possession of Dauphin Island, the "frightening sandbars" of which presented a constant threat to shipping.[19] The bay "where La Salle came down" ("the Bay of the Madeleine or St. Bernard's Bay") would have been a better choice, given the quality of the soil, the relative proximity to the Mississippi, and the opportunities offered for trade with the Spaniards. The Mobile position was certainly not without its uses, but Hubert would readily have given it up in favor of "La Salle's bay." This was also the view taken by Derbanne.[20]

As for Dauphin Island, it was no longer as interesting as formerly. In 1716–1717 it lost its role as an outpost of Mobile, which had been the chief reason for settling people there. Rémonville and Baron had already pointed out the danger to shipping constituted by the narrowness and shallowness of the entry channel and the poor protection that low-lying Spaniards Island offered against "blasts of wind." Although the bottom of the channel and the harbor, being made of "firm mud," enabled ships to anchor solidly and resist storms, alluvial deposits from the river were reducing year by year the width and depth of the passage available for navigation, especially when the practice of careening ships in the channel encouraged accumulations of

18. AN, AHM 3 JJ 201 4, Baron, Mémoire des observations sur la colonie française du Misisipy, 1714; Giraud, *History*, I, 283–84.

19. AC, C 13A 5, f. 140, 142, Hubert, Mémoire sur la colonie de la Louisiane, October, 1717; C 13C 1, f. 87v–88, Hubert, n.d.

20. AC, C 13A 5, f. 57v (P.S.), Hubert, Oct. 26, 1717; f. 123v–24, Hubert, Nov. 26, 1717; f. 139v–40, Hubert, Mémoire sur la colonie de la Louisiane, October, 1717; C 13C 4, f. 42–43, Journal d'un voyage que M. Derbanne a fait au Mexique, Nov. 1, 1717.

sand so thick that trenches had to be dug through them to allow traffic to pass.[21] And as the depth of the water diminished, ships found it harder to withstand the force of hurricanes. The *Dauphine* went down in these conditions at the beginning of 1716.[22]

In the following year the situation suddenly became worse. The bad weather that prevailed in March when the royal frigates arrived made it particularly difficult to approach the island. The *Ludlow* was unable to reach the narrow entrance to the harbor, and although the *Paon* managed to enter, thanks to a lull in the storm, it struck the shore while being towed and suffered serious damage. At the end of April, when the *Paon* was about to start off again, a storm broke; muddy waves completely blocked the channel linking Dauphin Island to Spaniards Island and closed the usual exit from the harbor. It was only after much sounding that the ship's master, Lieutenant Simon Du Sault, helped by Jacques Le Roux, a master shipbuilder from Rochefort, discovered eastward of Spaniards Island a fairway adequate for the *Paon* to get out of harbor.[23] But this new route, which Sieur Du Sault hoped might turn out to be an improved replacement of the henceforth impassable "western passage," was even more vulnerable, being more likely to become silted up. It was in an area congested with constantly shifting sandbanks, where even Crozat's brigantine, which drew very little water, was unable to get through. In fact, after this time there was no safe anchorage except at a point one-third of a league west of Spaniards Island, and unfortunately this "great roadstead" was too open and too remote from Dauphin Island to serve as a harbor for disembarkation.[24] There could be no ques-

---

21. AC, F 3 24, f. 85, Rémonville, Description du fleuve St Louis ou Mississipi, 1715; AC, C 13A 4, f. 971–72, Draft of *mémoire* from the king to Lépinay and Hubert, October, 1716; AN, AHM 3 JJ 201 4, Baron, Mémoire des observations sur la colonie française du Misisipy, 1714, and Observations touchant la colonie du Mississipy, 1715. Spaniards Island was originally called Ile Espagnolette.

22. AC, C 13A 4, f. 551, La Mothe, Jan. 23, 1716; f. 635, Duclos, Jan. 25, 1716.

23. AC, C 13A 5, f. 38v–39, L'Epinay, Dauphin Island, May 10, 1717; AM, B 1 21, f. 9v, 10–12, Du Sault, aboard the *Paon*, Aug. 29, 1717.

24. AC, C 13A 4, f. 597–99, Observations by La Mothe-Cadillac to the Council of the Navy, June 22, 1716; C 13A 5, f. 46, Hubert, Oct. 26, 1717; f. 140v, Hubert, Mémoire sur la colonie de la Louisiane, October, 1717; C 13C 2, f. 149–49v, Du Sault, aboard the *Paon*, Aug. 29, 1717; f. 156, Le Maire, Mémoire sur la Louisiane, 1718; C 13C 4, f. 75–75v, Mémoire des connaissances que le Sr Béranger a tirées de la province de Louisiane, AE, Mem. & Doc., America, I, f. 203v, Bienville, June 10, 1718; Giraud, *History*, I, Fig. 6, pp. 64–65.

tion of creating on the low shore of Dauphin Island, which was permanently threatened with submersion, an artificial harbor by building a series of locks like those at Dunkirk, to drain away the constantly renewed deposits of sand. Nor was it possible to open a new access channel to Port Dauphin by building a jetty or "palisade" long enough to cross all the interminable sandbars at the mouth of Mobile Bay.[25]

Among the people, the closing of the harbor inevitably confirmed the notion that Dauphin Island would soon be abandoned. Everyone believed that as soon as the Council of the Navy learned what had happened, it would order the place evacuated. Once again, therefore, the inhabitants, who had lost many of their cattle in the storm, gave in to discouragement and apathy. While awaiting the council's decision, they left unfinished the dwellings they had been building and did not even repair the ones they occupied, and the *ordonnateur* Hubert, convinced that a change was imminent, did nothing about this. As he saw it, the only thing to be done was to reoccupy Ship Island, the natural advantages of which had been underestimated, for it possessed, within reach of the Mississippi, a "roadstead steady and sure" in which, if it were fortified, all ships coming from France could anchor. And he believed it possible that the inhabitants might wish to return to that original position.[26]

Hubert's view was that the storehouses on Dauphin Island should be closed at once and moved to Mobile. From Ship Island, brigantines would convey direct to Fort Louis goods from France, while cargoes intended for the inland posts and the Illinois country would be taken to the Mississippi by *voyageurs* who would come across to fetch them as the ships arrived. It would even be possible to shorten the journey of these *voyageurs* by establishing new storehouses "at Biloxy on the Mississippi," to which boats would convey the goods from Ship Island. Hubert did not yet have an inkling of the birth of New Orleans. This "Biloxy," which meant both the site of the future capital and the zone of the portage and the upper end of Bayou St. John, was

---

25. AC, C 13A 4, f. 597–99, Observations by La Mothe-Cadillac to the Council of the Navy, June 22, 1716; C 13A 5, f. 140v–41, Hubert, Mémoire sur la colonie de la Louisiane, October, 1717; C 13C 1, f. 82v–83, Hubert, n.d.

26. AC, C 13A 5, f. 46, 49–49v, Hubert, Oct. 26, 1717; f. 140–41, Hubert, Mémoire sur la colonie de la Louisiane, October, 1717; C 13C 1, f. 82v–83v, Hubert, n.d.; AN, AHM 3 JJ 201 4, Baron, Mémoire des observations . . . , 1714; BN, FF 14613, f. 307, Pénigaut's report.

for him to be merely an entrepôt where the "traders who navigate the river" would pick up supplies.²⁷

Actually, Dauphin Island was never abandoned, and the question would not arise so long as France retained Fort Louis. Protected by a fort of stakes, with a good garrison and a battery of big guns, the fort could effectively defend the entry to Mobile Bay, and Hubert advised that it be kept for that purpose.²⁸ But the inhabitants were now convinced that Ship Island was going to take its place, and this feeling doomed every inclination to do anything and paralyzed the life of the settlement.

While justified by the closing of Dauphin Island's harbor, the plan to return to Ship Island was a fresh example of the instability that had up to now prevented definitive occupation of any point on the coast. Hubert regretted this indecisiveness and put it down to the confusion caused at Court by the diversity of opinions to which the colony was still subject.²⁹ On a coast, however, where the Spaniards held all the natural places of refuge, hesitation was inevitable. No decisive solution was in fact possible. The Ship Island position, though less "variable" than Dauphin Island, was itself a dubious choice from several angles, and the part of the coast to which it gave covered access did not offer any better prospects for agriculture than the Mobile region.³⁰

The weakness of agriculture was not made up for by trade in the last years of Crozat's regime. The desire expressed by the Council of the Navy to intensify relations between France and the overseas provinces could not affect Louisiana in the immediate future, since the financier's monopoly was as absolute there as ever.³¹ In any case, it is doubtful whether, even if Crozat had loosened his grip, the colony would have attracted merchants. Rémonville's sad example would have sufficed to put off any who might have felt inclined to fit out a ship to go to the Mississippi. Five years of lawsuits and proceedings had still not enabled him to settle his debts.³² When the Crown paid him the

27. AC, C 13C 1, f. 83–83v, Hubert, n.d.; Giraud, *History*, I, Fig. 1, p. 35, and p. 356.

28. AC, C 13C 1, f. 83, Hubert, n.d.; AE, Mem. & Doc., America, I, f. 200, Bienville, June 10, 1718.

29. AC, C 13A 5, f. 139v, Hubert, Mémoire sur la colonie de la Louisiane, October, 1717.

30. AC, C 13C 2, f. 156, Mémoire de Le Maire, 1718; AN, AHM 3 JJ 200 4, Le Maire, Mémoire sur la Louisiane, May 13, 1718.

31. See Chap. V.

32. Giraud, *History*, I, 137–40.

money it owed in the form of orders on the Treasurer of the Navy, he offered to hand this sum over to his creditors, but many of them refused to accept it, particularly since these notes lost four-fifths of their value when converted into state notes. Rémonville's situation was made worse by the difficulties he encountered in recovering a deposit of 4,500 livres that the treasurer of the navy had retained when Rémonville was awarded, for the Louisiana service, a British ship he had captured during the voyage of the *Renommée*. To escape the humiliation of arrest for debt, as his creditors threatened, Rémonville had continually to request the Regent for safe-conducts.[33]

Furthermore, the state of trade in the realm reduced the merchants' possibilities of action. Although the Regent's first financial measures eased the difficulties of the treasury for the time being, they worsened the commercial crisis that prevailed at the end of Louis XIV's reign. The inadequacy of the money supply, the "extraordinary scarcity of silver," and the absence of credit caused many a bankruptcy.[34] Consequently, there was no capital available for colonial enterprises. Merchants showed reluctance even where trade with the West Indies was concerned[35] and they were less interested still in a colony so poor as Louisiana. Even if the Council of the Navy had opened up the colony freely to

---

33. AM, B 1 19, f. 491–92, Rémonville, La Rochelle, April 17, 1717; f. 498–99, Gillot, Rochefort, April 18, 1717; f. 342v–45, Rémonville, La Rochelle, Feb. 6, 1717; B 1 20, f. 503v, Rémonville, La Rochelle, July 17, 1717; B 1 21, f. 17–19, Proceedings of the Council of the Navy, Sept. 7, 1717; B 1 30, f. 235–38, Proceedings of the Council of the Navy, Aug. 9, 1718; f. 323v–25, Proceedings of Sept. 24, 1718; f. 351–52, Beauharnais, Oct. 9, 1718; AC, B 39, f. 70v, 94v–95, to Beauharnais, July 7, Oct. 15, 1717; f. 161v–62, to Lusançay, Sept. 8, 1717; B 1 40, f. 55–55v, to Beauharnais, Sept. 30, 1718; f. 63, to Rémonville, Oct. 19, 1718; AC, F 1A 20, f. 53–53v, Order to pay to Sr de Rémonville, Nov. 26, 1718; AC, F 2C 1, f. 233–34, Proceedings of the Council of the Navy, Sept. 23, 1718; AC, C 13A 4, f. 25–27, Proceedings of the Council, Jan. 4, 1716.

34. BN, FF 6933, f. 20–33, the Regent to M. de Basville, Feb. 3, 1716; FF 11378, f. 144–46, Guynet, Caen, July 17, 1717; FF 23672, f. 179, Proceedings of the Regency Council, June 21, 1717; AE, Mem. & Doc., France, 1219, f. 110v–11, Jean Chaperon, Mémoire pour le rétablissement et l'augmentation du commerce de France, Oct. 28, 1715; AM, B 3 236, f. 347–28, 350–51, 396, Lusançay, March 3, March 28, May 14, 1716; Buvat, Journal de la Régence, I, 242; E. J. Hamilton, "Prices and Wages at Paris under John Law's System," *Quarterly Journal of Economics* (November, 1936), 43–44.

35. AC, B 39, f. 162v, to Champigny and Le Brun, Sept. 11, 1717; AM, B 1 21, f. 257v, Begue, Sept. 16, 1717; B 1 29, f. 415, 419v, Feuquières, Fort Royal, Feb. 19, 1718; AC, F 3 83, f. 68, Bénard, Mémoire pour le Conseil de marine, Dec. 1, 1720.

their initiatives, that would not have solved the question of return cargoes. "Louisiana," wrote the administrators of St. Domingue, "is not a place where merchants seek to do any trade. There are few inhabitants and no produce, and no money is to be seen there."[36] Although there was increasing speculation at Court about the colony's future prospects, all Louisiana could supply for the moment was the hides of deer and buffalo, planks, and tar, which was beginning to be made there. None of this, moreover, was in great quantity, and all of it crudely prepared, because the Mississippi still lacked a tar distillery, a tannery, or a sawmill. If Crozat had managed, as he tried, to build a sawmill in Louisiana he would have been introducing in the colony a technology still unknown in the home country, since it was only in 1717 that the Council of the Navy considered buying the first example from Holland.[37] At this elementary stage of its development, Louisiana could not have attracted merchants from France, whatever regime it was under.

The business done in Louisiana was still conducted on as narrow a basis as in previous years. Crozat's storehouse on Dauphin Island was poorly stocked. The trade goods most in demand were not plentiful enough to maintain a substantial traffic with the natives, and disposal of them was made difficult by the high prices the company imposed. The "reduction order" that Crozat sent to his agents, which arrived in March, 1717, only a few months before the end of his monopoly, had, as has been mentioned, no immediate effect. The result was a paradoxical situation in which, while the administrators complained of a shortage of goods, the financier's storehouse was cluttered with unsalable articles. In 1717 supplies that had arrived four years earlier on the *Baron de la Fauche* had still not been disposed of completely.[38] And yet with what they obtained from the storehouse, the inhabitants managed to carry on a certain amount of

36. AM, B 1 20, f. 419, Chateaumorant and Mithon, May 11, 1717.

37. AC, B 39, f. 129, 133, M. de Louches, May 5, June 7, 1717; f. 305v, to MM. de Costebelle and Soubras, July 5, 1717; AM, B 1 29, f. 377, Proceedings of the Council of the Navy, April 1, 1718; AC, C 13C 1, f. 118v, Mémoire sur la Louisiane; C 13C 2, f. 111v, Le Maire, Jan. 15, 1714; BN, FF 12105, f. 16, Le Maire, Mémoire sur la Louisiane, March 1, 1717; Giraud, *History*, I, 286–87.

38. See p. 64 above. AC, C 13A 5, f. 27–28v, L'Epinay and Hubert, May 30, 1717; f. 49, Hubert, Oct. 26, 1717; AM, B 1 9, f. 100–100v, Proceedings of the Council of the Navy, Aug. 4, 1716; f. 424, Duclos, June 3, 1716; AE, Mem. & Doc., America, I, f. 293–93v, List presented by Sr Crozat . . . for the liquidation, estimate of the merchandise he surrenders to the king.

trade with the Indians, which brought them in return foodstuffs and buckskins. This trade was practiced by the officers and soldiers, many of whom had, moreover, stocked up with trade goods before they left France. Spirits in particular served for especially lucrative barter transactions, despite the restrictions that Lépinay tried to enforce against their sale.[39]

It was to these few exchanges that the colony's internal trade was reduced, and its external trade was no more active. The commercial relations established with the Illinois country were becoming more and more modest. The *voyageurs* still kept up, via the Mississippi, the link with Dauphin Island. They chose for their descent of the river the season of floods (January–May), which enabled them to use comparatively spacious "vehicles," replacing these with lighter craft when they returned up river at the time of low water in the autumn. Through Bayou St. John and Lake Pontchartrain they made their way to the coast, and so to Mobile Bay. The products they brought with them might have given rise to a fairly variegated trade, but alas, the insufficient quantity of goods available on Dauphin Island and the excessive prices asked for them restricted the possibilities for trade, and in many cases the *voyageurs'* pirogues had to go back empty.[40]

At the same time, the trade that had begun to develop with St. Domingue and the Islands dried up. No mention of any such activity is found in the last years of Crozat's monopoly. From time to time we learn that a ship is being fitted out at St. Domingue to sail to Mobile, but it usually fails to arrive. The St. Domingue settlers seem even to have stopped buying timber in Louisiana, preferring to get it from New England.[41] For their part, the inhabitants of Mobile and Dauphin Island communicated only with difficulty with the markets in the Islands, since they lacked the necessary vessels. The British ship that Rémonville had put at their disposal, the *Catherine,* was soon seized by

39. AC, C 13A 5, f. 47v, 57, Hubert, Oct. 26, 1717; C 13A 6, f. 328v, Leblond de la Tour, Aug. 30, 1722; AC, F 3 241, f. 141, Ordinance by Lépinay, May 24, 1716.

40. AC, C 13A 4, f. 787, 789–91, 795, 803–804, Mémoire en forme de journal . . . ; C 13A 5, f. 27–28, L'Epinay and Hubert, May 30, 1717; f. 65, Bienville, May 10, 1717; C 13C 1, f. 351v (Véniard de Bourgmont), Exacte description de la Louisiane; AN, AHM 3 JJ 201 8, Report on the Mobile River, n.d.; Giraud, *History,* I, 344–46.

41. AC, C 9A 13, Petition to the marquis de Chateaumorant, Léogane, Oct. 15, 1717; AM, B 1 5, f. 102v–103, Laudreau, Rochefort, Aug. 1, 1716; B 1 21, f. 168v, 170, M. de Charitte, at Cap Français, Aug. 12, 1717.

the Spaniards, and Charles Fleury's brigantine, the *Marguerite*, was abandoned at Vera Cruz, where it had been "found unserviceable."[42]

The problem of communications by sea thus continued to be as serious as in the period of isolation during the War of the Spanish Succession. For the crossing to St. Domingue, Louisiana possessed only a "ferryboat," the *Heureux*, which appears to have made its last trip in February, 1716. And when Crozat surrendered his monopoly, the colony's "seagoing vessels" consisted only of some "flatboats" of no more than fifteen tons burden. To an even greater extent, navigation was confined to the immediate neighborhood of Dauphin Island and Mobile Bay. The Council of the Navy assigned no greater role than this to their ferryboat, and considering it pointless to retain a relatively large crew on the payroll, it reduced their numbers to ten.[43]

The monetary situation also helped to keep the colony's commercial life in permanent stagnation. The country's channels of trade were congested with valueless notes, and given the lack of specie, only exchanges effected in kind were possible. The almost complete lack of money in circulation was not only a source of discontent; it also restricted Crozat's operations, since the inhabitants were not keen to hand over to the company's storehouse, which would not pay for them in money, the produce and skins that the Indians supplied.[44] The Council of the Navy intended to provide a partial solution to the problem by issuing some copper coins, which would at least bring small-denomination currency into colonies where money was particularly scarce. Marshal d'Estrées proposed this to the Regency Council in November, 1716, and an edict was duly promulgated to circulate six-denier and twelve-denier coins in the American

---

42. AC, C 9A 12, Statement by François Gabaret, Jan. 3, 1715; C 13A 5, f. 257–57v, Proceedings of the Council of the Navy, March 25, 1719; AM, B 1 9, f. 75v, 342, 346, Proceedings of the Council, July 28, Sept. 1, 1716. See p. 141 above. Giraud, *History*, I, 174.

43. AM, B 1 9, f. 266–67v, 492, Proceedings of the Council of the Navy, Aug. 29, Oct. 20, 1716; AC, C 13A 4, f. 305, 445, Proceedings of the Council, Sept. 8, Oct. 20, 1716; f. 665, Draft of the expenditure thought by Duclos to be indispensable for maintaining the colony, June 5, 1716; f. 985, Draft of *mémoire* by king to Lépinay and Hubert, October, 1716; C 13A 5, f. 54, Hubert, Oct. 26, 1717; f. 182, General inventory of all the effects . . . found in the royal storehouses . . . , March 1, 1718; AC, F 1A 19, f. 70, List of expenditure to be undertaken for the colony of Louisiana, 1716.

44. AC, C 13A 5, f. 57, Hubert, Oct. 26, 1717.

possessions. But the letters patent putting this decision into effect were not completed until March, 1717, and the first consignment of coins, intended for the year 1718, had to be held back for a later date because of a mistake made in striking them.[45]

The little money that did circulate in the colony came from pay and salaries, and we know how irregular that source could be because of Crozat's default. Trade with the Spanish possessions was too uncertain to make much contribution to Louisiana's money supply.[46] Saint-Denis' enterprises had recently shown that it was useless to expect to overcome the Spanish authorities' opposition to a commercial understanding between the colonies of the two kingdoms.[47] It seemed increasingly clear, as La Mothe had forecast, that only clandestine transactions could be effected with the places under Spanish rule. The voyage that Crozat's agent Chastelain made to Havana on the *Ludlow* in the weeks following that ship's arrival at Dauphin Island served as proof of that. Although Chastelain succeeded in arranging to sell to two Spanish merchants some textiles from Rouen and Brittany, to be delivered at Mobile in one case and in Cuba in the other, this was done behind the back of the authorities, who had immediately informed the captain of the frigate that they would not receive any French vessel. Before leaving Havana Chastelain even managed secretly to sell three thousand buckskins, receiving their price in specie and tobacco, and he returned convinced that the Spaniards would willingly make more purchases of the same order (provided the governor remained in ignorance) in exchange for the tobacco that was so plentiful in the island.[48] In the previous year the French consul at Teneriffe had suggested to Crozat's company that they introduce French goods into the ports of Spanish America via the Canary Islands, conveying the proceeds from their sale, with the complicity of the Spanish merchants, either to Havana, where

---

45. AC, A 22, f. 24v, Letters patent for giving currency in America to 12-denier and 6-denier coins, March 9, 1717; BN, FF 23664, f. 81v, 143, Proceedings of the Regency Council, Nov. 16, 1716, March 14, 1718; AM, B 1 19, f. 281v–82v, Draft of letters patent for giving currency in America . . . , Council of the Navy, March 20, 1717; AC, 39, f. 177v, to the duc de Noailles, Dec. 18, 1717; f. 243v, to Vaudreuil and Bégon, July 6, 1717; f. 341, Letters patent for giving currency in America. . . .
46. AM, B 1 9, f. 423v–24, Duclos, June 3, 1716; Giraud, *History,* I, 296–97, 301.
47. Giraud, *History,* I, 367–68; p. 185f. below.
48. AC, C 13C 1, f. 84–86v, Hubert, n.d.

the financier's representatives could pick them up in passing, or else direct to Dauphin Island.[49]

However, trade of this sort involved too many risks and uncertainties to result in regular transactions that might ensure periodic arrivals of piastres in Louisiana. The consul at Teneriffe, while declaring that "with the Spaniards, payment makes everything easy," agreed that it was hard "to obtain entry to Havana" and harder still "to take a cargo on board there."[50] And Crozat was too cautious to risk letting his ships or their cargoes get confiscated, especially at a moment when the governor of Havana did not conceal the aggressive designs that the King of Spain[51] entertained on Louisiana. The trade Crozat would have liked to carry on with the Spanish provinces could not amount under these conditions to anything more than casual operations subject to the skill shown in evading the governors' vigilance. The resultant profits, moreover, would benefit the financier alone: he and nobody else would take possession of the metal coins collected in Havana, and Louisiana's monetary circulation would gain nothing from the activity.

The decision of the Council of the Navy to forbid the king's officers to engage in private trade of any sort in the colonies, however justified, had the effect of restricting still further the population's commercial opportunities. By way of exception, the council allowed Lieutenant Du Sault to take out a limited quantity of goods so as to be able to procure at Dauphin Island the "refreshments" his sailors needed. All other transactions, however, were banned. The enquiry the council ordered into the trading activity of which the offices of the *Ludlow* and the *Paon* were accused when they returned to France was carried out in a spirit that testified to the council's determination no longer to tolerate such practices.[52]

The facilities that Crozat seems to have wished to offer to merchants wishing to undertake barter dealings with the Indi-

49. AM, B 7 267, Mémoire joint à la lettre du Sr Porlier, conseul de France à Ténérife, June 26, 1716.
50. *Ibid.*
51. AC, C 13C 1, f. 86, Hubert, n.d.
52. AC, B 38, f. 173v, to Du Sault, Sept. 14, 1716; f. 311, Mémoire du Roy pour servir d'instruction au Sr de L'Epinay, Oct. 20, 1716; B 1 39, f. 85v–86, to Beauharnais, Oct. 20, 1717; AM, B 1 9, f. 361v–62, Proceedings of the Council of the Navy, Sept. 8, 1716; B 1 21, f. 69–70, Du Sault, Rochefort, Sept. 18, 1717; f. 98v–100, Beauharnais, Oct. 12, 1717; AM, B 2 249, f. 225–25v, to Beauharnais, Dec. 8, 1717.

ans had no effective result for the moment. When they arrived at Fort Louis in Mobile, Vincent Dubreuil, Jean-Baptiste Massy, and the brothers Guénot de Tréfontaine informed the governor of their intention to go to trade "among the Alabamas and in the villages round about," accompanied by their servants.[53] Their presence in a sector that had been frequented for so long by British traders would have been singularly useful to the French cause. Unfortunately, their freedom of action was frustrated by the restrictive conditions imposed upon them: they were required to obtain permission for their movements not merely from the governor but also from the officer commanding the post in the area where they were traveling, which was contrary to their agreement with Crozat exempting them from all formalities. Discontented with the ensuing delays and the prejudicing thereby of plans the "secrecy" of which had not been respected, the merchants threatened, after several months of an experience that was disappointing and costly, to appeal to the Council of the Navy if the agreement they had made with the financier was not honored. But Crozat's resignation made their protests pointless.[54] Although their initiative was not an isolated case—two other merchants obtained in August, 1717, authorization from Lépinay to engage in trading operations among the Chickasaws and the Conchaques[55]—it could do very little to quicken the colony's trade. Barter with the Indians continued to be carried on mainly by the inhabitants, whose means were too slight for them to be able to take among the native tribes the place that the British had held before the revolt of 1715.

The *ordonnateur* Hubert therefore expressed a pessimistic view at the end of these years of transition. As he saw it, the colony lacked everything it needed. "We do not observe," he said, "any progress to have been made since it was established."[56] Neither of the two built-up areas between which the population was divided was adequate for the needs of govern-

53. AC, C 13A 5, f. 120, Copy collated by Raguet, royal notary, June 8, 1718, of permits granted by M. de Lépinay.

54. AC, F 3 241, f. 127v–28, Agreement of July 16, 1716, between Crozat and Dubreuil, Massy and Guénot.

55. AC, F 3 241, f. 149, Permit given to Srs Des Brosses and La Chaume, at Fort Louis, Aug. 30, 1717.

56. AC, C 13Aa 5, f. 139v, Hubert, Mémoire sur la colonie de la Louisiane, October, 1717; f. 188v, Hubert, Louisiane, June 10, 1718; AE, Mem. & Doc., America, I, f. 138, Hubert, Mémoire au sujet de l'établissement de la colonie de la Louisiane, 1717.

ment. The closing of the harbor of Dauphin Island and the fear that it would soon be abandoned meant that any hope of further growth was extinguished there, and seemingly rendered pointless the measures taken by Lépinay to erect a hospital and enlarge the royal storehouse and the governor's residence. The Mobile position was still no more than an isolated establishment in a hostile setting, separated from the post recently set up among the Alabamas by a considerable territory occupied by different groups of Indians.[57]

Material life was as difficult as in the past. Prices exceeded even those that prevailed in the first years of the monopoly, and the *ordonnateur* did not know how he was going to ensure the feeding of the sick when eggs and chickens, which alone could make up for the lack of meat, cost respectively 50 sols a dozen and 3 livres 12 sols each.[58] La Mothe's attempt in 1716 to fix the price of butchers' meat seems to have had no effect, because when the inhabitants slaughtered an animal, not only did they never manage to sell all the meat, but what they did sell was paid for in goods and produce of the country, the high cost of which frustrated all possibility of fixing prices at a reasonable level.[59] The shortage of local resources of food, the constant shrinking of the amount of money in circulation, and the discrediting of the notes of all kinds that choked the country's channels of trade determined, in fact, a permanent upward movement of prices that the governor was helpless to combat and which was reflected in its turn in a constantly rising level of wages. The workmen, who were paid in goods, trebled the payment they required for their day's work, doing this all the more easily because their small numbers enabled them to impose conditions.[60] The only way to stabilize prices, to some degree at least—and because of the inadequacy of what the ships brought in, this was impossible anyway—would have been to make payments, in lieu of specie, in foodstuffs from France.[61]

---

57. AC, C 13A 5, f. 52v, Hubert, Oct. 26, 1717; f. 182v, List of buildings on land situated on Dauphin Island that belong to the king, March 1, 1718; AN, AHM 3 JJ 200 4, Le Maire, Mémoire sur la Louisiane, May 13, 1718; 3 JJ 201 8, Report on the Mobile River [1720 ?]; on Fort Toulouse, see p. 157 below.

58. AC, C 13A 5, f. 47v–48, Hubert, Oct. 26, 1717; Giraud, *History*, I, 313–14.

59. AC, A 23, f. 6–6v, Ordinance, by La Mothe-Cadillac and Duclos, Aug. 23, 1716; AM, B 1 9, f. 423–23v, Duclos, June 3, 1716.

60. AC, C 13A 5, f. 254, Bienville, Sept. 25, 1718; AE, Mem. & Doc., America, I, f. 145, Hubert, Mémoire au sujet . . . de la colonie de la Louisiane, 1717.

61. AC, C 13A 5, f. 52v, Hubert, Oct. 26, 1717.

It was the salaried personnel at all levels who inevitably suffered the most immediate consequences of a situation to which their pay bore no relation. But discontent was general throughout the colony, being shown also among the inhabitants. While making the high prices that prevailed a pretext for increasing their own demands beyond all bounds, the inhabitants would not accept the refusal by the Council of the Navy to submit to their conditions for purchases it wished to make in Louisiana. This refusal constituted in their eyes, given Crozat's usurious demands, a profound injustice to them. Hubert noted the same "seditious complaints" among the population as were heard in Duclos' time.[62] The inhabitants and the salaried personnel alike held both the Crown's representatives and Crozat responsible for living conditions that seemed impossible to improve. Less and less respect did they show, consequently, for the financier's rights. And since the latter, in the last months of his monopoly, suspended the dispatch of ships to Louisiana, the governor considered it pointless to protect a privilege that no longer possessed any justification. When two British ships, one of which came from Jamaica, put in at Dauphin Island in the summer of 1717, Lépinay, while claiming to allow them only to "take in water and wood," actually gave them complete freedom to sell their goods, which included woolens, in order to mitigate the discontent among the population at a moment when the reserves of Crozat's storehouse were being exhausted.[63]

Nevertheless, despite the poor results achieved, Hubert believed that the coming of the Council of the Navy had made it possible to rescue the colony from its "deplorable condition." The initiatives taken in 1716, and the interest in colonial matters that they reflected, marked perhaps the beginning of a different future.[64] In any case, Louisiana no longer looked, as in the past, like a colony that had been sacrificed. The disquiet felt by the Spaniards at the arrival of military reinforcements and ships in greater numbers seemed to Le Bart to prove that this was so. The Spaniards, he said, were becoming aware of the country's commercial possibilities and of the role that Louisiana could play

62. *Ibid.*, f. 49, 57; AC, C 13A 5, f. 139, Hubert, Mémoire sur la colonie de la Louisiane, October, 1717; BN FF 12105, f. 20, Le Maire, Mémoire sur la Louisiane, March 1, 1717; Giraud, *History,* I, 313–14.
63. AC, C 13A 5, f. 48v–49, Hubert, Oct. 26, 1717; f. 209, Bienville and Larcebault, April 15, 1719.
64. AC, C 13A 5, f. 83v, Mémoire sur la Louisiane, 1717; f. 143, Hubert, Mémoire sur la colonie de la Louisiane, October, 1717.

when it had acquired a population capable of exploiting it.[65] For many people, indeed, trade and especially mineral resources ensured for the colony a future better than it could expect from agriculture,[66] and the Spaniards' fears were due less to the increase in the French garrison than to the progress France was making in the interior of the continent, to apprehension that it might discover mineral resources there that had hitherto remained unknown, and to the repeated attempts made by the French to develop trade relations with the neighboring Spanish colonies.

65. AE, Mem. & Doc., America, I, f. 156v, Le Bartz, 1717.
66. AC, C 13A 5, f. 142v–43, Hubert, Mémoire sur la colonie de la Louisiane, October, 1717; AN, AHM 3 JJ 201 4, Baron, Mémoire des observations, 1714; BN, FF 12105, Le Maire, March 1, 1717.

Occupation of the Hinterland XI

WHEN LOUIS XIV's reign ended, Pontchartrain's program for expanding France's zone of domination was not yet being put into effect.[1] The Council of the Navy at once took an interest in the question, and drawing upon Duché's counsel, set about forming a plan for occupying the interior of Louisiana. In doing this, it was moved, more than the secretary of state had been moved, by desire to take possession of the regions where there were minerals, the existence of which had been affirmed in many a *mémoire*. Crozat, Duché, La Mothe, Le Maire, all constantly talked of the wealth of the colony and said that this was not confined to the cursorily prospected area near the posts in the Illinois country but was also certain to be found in several other sectors, such as the Red River Valley and the Alabama country.[2] This was what largely lay behind Crozat's proposal to establish posts in the valleys of the Red River and the Arkansas River, and when he advocated a thorough occupation of the Wabash (lower Ohio) Valley, this was to ensure access to the Missouri, which would bring the French closer to "the Spanish mines."[3]

It may be that the Council of the Navy saw in these promises the means of remedying France's shortage of real money. From this time onward, in any case, the council showed an interest in minerals that found expression in its intention to make the Chevalier Jean-Charles de Follart commander-in-chief of the troops in Louisiana and especially in the curiosity it voiced regarding La Mothe's journey to the Illinois country. The council instructed Lépinay to inform himself of the precise location of the deposit that his predecessor had briefly noticed, to study the

1. Giraud, *History*, I, 349–50.
2. AC, C 13A 4, f. 509–510, La Mothe, Jan. 2, 1716; AM, B 1 9, f. 463v–64, Proceedings of the Council of the Navy, Oct. 11, 1716; AC, Fortifications records, Louisiana, 20, Crozat, Mémoire pour faire connaître . . . , 1715.
3. AC, C 13A 4, f. 443, Proceedings of the Council, Oct. 20, 1716; f. 501, Mémoire de Crozat, 1716; f. 1023–24, Mémoire de Crozat à S.A.S. [December, 1715?].

conditions for exploiting it, and to carry out deep drilling to obtain reliable knowledge of the quality of the mineral. The decision to reinforce the colony's garrison itself proceeded originally from concern to protect its mineral wealth.[4] The posts that the council planned to establish corresponded to the localities where great possibilities for mining were predicted. This was the case with the post that the council thought briefly of setting up "in the Arkansas country," on the basis of Crozat's mistaken reports; with the post it ordered to be set up in the Alabamas' territory, where young Saint Michel, who had spent many years in this region in order to learn the language of the natives, said that silver was to be found; and also with the posts to be placed among the Natchez and the Yazoos, which were thought to be near enough to the mineral areas of the Illinois country for their garrisons to help in the exploitation of these areas.[5]

The strategical argument was not, of course, overlooked by the Council of the Navy. It saw, as Pontchartrain had seen, more effective control of the interior as the surest shield against the intentions of the British in the direction of the Mississippi. Hence the plan to guard the lower valley of the Ohio and "the branch of the river that comes in from Carolina" by means of two detachments under Bienville's command. However, though both arguments were combined in the council's thinking,[6] it gave increasing weight to mining in its plans for penetration of the interior.

Having decided that the number of posts laid down in the instructions of 1714 was insufficient,[7] the council decided at the beginning of 1716 that it should add two additional establishments, one in the Arkansas country and the other on the lower Tennessee, where Crozat, making provision against an offensive

---

4. AC, B 38, f. 287, to La Mothe and Duclos, Feb. 15, 1716; AC, C 13A 4, f. 974–77, Draft of the king's *mémoire* to Lépinay and Hubert, October, 1716; C 13A 5, f. 143, Hubert, Mémoire sur la colonie de la Louisiane, 1717; AE, Mem. & Doc., America, I, f. 180v, Mémoire sur la Louisiane, 1717.

5. AC, C 13A 4, f. 501–504, Mémoire de Crozat, 1716; f. 700, Duclos, June 24, 1716; AM, B 1 9, f. 268, 283, Proceedings of the Council of the Navy, Aug. 21, 1716; f. 358v–60, Proposals by M. Duché, Council, Sept. 8, 1716; f. 419–19v, La Mothe and Duclos, July 15, 1716; AC, B 38, f. 287–88, to La Mothe and Duclos, Feb. 15, 1716; on St. Michel, see Giraud, *History*, I, 84–85.

6. AC, B 38, f. 287–89, to La Mothe and Duclos, Feb. 15, 1716; AC, C 13A 4, f. 624, La Mothe, Feb. 7, 1716; f. 673–75, Duclos, June 7, 1716; f. 1022, Mémoire de Crozat à S.A.S. [December, 1715?].

7. AM, B 1 9, f. 273–80, Proceedings of the Council of the Navy, Aug. 29, 1716; Giraud, *History*, I, 350.

by British traders, proposed to install a storehouse that would relieve the Indians of any need to buy the enemy's goods.[8] A few months later, however, convinced by letters from La Mothe and Duclos that this program was beyond the colony's means, the council agreed with Duché on a more restricted plan. One post, placed among the Alabamas, would stand guard over access to Fort Louis at Mobile, while the Mississippi, on which France still had nothing except the isolated position at Biloxi, would be protected by a fort to be situated either in the Natchez territory or in that of the Yazoos. On Duché's advice, which was probably based on information sent by *major* de Boisbriant and also on the fertility claimed for the land of this region, the council opted for the Yazoo country, resolving to leave occupation of the Natchez country and the Wabash Valley for later.[9] Meanwhile, the Yazoo garrison would suffice to protect the Natchez storehouse.[10]

The council thus settled on a formula for occupation that was narrower than Pontchartrain's and failed to provide for defense of the important Wabash "crossroads," that "second key to Louisiana." It did not even take over responsibility for feeding the troops, considering that local resources—big game, maize— would suffice until the men were able to grow wheat. And it dealt no less summarily with the question of "medical aid" when it provided that a surgeon would be attached to the Yazoo garrison and an "assistant-surgeon" to the one in the Alabamas' country. For the needs of the sick the council failed to supply either the "refreshments" or the "cots" or palliasses that the surgeon–medical officer of the colony had requested, merely instructing Lépinay to say whether he thought this additional expense appropriate.[11]

---

8. AC, B 38, f. 287–89, to La Mothe and Duclos, Feb. 15, 1716; AC, C 13A 4, f. 499–506, Mémoire de Crozat, 1716.

9. AC, C 13A 4, f. 567–68, 570, La Mothe, Jan. 31, 1716; f. 647–48, Duclos, Jan. 25, 1716; f. 972–74, Draft of the king's *mémoire* to Lépinay and Hubert, October, 1716; AM, B 1 9, f. 273–83v, Proceedings of the Council of the Navy, Aug. 29, 1716; f. 419–19v, La Mothe and Duclos, July 15, 1716; f. 358v–60, Proposals by M. Duché, Council of Sept. 8, 1716.

10. AM, B 1 19, f. 164v, Letter from Father Leblanc, note by the Council, Feb. 26, 1717; AC, C 13A 5, f. 86v–87, Mémoire sur la Louisiane, 1717; f. 141, Hubert, Mémoire sur la colonie de la Louisiane, October, 1717; C 13C 2, f. 162, Le Maire, Mémoire sur la Louisiane, 1718.

11. AC, C 13A 4, f. 979–80, Draft of the king's *mémoire* to Lépinay and Hubert, October, 1716; AC, B 38, f. 327–28, to L'Epinay and Hubert, Oct. 28, 1716; AM, B 1 9, f. 268, Proceedings of the Council, Aug. 29, 1716; f. 328v, Duclos, Dec. 25, 1715; f. 420, La Mothe and Duclos, July 20, 1716.

However, by the time the king's ships brought to Louisiana the order to postpone occupation of the Natchez country, events had decided that question otherwise. Bienville had made himself master of the Natchez territory months earlier after obtaining due satisfaction for the attacks on the Canadian *voyageurs*.[12] He had not originally contemplated inflicting a signal act of vengeance on the Natchez Indians. The one and only company he possessed would not have been enough for that, especially since he lacked wholehearted support from his subordinates. His disputes with Derbanne and with Captain Chavanne de Richebourg show that even the limited plan of action to which he had to resign himself failed to win their approval.[13]

In face of the disproportionate balance of forces, Bienville had in fact given up any idea of attacking the Natchez. When he drew near the Tunicas' village[14] above the confluence of the Red River with the Mississippi, he entrenched his forces on an island in the great river where he quickly erected three crude shelters behind a "ring of stakes" to serve as prison, guardhouse, and storehouse.[15] In this "Fort Saint-Joseph-des-Tunicas" the garrison's situation soon became extremely precarious. The spring flood quickly covered the surface of the island, and illnesses spread among the men because of the humidity and the heat, while food supplies were rapidly exhausted despite some supplements of meat and flour contributed in passing by "inhabitants from the Illinois country." Deprived of the services of some of his men and obliged to evacuate the sick to the more highly situated village of the Tunicas, Bienville resolved, given the conditions, to content himself with what satisfaction he could get that was not beyond his actual power. Accordingly, he captured a number of Natchez chiefs whom he lured into the fort by concealing any unfriendly intentions toward them. At his request, one of these chiefs got his people to execute two of the murder-

---

12. See p. 78 above.
13. AC, F 3 24, f. 79v–80, Derbanne to M. de Lamothe, April 27, 1716.
14. The Tunicas, driven by intertribal wars from the place they were living when the French arrived (Giraud, *History*, I, map, pp. 74–75), had taken possession of territory beside the Mississippi that had previously belonged to the Oumas, two or three leagues above the confluence of the Red River (AC, C 13C 1, f. 351 [Véniard de Bourgmont], Exacte description de la Louisianne; C 13C 2, f. 127, 128v, Le Maire, Jan. 15, 1714; f. 162, Le Maire, Mémoire sur la Louisiane, 1718; BN, FF 12105, Mémoire de Le Maire, March 1, 1717).
15. AC, C 13A 4, f. 678–80, Duclos, June 7, 1716; f. 788–89, Mémoire en forme de journal . . . .

ers of the Canadians. After that, by brazenly claiming that he was in a position to form a coalition of tribes that could annihilate the Natchez, Bienville made his hostages give him the names of four other guilty men, two warriors and two chiefs, who happened to be among the prisoners held in the fort. He at once took steps to "crush the heads" of the warriors and had the chiefs sent off toward Mobile with an escort of Canadians whom he ordered to kill them en route, sufficiently far from the Natchez territory for no "rumor" of this to reach their villages.[16]

The vengeance exacted was not complete, since the chief most deeply compromised, Terre Blanche ("White Earth"), had escaped and was all the more to be feared because he had openly declared for the British. Nevertheless, Bienville, by speculating skillfully on the natives' reactions and making up for the inadequacy of his means by a policy of cunning and audacity, had succeeded, without putting his men at risk, in punishing most of the guilty. He even insisted on restitution of the goods that the Natchez took from the Canadian *voyageurs* and from "Crozat's storehouse." And he obtained at last the right to erect on their territory a fort that he required them to help build.[17] The Natchez accepted Bienville's conditions without difficulty, and the *aide-major* Pailloux de Barbezan went with two soldiers to find the most suitable site for this "Fort Rosalie," which was to consecrate the military occupation of this region. He selected a "small hill" that dominated the Mississippi not far upstream from the "disembarkation point" of the Natchez, and obtaining from Bienville's camp the tools needed—axes, spades, picks, ironwork—he began construction of the fort without delay. The natives were employed to cut down and carry the "acacia-wood stakes" and to prepare the pieces of bark that would roof the buildings. Helped by a dozen soldiers, they quickly erected the four-sided palisade of the fort, within which were placed a guardhouse, a powder magazine, a storehouse, and a barracks. Started during June, 1716, the work was completed at the beginning of August, in the presence of Bienville, who had come to join the *aide-major* with the few "soldiers in good health" who were at his disposal.[18]

Actually, Fort Rosalie was nothing but a mere "upright pali-

---

16. AC, C 13A 4, f. 678–80, Duclos, June 7, 1716; f. 789–804, Mémoire en forme de journal . . . .
17. AC, C 13A 4, f. 800–801, Mémoire en forme de journal . . . .
18. *Ibid.*, f. 800–806.

sade" made of "stakes as thick as a leg," with four bastions, one at each corner, and it stayed like that until the year it was destroyed (1729), as the engineer Broutin was able to record at that time. The double escarpment by which the "little mountain" on which it stood dominated the Mississippi was itself relatively accessible: Broutin noted that "it was possible to walk into the fort from any side with the greatest of ease." As for the buildings it contained, from the guardhouse to the barracks, these were nothing but "wretched huts."[19] For the moment, however, given the apparent attitude of the Natchez, who had just been celebrating with public rejoicing their reconciliation with the French, this rudimentary edifice seemed enough to ensure occupation of the territory. Crozat's agent recovered possession of much of his merchandise and set up afresh the storehouse he had temporarily abandoned. The exchanges with the natives that took place there now recommenced. The Natchez position became once more a port of call for the *voyageurs* who traveled the Mississippi, and the little French settlement there was reconstituted under the protection of the fort. Its few inhabitants kept a small number of cattle but soon successfully undertook the growing of wheat. Increasingly the idea became established that the fertility of this region would ensure great agricultural possibilities as soon as it acquired settlers enough "to develop these."[20]

Lépinay's arrival with instructions from the Council of the Navy made no change in the situation. For lack of credits and also lack of goods in Crozat's storehouse, the governor was unable to fulfill the plan for a fort in the Yazoo country.[21] With the means he had, all that was possible was to send clothes and munitions to Fort Rosalie for the few men who remained there under Sieur Pailloux's command and to organize a detachment to set up a post among the Alabamas, whose territory, because of its strategic importance, called for an immediate military ef-

19. AC, C 13C 2, f. 220v, Journal de Diron; AC, Fortifications records, Louisiana, 35, Broutin, Map of the environs of Fort Rosalie among the Natchez and of the provisional fort.
20. AC, C 13A 4, f. 694, Bienville to La Mothe, Fort Joseph among the Tunicas, June 23, 1716; f. 806, Mémoire en forme de journal . . . ; C 13A 5, f. 141v, Hubert, Mémoire sur la colonie de la Louisiane, October, 1717; C 13C 1, f. 350–50v (Véniard de Bourgmont), Exacte description de la Louisianne.
21. AC, C 13A 5, f. 27–27v, L'Epinay and Hubert, May 30, 1717; f. 62v, Bienville, May 10, 1717; f. 141v, Hubert, Mémoire sur la colonie de la Louisiane, October, 1717; AE, Mem. & Doc, America, I, f. 205, Bienville, June 10, 1718.

fort. Twenty men set off with an interpreter, led by Lieutenant de La Tour, and during the summer they erected, in the "big village of the Alabamas" on the river of that name, Fort Toulouse, which was intended to protect Fort Louis by barring the British from access to the Mobile River.[22]

In 1717, then, the military occupation of inland Louisiana was confined to these two positions in the Natchez and the Alabama countries. They were but weak points of support for French domination of the territory. The garrisons were meager and did not include the specialized personnel needed for their auxiliary duties. The lack of a clerk and an armorer made impossible any regular system of administration and hindered relations with the natives, who regarded repairing of their weapons free of charge as a proper reward for their alliance.[23] The picture of the occupation thus remained more or less as it had been at the end of Louis XIV's reign. Between the coastal zone and the establishments in the Illinois country there were only isolated "pickets" on which no definitive occupation could base itself.

The Illinois establishments themselves, although they made an effective contribution to colonization, played no strategic role because they lacked any military protection. They were still located around the two missions to the Tamaroas and the Kaskaskias. The former, under the ministry of a Father Varlet, seems to have made no progress.[24] He approached his apostolate without conviction; disappointed by the country and angry at the religious indifference of the population of Fort Louis, whom he considered incorrigible, he turned his back on them, even though he was their "appointed parish priest," and confined his attention to his work among the Tamaroas.[25] His stay in Illinois coun-

---

22. AC, C 13A 4, f. 673–74, Duclos, June 7, 1716; C 13A 5, f. 27v, 29v–30, L'Epinay and Hubert, May 20, 1717; f. 56, Hubert, Oct. 26, 1717; f. 120, Copy collated by Raguet, royal notary, June 8, 1718, of permits granted by M. de Lépinay; AN, AHM 3 JJ 201 8, Report on the Mobile River; AE, Mem. & Doc., America, I, f. 199v, Bienville, June 10, 1718. It is not possible to give an exact figure for the garrison of Fort Rosalie. We can only note what Bienville said later, namely, that he left thirty-five men there, which must have been nearly the entire force he had for his campaign (AC, C 13C 4, f. 46v, Mémoire sur les services du Sr de Bienville [1724?]).

23. AC, C 13A 5, f. 29, 31–31v, L'Epinay and Hubert, May 30, 1717; f. 48–48v, Hubert, Oct. 26, 1717; f. 66, Bienville to Hubert, Sept. 19, 1717; f. 117, La Tour to Hubert, Fort Toulouse, March 17, 1718; f. 141v, Hubert, Memoire sur la colonie de la Louisiane, October, 1717.

24. On Dominique-Marie Varlet, see Giraud, *History*, I, 339.

25. Sem., Missions, no. 45, M. de Brisacier to M. Varlet, Paris, Oct. 31, 1716.

try, which ended in 1717, was brief, and he appears to have had no personal influence there. With him ends the rich correspondence that his predecessors had kept up with the seminaries of Paris and Quebec.[26]

The official documents tell us nothing more about the mission to the Tamaroas. They are more informative about the mission to the Kaskaskias, which was directed by Father Jean Mermet, helped by Father Louis de Ville. The little colony over whose life these two religious presided seems to have been recruited to an increasing extent from Canadians, especially the nomadic elements of the region, and because of the large number of marriages with Indian women, the population included a growing proportion of half-breeds.[27] It was natives, however, who constituted the largest number: Etienne Véniard de Bourgmont mentions about four hundred Kaskaskias and twenty Canadians. This was the situation that caused Bienville to say that the colony was not yet "established."[28] All the same, agricultural activity still went on, the Crown was thinking of granting the Jesuits a concession of four leagues of land around the church they had built, and the inhabitants were playing a role that was increasingly useful to France—some through the influence they had won over the natives, others, like the Canadian Bourdon, through the help they gave in prospecting for the region's mineral resources.[29] In these lonely spots, too, the Jesuit mission was the place where an assured welcome awaited officers whose

26. Sem., Mgr Taschereau, Mission de Séminaire de Québec chez les Tamarois ou Illinois, 1849; Auguste Gosselin, *L'Eglise du Canada depuis Monseigneur de Laval jusqu'à la conquête* (3 vols.; Quebec, 1911–14), I, 331ff.; A. Rhéaume, "Mgr Dominique-Marie Varlet," *Bulletin des Recherches Historiques* (February, 1897), 18–20; BN, FFNA 5398, f. 50–52, Extract from a letter from M. Varlet, missionary, to M. Varlet, his brother, from Fort Louis, Jan. 5, 1714 (reproduced in part in Delanglez, *The French Jesuits in Lower Louisiana*, 74).

27. AC, C 11A 35, f. 254v, Bishop of Quebec to the Minister, Aug. 14, 1715; C 11A 38, f. 101, Vaudreuil, Oct. 12, 1717; C 13A 4, f. 926, Mémoire sur l'importance d'envoyer des habitants à la Louisianne [written in Louisiana], Oct. 8, 1716; AM B 1 9, f. 65, Vaudreuil and Bégon, Oct. 14, 1716. AE, Mem. & Doc., America, I, f. 315v, Duché to [comte de Toulouse ?], Paris, May 19, 1717; "Kaskaskia Church Records, 1717," *Transactions of the Illinois State Historical Society for the Year 1904* (Springfield, 1904).

28. AC, C 13C 1, f. 353 (Véniard de Bourgmont), *Exacte Description de la Louisianne*; AE, Mem. & Doc., America, I, f. 201v, Bienville, June 10, 1718.

29. AM, B 1 9, f. 627v–28, Vaudreuil, Oct. 14, 1716; AE, Mem. & Doc., America, I, f. 277–78, Crozat to comte de Toulouse, Sept. 28, 1716. See p. 40 above, and Giraud, *History*, I, 352n12.

state of health called for immediate help or traders who were trying to escape from attacks by the natives.[30]

Unfortunately, the lack of a fort and garrison reduced the usefulness of these concentrations of population. Their remoteness from the posts in the Great Lakes region, the importance that the Council of the Navy attached to the mineral resources of the neighborhood, and the advantage there would be in guarding against possible incursions by the British and in supervising more closely the *coureurs de bois* who operated in the Illinois country, would all have justified the taking of protective measures.[31] Such measures would have been all the more necessary in that relations with Dauphin Island and Mobile became temporarily less active than in previous years. Lépinay was in Louisiana for too short a time to visit the settlements in the interior, and he sent no military detachments there. The direction of these groups of people consequently fell even more completely than before to the charge of the missionaries alone: the Jesuits, especially—who were more closely involved with the country and its population than the representative of the Seminary of Foreign Missions—wielded the principal authority there.

The Jesuits' ambition extended beyond their mission to the Kaskaskias. In 1716 Crozat had urged the Council of the Navy to realize the need to increase the number of missionaries to meet the needs of the posts it intended to create. He had proposed that the Seminary be assigned the missions of southern Louisiana between the coast and the lands of the Natchez and Alabamas, reserving to the Jesuits the positions in the Illinois, Wabash, and Arkansas countries. As masters of the Kaskaskia country and the lower valley of the Ohio, these religious would then command sufficient agricultural resources to ensure the food supply for the new post among the Arkansas.[32] For that last-mentioned mission, Crozat suggested that the Capuchins might be enlisted. Two who had already served in India and in Egypt expressed a desire to go to Louisiana, and one, Father Alexis de Loches, could claim scientific qualifications—while in India, he had taught mathematics and piloting, and so pos-

---

30. AC, C 11A 36, f. 71, Vaudreuil, Oct. 14, 1716; C 11A 38, f. 101–101v, Vaudreuil, Oct. 12, 1717; AM, B 1 9, f. 627–28, Vaudreuil, Oct. 14, 1716.

31. AM, B 1 8, f. 274, Ramezay and Bégon, Nov. 7, 1715; AC, C 13A 4, f. 443, Proceedings of the Council of the Navy, Oct. 20, 1716.

32. AC, C 13A 4, f. 119–20, Proceedings of the Council of the Navy, June 23, 1716.

sessed sufficient knowledge of cartography and land surveying to do the work of an engineer. Bringing the Capuchins into this middle zone, said Crozat, would form "a sort of barrier" between the Seminarians and the Jesuits, and the good relations that the Capuchins enjoyed with the latter would probably prevent any possible conflict with the religious in the Illinois country.[33]

The financier's suggestions (which there is no reason to suppose were directly inspired by Bienville) implied that the Seminary was to give up its establishment among the Tamaroas.[34] However, the Council of the Navy declined to deprive the Seminary of this last vestige of authority. It also rejected, after first showing some slight inclination to adopt it, the proposal that new missionaries be recruited among the Capuchins—not so much from prejudice against their order, it appears, but rather from fear of the conflicts that might one day result from such a measure.[35] The council also hesitated, out of considerations of economy, to entrust the Arkansas to the Jesuits. That task it thought should fall to the Seminary, in view of the subsidy it received for the missions in Louisiana.[36] When at last the council did choose the Jesuits and provided a special credit for them, this was because of Crozat's insistence and the desire he expressed for a "correspondence" to be created between the missions in the Arkansas and Illinois countries, for which unity of spiritual leadership would constitute the best guarantee.[37] And when the council renounced the idea of occupying the Arkansas country, it chose at Duché's request a Jesuit missionary for the Yazoos, attaching to him, after representations from the bursar of his order, two others for the Illinois and the Wabash area, although the council had no plans for a post on the lower Ohio in the immediate future.[38] However, only two Jesuits, Fathers Guillaume Loyard and Jean Le Boullenger, came to Louisiana in the

33. *Ibid.*, f. 120–21.

34. Contrary to what is said by Delanglez, *The French Jesuits in Lower Louisiana*, 75.

35. AC, C 13A 4, f. 121, Proceedings of the Council of the Navy, June 23, 1716; AC, B 38, f. 424v, Instructions to Sr de La Varenne, Aug. 17, 1716; AM, B 1 20, f. 298–99, M. de La Varenne, April 10, 1717.

36. AC, C 13A 4, f. 121–22, Proceedings of the Council of the Navy, June 23, 1716.

37. AC, C 13A 4, f. 131, Proceedings of the Council of the Navy, July 6, 1716; AC, B 38, f. 45, to marshal de Villeroy, July 11, 1716.

38. AM, B 1 9, f. 360–60v, Proceedings of the Council, Sept. 8, 1716; AC, B 38, f. 177v, to Beauharnais, Sept. 30, 1716.

frigates of 1717. According to Bienville, they were assigned to missionary work among the Yazoos and the chaplaincy of the fort that the council proposed to erect on their territory.[39]

We know how much the Jesuits' arrival worried the priests of the Seminary, who considered themselves despoiled of a position that they regarded as belonging to their missions. Le Maire accused the Jesuits of having given a "false account" of the situation in order to justify before the Council of the Navy their claims in relation to the Yazoos and the peoples of the Red River Valley.[40] The Seminary was in no position to react against what was being done. In Paris, Crozat, who they thought was on their side, supported the Jesuits' claims, and in Louisiana itself the Seminarians had no one on whom they could rely to oppose their rivals. Father Antoine Davion, the only representative of the Seminary who was doing missionary work among the natives, was kept busy with the Tunicas and was in any case too conciliatory by temperament to contend with the new missionaries about responsibility for work among the Yazoos.[41]

For the moment, being obliged to wait at Fort Louis for an opportunity to begin their journey to the Yazoo country, the Jesuits were unable to enter the domain that had been allotted to them. That was regrettable, for the gradual progress of French expansion and the more extensive contacts with the natives that resulted would have called for closer collaboration on the part of these spiritual workers, whose personal influence might have made up for some of the most glaring defects of the French occupation.

39. AM, B 1 19, f. 164v, 167, Father Leblanc, bursar of the Jesuit missionaries in Canada, to the Council of the Navy, n.d.; AE, Mem. & Doc., America, I, f. 83v, Legac, Etat dans lequel a été trouvée la colonie de la Louisiane le 25 août 1718; Sem., Missions, no. 45, M. de Brisacier to M. Varlet, Paris, Oct. 31, 1716; Delanglez, *The French Jesuits in Lower Louisiana*, 80; Camille de Rochemonteix, *Les Jésuites et la Nouvelle-France au XVIIIe siècle* (Paris, 1906), I, 263.

40. Sem., Missions, no. 47, F. Le Maire, Dauphin Island, May 28, 1717.

41. *Ibid.*, Missions, no. 45, M. de Brisacier to M. Varlet, Paris, Oct. 31, 1716; Letters 0, no. 53, M. Tremblay to M. Glandelet, June 5, 1712.

XII Native Policy and the Conflict with the British

THE REBELLION OF the Indian tribes against the British traders improved France's position for a moment only.[1] In order to win a lasting alliance with the natives France would have needed extensive financial resources backed by an active and generous commercial policy. The Council of the Navy had been convinced from the outset that "constantly repeated" distributions of gifts would be the surest guarantee of the natives' support. It recommended that "kind actions" toward them should not be stinted, and that they should be reminded that France had not set foot in Louisiana "with a view to conquering them" but so as to "trade with them" and to offer them the protection of her arms against the British and the Spaniards.[2]

Unfortunately, the council failed to live up to these statements of principle. While instructing Lépinay to exploit the natives' break with Britain to divert toward Mobile the trade that the Indians had formerly carried on with Carolina, the council did not increase the stock of gifts, and—since Crozat also supplied the colony poorly with trade goods, and his price policy underwent no decisive change—the natives soon had reason to regret the departure of the British merchants.[3]

In Canada the council at least made an effort to correct the main shortcomings of French commercial policy by seeking from the manufactories of the home country fabrics that could compete with those offered by the British, or by providing larger credits for gifts to the Indians, or by indemnifying the officers for the expenditure they incurred in "being kind to the Indi-

---

1. Giraud, *History*, I, 329–31.
2. AC, C 13A 4, f. 78–80, Mémoire du Conseil de Marine, presented to the Regency Council, Feb. 11, 1716.
3. AM, B 1 9, f. 465v, Proceedings of the Council of the Navy, Oct. 11, 1716; AC, C 13A 4, f. 855–57, L'Epinay, Rochefort, Aug. 6, 1716.

ans."[4] In Louisiana, on the contrary, the council's failure to act reduced severely the resources available to its subjects. The practice, which went back to the first years of colonization, of employing some young men to live among the natives to learn their languages and understand their outlook certainly served the interests of France, but this personal link applied in only very few cases.[5] The colony should have had, over and above these intelligence agents, a leader capable of conceiving and applying a native policy. But Lépinay came to the country as a stranger knowing nothing of these natives whose loyalty he had to regain, yet invested with greater authority than his predecessor—authority that gave him, to the exclusion of the *lieutenant de roy,* supreme control over the distribution of gifts. Bienville thus lost one of his oldest prerogatives at a moment when his experience might have usefully guided a governor who possessed no defined principle for native policy.[6]

Lépinay seems, indeed, not to have used his powers at all to the Indians' satisfaction. Although the *ordonnateur*'s charge that he treated them uncivilly and was clumsily stingy with his gifts may have been partly inspired by ill will, Lépinay's almost complete silence on these matters in his correspondence and the extreme scarcity in it of allusions to the natives does seem to indicate that he "gave little importance" to the latter.[7] He may have upset the delegations who came soon after his arrival, in accordance with custom, to hold the ceremony of "the pipe of peace" with him, by distributing to the chiefs (overlooking their escorts) gifts that were insufficient even to meet their material needs.[8] In his concern, moreover, to be the sole dispenser of gifts, Lépinay gave them only to those Indians who visited him personally. The commandants of the inland posts, such as Lieutenant de La Tour among the Alabamas, had no choice but to draw on their own resources or on the goods belonging to merchants passing

---

4. AM, B 1 19, f. 155, Vaudreuil, Oct. 14, 1716; f. 294, Proceedings of the Council, March 17, 1717; B 1 20, f. 166, Draft of *mémoire* from the king to Vaudreuil and Bégon.

5. AM, B 1 9, f. 464, Mémoire de Crozat, Council of Oct. 11, 1716; AC, C 13A 4, f. 789–91, Mémoire en forme de journal . . . ; AC, F 1A 18, f. 183 ff., List of expenditure for Louisiana, 1715.

6. AC, C13A 5, f. 56–56v, Hubert, Oct. 26, 1717; f. 62–63; Bienville, May 10, 1717.

7. AC, C 13A 5, f. 55v–56, Hubert, Oct. 26, 1717; f. 189, Hubert, June 10, 1718.

8. AC, C 13A 5, f. 55–56, Hubert, Oct. 26, 1717; BN, FF 14613, f. 306–307, Report by Pénigaut.

through in order to respond to the natives' requests. This was a precarious solution to the problem, and one that satisfied only imperfectly the expectations of the natives, especially in areas where the British traders had accustomed them to more liberal conditions.[9]

Shut up in his residence in Fort Louis at Mobile, the governor had only infrequent contacts with the Indians. In their eyes he lacked the prestige of a man of action and lost those opportunities for mediation between tribes that Bienville had been able to utilize when he was in command of the colony.[10] When La Mothe was in charge, the *lieutenant de roy*, making use of his right to allot some of the gifts, had still been able to intervene successfully in relations with the Indians. Lépinay's arrival meant the annulment of Bienville's influence for the benefit of a man who, essentially concerned not to yield any of his prerogatives, neglected a task of capital importance. The only record of action by Lépinay where native matters were involved consists of a few minor measures, such as his ban on Frenchmen selling brandy in the "savage villages."[11]

With the tribes who lived on the coast or beside the lower Mississippi, Lépinay's attitude did not harm the interests of France. These were peaceful tribes who had long been used to the presence of the French. In the immediate neighborhood of Mobile, the Chaktaux or Chatot of the Dog River and the Apalachee of the Saint Martin River were hard-working people who lived by hunting, fishing, and agriculture. Both tribes enjoyed friendly relations with the French that were fostered by their Catholicism and by visits from the missionaries.[12] The small nations who were the Apalachees' neighbors on the Mobile River and the lower Tombigbee—the Tawasa, Mobilians, Taensa, Toomé (or Tohomé)—were similar in attitude. By choosing in

9. AC, C 13A 5, f. 55v, Hubert, Oct. 26, 1717; f. 66, Bienville to Hubert, Fort Louis, Sept. 19, 1717.
10. AC, C 13A 5, f. 55–56v, Hubert, Oct. 26, 1717; AE, Mem. & Doc., America, I, f. 140v–41, Hubert, Mémoire au sujet de l'établissement de la colonie de la Louisiane, 1717.
11. AC, F 3 241, f. 141, Ordinance by Lépinay, May 24, 1717.
12. The Chaktaux or Chatot had come from St. Joseph's Bay, where they served the Spaniards. Bienville had "attracted" them into French territory in 1703. AC, C 13C 1, f. 347v–48 (Véniard de Bourgmont), Exacte description de la Louisianne; f. 309v–70, Bienville, Mémoire sur la Louisiane, 1725; BN, FF 12105, f. 4, Le Maire, Mémoire sur la Louisiane, March 1, 1717; Parish register of Mobile, Ala., May 23, 1716.

1715 to settle, at Bienville's invitation, close to Fort Louis, the Taensa had indeed chosen precisely to seek French protection.[13]

The French had nothing to fear, either, from the tribes whose territory lay between Mobile Bay and the Mississippi—the Pascagoula, Capina, Biloxi, and Colapissa, who occupied, not far from the coast, the banks of the Pascagoula and Pearl rivers and the northern shore of Lake Pontchartrain. All of these were regarded as "friends of the French." They supplied agricultural produce, fish, and "wild meat," playing a role in feeding the French positions that would become more and more useful as these positions became more numerous.[14]

Along the lower Mississippi, the French received some service from the Tawasa (or Chawasha), Biloxi, and Washa who lived above and below the future site of New Orleans. Their relations were also good with the Tchoupitoula, Bayougoula, and Houma who were spread out between the Washa and the confluence of the Red River, as they were also with the Tunica. The latter were about to be reconciled with the Chitimacha; this happened in 1718, when that tribe acceded to Bienville's request and adopted a partly settled way of life.[15]

To be sure, all these peoples were declining in numbers. Since 1714 Le Maire had been observing their rapid shrinkage, which was caused by the wars they waged among themselves and also by the diseases introduced by the Europeans. The Chitimacha now numbered no more than a hundred men, instead of the six hundred Bienville had counted in 1704, and the groups living near Mobile—Chatot, Apalachee, Tawasa, Mobilian—consisted of tiny groups of between ten and thirty families.[16] Some years

---

13. AC, C 13C 1, f. 348–48v (Véniard de Bourgmont), Exacte description de la Louisianne; f. 370–70v, Bienville, Mémoire sur la Louisiane, 1725; Giraud, *History*, I, 329–30.

14. AC, C 13C 1, f. 349 (Véniard de Bourgmont), Exacte description de la Louisianne; f.415v–16, Bienville, Mémoire sur la Louisiane, 1725.

15. AC, C 13C 1, f. 349v, 351 (Véniard de Bourgmont), Exacte description de la Louisianne; f. 408v–10v, Bienville, Mémoire sur la Louisiane, 1725; BN, FF 12105, f. 9, Le Maire, Mémoire sur la Louisiane, March 1, 1717. For the locations of these tribes I have used the data given by V. de Bourgmont, Le Maire, and Bienville, which complement each other. There is, however, some uncertainty in the picture, owing to the mobility of some of these groups. AN, AHM 3 JJ 201 8, Report on the Mobile river [1720 ?].

16. AC, C 13C 2, f. 125–26, 134, Le Maire, Jan. 15, 1714; BN, FF 12105, f. 10, Le Maire, Mémoire sur la Louisiane, March 1, 1717; AC, C 13C 1, f. 409–409v, Bienville, Mémoire sur la Louisiane, 1725.

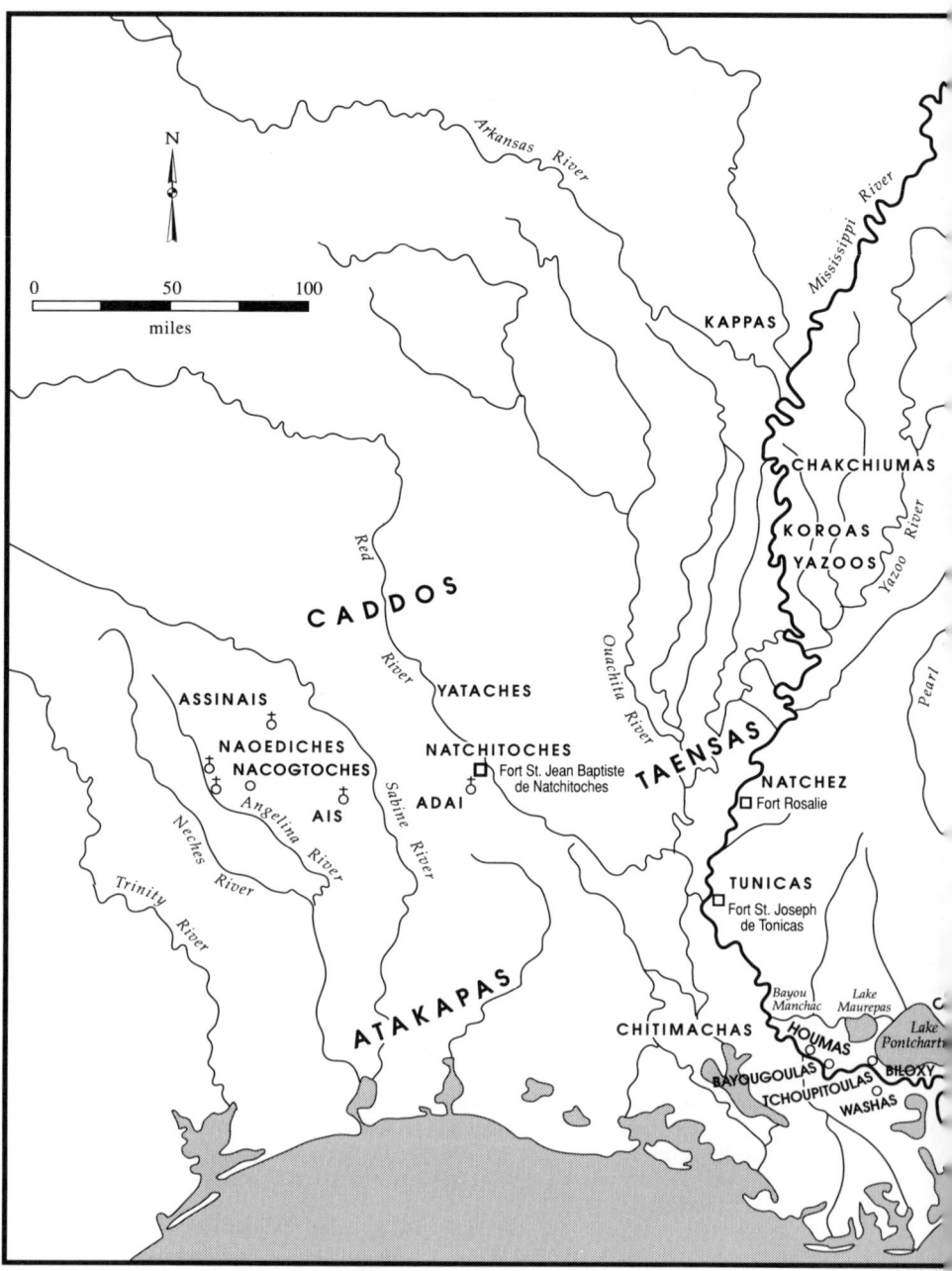

Native Peoples of Southern Louisiana Map by John Snead

later Bienville was to supply more exact figures relating to this decline.[17] For the isolated French positions, it constituted a factor of weakness rather than the reverse, since these insubstantial groups of Indians would not be able, in the event of danger, to provide effective military help. But there was no "native problem" in the strict sense in the area near the coast: relations were everywhere based on friendly trust, excluding any possibility of conflict.

The situation became more complex farther inland, especially in that intermediate zone occupied by the Alabama, Creek, Choctaw, Chickasaw, and Natchez, where the British offensive had developed. Here the nations were not only stronger; they had also been subject for too long to British influence to provide the French with such ready allies as the coastal communities. It was in this sector, where a particularly active native policy was needed, that the governor's negligent attitude became harmful to France.

The game with the Natchez had not been entirely won. Although Bienville had secured the execution of a famous "war leader" (Barbu, "the Bearded One") who was among the chief instigators of the "death of the French," he feared that the fact that Terre Blanche was still at large might make trouble among the allied tribes, who could reproach him with having made peace before he had obtained full satisfaction for the French grievances. Although the Natchez were not to be feared for the moment, their relations with the French lacked the confidence of earlier years.[18] Distributions of gifts would have easily reconciled the wavering chiefs, but Lépinay supplied nothing to the commandant of Fort Rosalie,[19] and the small garrison there was not strong enough in the event of renewed difficulties to keep so numerous a population at bay. Moreover, the Yazoo, Koroa, and Chakchiuma who extended beyond the Natchez along the Yazoo River were all unreliable, so France's position on the Mississippi was still to some extent one of uncertain stability.[20]

On the other hand, the Choctaw and the Chickasaw were showing a conciliatory attitude. But where relations with these

17. AC, C 13C 1, f. 408, ff., Bienville, Mémoire sur la Louisiane, 1725.
18. AC, C 13A 4, f. 694–95, Bienville to La Mothe, Fort St. Joseph among the Tunicas, June 23, 1716; AC, F 3 24, f. 78, Mémoire de ce que Richebourg a ordre de Bienville de représenter à Lamothe-Cadillac.
19. AC, C 13A 5, f. 55, Hubert, Oct. 26, 1717.
20. AC, C 13C 1, f. 351 (V. de Bourgmont), Exacte description de la Louisianne.

nations were concerned, the absence of a missionary was a serious weakness for France, and Lépinay took no measures to ensure their loyalty.[21] He seemed unaware that although the Chickasaw had taken part in the rebellion of 1715, they preferred a policy of neutrality to any fixed commitment and had not completely abandoned their amicable feeling toward the British colonies, and he forgot that the Choctaw had been on the point of yielding to the approaches of the British and that to an increasing extent their reactions would depend on the commercial advantages the French could offer them.[22]

Seemingly, the difficulties that paralyzed South Carolina after 1715 and, despite the vigorous measures taken by Governor Craven,[23] made impossible such large-scale enterprises as the British had carried out in previous years, now laid open to French initiative the region bordering on the British colony. The Yamasee War[24] was waged, in fact, on the borders of South Carolina with the support of the Spaniards of St. Augustine. The Indians increased their attack on the British plantations, and the South Carolinians were unable to assemble the forces and financial means needed to defend themselves or to obtain from Virginia the material help they sought. The commercial rivalry between the two colonies destroyed any possible feeling of solidarity, and such gestures as Virginia made toward coming to the aid of its neighbor only created further misunderstandings. South Carolina soon accused the Virginians of trying to prolong the war for the sole purpose of favoring the interests of their merchants. These local animosities, which the governor of Pennsylvania contrasted to the more national spirit of the French establishments, were observable, moreover, in most of the British possessions on the Atlantic coast.[25] The discontented

---

21. AC, C 13C 1, f. 400, Bienville, Mémoire sur la Louisiane, 1725.

22. AN, AHM 3 JJ 201 8, Report on the Mobile River [1720?]; AC, F 3 24, f. 86v–87, Rémonville, Description du fleuve St. Louis, 1715; PRO, CO 5, f. 65, The Lords Proprietors of Carolina to the Board of Trade, July 27, 1716; f. 72, Richard Beresford, Feb. 6, 1716–17.

23. Verner W. Crane, *The Southern Frontier, 1670–1732* (Durham, N.C., 1928), 169–72.

24. Giraud, *History*, I, 329–31.

25. PRO, CO 5, 382, f. 34, The most humble petition . . . of . . . the Lords Proprietors of the Province of Carolina in America, July, 1717; f. 36, The humble address of the General Assembly of South Carolina, May, 1715; f. 40, Boon and Beresford's memorial; CO 5, 1265, f. 11 (I), [?] to John Duddleston, merchant in Bristol, Charlestown, Sept. 16, 1715; f. 25, The commissioners appointed by the Commons House of Assembly of South Carolina to their agents in England,

population of South Carolina blamed its ordeals on the government of the Lords Proprietors on whom the province's fate depended and charged them with indifference. The South Carolinians begged the king to take over the proprietors' faltering authority, pointing out the importance of the province's geographical position at the extreme limit of the British colonies, which South Carolina was defending against the Indians, the French, and the Spaniards.[26]

Being obliged to concentrate on the defense of its own territory and preoccupied with the change of regime that it hoped to see, South Carolina was intervening less actively in the interior. Consequently, it left opportunities for the French of Mobile that Bienville saw as his duty to exploit immediately after the rebellion.[27] By securing the alliance of the Alabama who had massacred the British traders, the French established their first trading link with the Creek tribes. In 1716 they promised to support them against South Carolina in the event of a clash between France and Britain and meanwhile to strengthen them "to the full extent of their resources" by supplying arms.[28] As a result of this *rapprochement*, Fort Toulouse acquired new importance for the French colony. The great numbers of the Alabama, their war-

---

Charlestown, March 15, 1715–16; f. 44 (II-III), Letters from South Carolina; f. 69, Joseph Boone, Charlestown, April 25, 1717; f. 79, Joseph Boone, South Carolina, June 8, 1717; f. 99, A Committee of the Assembly of Carolina to the Lords Commissioners, Carolina, March 8, 1717; f. 102, Memorial of Joseph Boone, May 13, 1718; f. 124 (1), Report of William Keith, Governor of the province of Pensilvania to the Lords Commissioners for Trade and Plantations, Feb. 16, 1718–1719; CO 5, 1293, f. 1–3, Stanhope to the Commissions for Trade and Plantations, June 14, 1716; f. 45–47, Boon and Beresford, Memorial to the Lords of Trade and Plantations, Dec. 5, 1716; CO 5, 1317, f. 59, 292–93, Alexander Spotswood to the Board of Trade, July 15, Oct. 24, 1717; CO 5, 1318, f. 76, To the Lords Commissioners . . . The Memorial of the Virginia Indian Company; CO 5, 1342, f. 5v, A. Spotswood to the Secretary of State, Oct. 24, 1715.

26. PRO, CO 5, 382, f. 32, 55, The . . . humble address of the Commons House of Assembly, Charlestown, August, 1715, February, 1717; f. 34, The most humble petition of . . . the Lords Proprietors of the Province of Carolina, July, 1715; f. 59v, The Council and Assembly . . . of the Settlement in South Carolina, Feb. 3, 1719–20; CO 5, 383, f. 1v, The Lords Commissioners to Stanhope, July 19, 1715; CO 5, 387, f. 34, The Assembly of South Carolina to the Province's Agents in London, Nov. 30, 1716.

27. Giraud, *History*, I, 329–30.

28. PRO, CO 5, 1265, f. 31 (I) The Assembly of South Carolina to the king, April 28, 1716; f. 149 (I), Replies by a Committee appointed by the Assembly to the Lords Commissioners' questions about the state of the colony, January, 1719–20.

like qualities, and the trade they could provide might well endow the fort with a first-class role, both strategic and commercial. Being situated near the Coosa and Tallapoosa rivers, it could dominate the Creeks' territory and expand in that direction the defensive zone of Fort Louis, which till then had not exceeded its immediate neighborhood. This "post among the Alabamas," this "advanced fortification" of Mobile, was thenceforth to be the limit set to the movement of the "English of Carolina."[29]

However, the latter did not leave the field entirely free to their enemies. In order to reduce the Indians' discontent and prevent traders from repeating the mistakes of earlier years, the government of South Carolina established a short-term monopoly of trade with the Indians. The "commissioners of the Indian trade" received into the "public storehouse" at Charleston buckskins and slaves obtained from the natives and sold them at auction. Through distributions of gifts, they endeavored to keep on their side those nations whose loyalty was not completely dead. At the end of 1715 they succeeded in winning over the Cherokee to the British side and obtained from them a promise of military help against the Creeks. Then in 1716, and again in 1717, they tried to make peace with the latter. They might have regained control of the Tallapoosa if the Tréfontaine brothers, who happened to be in that region, had not resisted the attempt of the British officers to "plant their flag" there, preventing the chiefs' defection by means of a "gift of goods." The commandant of Fort Toulouse, having nothing to offer the Indians, not even so much as a "quarter-pound of powder," would himself have been unable to react. Yet in spite of Bienville's appeals, Lépinay persisted in his inertia.[30]

29. AC,C 13C 1, f. 358–60, List of the savages who live between the Alabamas and Carolina [1716–17?]; f. 370v-71, Mémoire de Bienville sur la Louisiane, 1725; AE, Mem. & Doc., America, I, f. 20v, Mémoire de Bienville, 1725; f. 199v–200, Bienville, June 10, 1718.

30. AC, C 13A 5, f. 66, Bienville to Hubert, Sept. 19, 1717; f. 117v, La Tour, commandant of Fort Toulouse among the Alabamas, to Hubert, Fort Toulouse, March 17, 1718; f. 119, Extract from a request and ordinance presented to M. de Lépinay, Oct. 8, 1717; PRO, CO 5, 382, f. 61, The Council and Assembly . . . of the Settlement in South Carolina . . . , Feb. 3, 1719–20; CO 5, 1265, f. 25, Assembly of South Carolina to Board of Trade, March 15, 1715–16; f. 30, Memorial by the Colony's agents to the Board of Trade, June 23, 1716; f. 62, The Lords Proprietors of Carolina to the Board of Trade, July 27, 1716; f. 99, The Assembly of South Carolina to the Lords Commissioners, March 8, 1717; W. L. McDowell, *Journals of the Commissioners of the Indian Trade*, Sept. 20, 1710–Aug. 29, 1718, The Colonial Records of South Carolina, Series 2 (Columbia, S.C., 1955).

Actually, both camps tended to exaggerate the other's resources and achievements. The settlers of South Carolina were convinced that the French were masters of the interior. Concealing the basic reasons for the rebellion, which was caused by the excesses of their traders—as the Board of Trade had suspected from the outset was the case—the South Carolinians attributed to the intrigues of the "governor of Mobile" the war that had ruined their plantations and the massacres committed by the Alabamas, whereas Bienville had merely taken advantage of the Indians' discontent to urge them to drive the British from their villages.[31] The British ascribed to Fort Toulouse pieces of artillery that in fact it lacked and, convinced that the French colony was continually receiving fresh contingents of immigrants, accused Louisiana of preparing a coalition of the tribes of the interior to attack Carolina, so that France, mistress of Canada and assured of access to the Florida peninsula, would put herself in a position to threaten all the British possessions.[32]

The French for their part believed that the British had already regained the goodwill of "all their savages." Lieutenant de La Tour feared that the Alabama would soon defect from France through disappointment in an alliance that had not produced the promised results, and the *ordonnateur* Hubert thought that the Indians no longer had any confidence in the settlers at Mobile, whom the British had as usual described to them as living in poverty. In Hubert's view, Louisiana must, after a short respite, expect fresh aggressions, for the British would soon resume their schemes of conquest, and it would be easy for them

---

31. PRO, CO 5, 382, f. 60v, The Council and Assembly . . . of the settlement in South Carolina, Feb. 3, 1719–20; CO 5, 383, f. 2, The Lords Commissioners to Stanhope, July 19, 1715; CO 5, 387, f. 16, George Rodd to a gentleman in London, May 8, 1715; CO 5, 1265, f. 2, David Crawley to William Byrd, July 30, 1715; f. 25, The Commissioners appointed by the Commons House of Assembly of South Carolina to their agents in England, March 15, 1715–16; f. 30, Joseph Boon and Richard Berrisford, Memorial to the Board of Trade, June 23, 1716; f. 124 (I), Report of William Keith, Feb. 16, 1718–19; f. 149(1), Replies by a committee appointed by Assembly to the Lords Commissioners, January, 1719–20; AE, Mem. & Doc., America, I, f. 20v, Bienville, Mémoire sur la Louisiane, 1725; Francis Le Jau, *The Carolina Chronicle of Dr. Francis Le Jau*, ed. Frank J. Klingberg, University of California Publications in History, LIII (Berkeley, 1956), 151ff.

32. PRO, CO 5, 1265, f. 11 (I), [?] to John Duddleston, merchant in Bristol, Charlestown, Sept. 16, 1715; f. 25, The Commons House of Assembly to the Board of Trade, March 15, 1715–16; f. 31 (I), Address by the Assembly of South Carolina to the king, April 28, 1716; f. 30, Joseph Boon and Richard Berrisford, Memorial to the Lords of Trade, June 23, 1716; f. 99, A Committee of Carolina to the Lords Commissioners, March 8, 1717.

to capture positions that were still virtually defenseless. "Never," he said "has a matter called for more prompt and serious decisions."³³

But whatever the *ordonnateur* might think, the British were for the moment in no position to recover the initiative in the interior. The military support of the Cherokee on which they relied was not only subject to burdensome conditions but had been deprived of much of its effectiveness because of the losses the tribe had suffered through diseases and wars.³⁴ The policy that consisted of stirring them up against the Creeks and exploiting the hatred that existed between these tribes was itself a two-edged weapon, for it caused the Creeks to seek the protection of the French and also compromised any attempt by the British to influence them.³⁵ Despite a few successes, the settlers of South Carolina often as a consequence found that their efforts among the tribes of the interior came to nothing. In 1717, faced with the poor results of their policy, many looked for salvation only to divine help, or else to the antagonism between the Creeks and the Cherokee. South Carolina's agent in London argued before the Board of Trade that the most reliable way to safeguard the colony would be, with seeming friendship, to distribute to both tribes weapons that would enable them to destroy each other.³⁶ Carolina had been too seriously weakened and its standing among the Indians was still too precarious for the inhabitants of Mobile to have real grounds for fearing the offensive foreseen by the *ordonnateur*.

33. AC,C 13A 4, f. 673–75, Duclos, June 7, 1716; C 13A 5, f. 28, L'Epinay and Hubert, May 30, 1717; f. 55v–56, Hubert, Oct. 26, 1717; f. 66, Bienville to Hubert, Sept. 19, 1717; f. 117v–18, Sr de La Tour, commandant of Fort Toulouse among the Alabamas, to M. Hubert, March 17, 1718; f. 139, Hubert, Mémoire sur la colonie de la Louisiane, October, 1717; f. 57 v, (P.S.) Hubert, Oct. 26, 1717; AE, Mem. & Doc., America, I, f. 141v–42; Hubert, Mémoire au sujet de l'établissement de la colonie de la Louisiane, 1717.

34. PRO, CO 5, 1265, f. 69, Joseph Boone, Charles Town, April 25, 1717; f. 144, Robert Johnson to the Board of Trade, Charles Town, Jan. 14, 1719–20.

35. PRO, CO 5, 1265, f. 31(I), Address of the Assembly of South Carolina to the king, April 28, 1716; f. 65, The Lords Proprietors of Carolina to the Board of Trade, June 4, 1717; f. 70, Richard Beresford, Charles Town, April 27, 1717; f. 79, Joseph Boone, South Carolina, June 8, 1717; f. 99, A Committee of the Assembly of Carolina to the Lords Commissioners, Carolina, March 8, 1717.

36. PRO, CO 5, 1265, f. 65, The Lords Proprietors of Carolina to the Board of Trade, June 4, 1717; f. 69, Joseph Boone, Charles Town, April 25, 1717; f. 70, Richard Beresford, Charles Town, April 27, 1717; f. 79, Joseph Boone, South Carolina, June 8, 1717; f. 99, A Committee of the Assembly of Carolina to the Lords Commissioners, Carolina, March 8, 1717.

But Carolina had no reason, either, to fear a French invasion launched from Fort Toulouse, whose little garrison would have been hard put to resist an attack by the Alabama.[37] The French had not yet undertaken any important action farther into the interior than this "barely begun establishment." Their only enterprises were those carried out by the Tréfontaine brothers and their associates, about which all we know is that they reached as far as the Tallapoosa villages "two leagues from the Alabamas."[38] The trade links that the French had been able to form with the Creeks bore no proportion to what was written about them in the British documents. According to the latter, British ships, no longer finding anything of interest in South Carolina, turned away from Charleston to go and take on board at Mobile and Pensacola the pelts from the interior that henceforth would be acquired by the French and the Spaniards, and the merchants of Bristol even contemplated, at the end of 1717, sending their ships directly to those foreign ports.[39] What is alluded to here is perhaps the voyage of two vessels that put in during that year at Dauphin Island.[40] But the transactions that took place on that occasion did not show in the least that the French colony was better supplied with buckskins than in previous years. From the French documents it emerges, on the contrary, that though trade was being carried on, it was on the same restricted scale as before, because of the lack of goods for exchanging with the natives. The closer relationship established with the Alabama and other "up-country nations" had not yet ensured their alliance with France. Lieutenant de la Tour considered that the Alabama and the Creeks, for all their seeming amicableness, were actually waiting upon events. They would soon withdraw, like the Chickasaw, into a neutrality that would enable them to trade with the side that had the most to offer.[41]

37. AC, Mem. & Doc., America, I, f. 82, Legac, Etat dans lequel été trouvée la colonie de la Louisiane le 25 août 1718.
38. AC, C 13A 5, f. 48v–49, Hubert, Oct. 26, 1717; f. 119–20, Extract from a petition and ordinance presented to M. de Lépinay, Guénot de Tréfontaine, at Fort Louis, Oct. 8, 1717, and Permits given by Lépinay to Srs Dubreuil and de Tréfontaine, Nov. 12, 1717.
39. PRO, CO 5, 1265, f. 31 (I), Address of the South Carolina Assembly to the king, April 28, 1716; f. 72, Richard Beresford, Feb. 6, 1716–17; f. 107, Letter to the Board of Trade, South Carolina, Dec. 17, 1717; f. 144, Robert Johnson to the Board of Trade, Charles Town, Jan. 14, 1719–20.
40. See p. 149 above.
41. PRO, CO 5, 1265, f. 144, Robert Johnson to the Board of Trade, Charles Town, Jan. 14, 1719–20; AC, C 13A 5, f. 117v–18, La Tour to Hubert from Fort Toulouse, March 17, 1718.

The conflict that was going on in the zone between the French and British spheres of influence was certainly not getting any less intense, and its causes, because of the proximity of the two colonies, were as much alive as ever. The British could still fight successfully on the plane of trade, and Hubert expressed certainty that so long as France was not in a position to provide, like them, good-quality merchandise at low prices, it would be compelled to give up any hope of winning the respect and trust of the Indians.[42] But neither of the adversaries possessed the means of launching the offensive that each believed the other was planning.

In the northern zone adjoining the sector dependent on Canada, France's position was rather weak because of the lack of a fortified post. The idea put forward in 1714 of setting up a general command under Bienville's authority for the whole valley of the Mississippi had not been put into effect. Although the proposal still appeared in the "project for expenditure in Louisiana for 1717," no decision had been made to do anything about it.[43] Consequently, there was in this remotest region of the Illinois country no officer with responsibility for relations with the Indians. Native policy was the concern of the missionaries who looked after the Tamaroa and Kaskaskia settlements, and Fathers Jean Mermet and Louis de Ville were undoubtedly qualified by their experience to direct this branch of policy.[44] But without military support they could not prevent conflicts between tribes or impose peaceful solutions. Yet the incursions of the Cherokee into the territory of the Kaskaskias and the losses these inflicted on the latter and on the Canadian officers—two fell in 1717 during one of these clashes—showed how very necessary it was to take measures of defense.[45]

Until the decision to recover possession of the "old fort" called Crèvecoeur was executed,[46] the fortified posts occupied by Canadian detachments at the edge of the Great Lakes were all that protected the Illinois country and the settlements there. France's recent return to these "up-country areas" had made it possible to strengthen the position at Michilimackinac, Detroit,

42. AE, Mem. & Doc., America, I, f. 141v–42, Hubert, Mémoire au sujet de l'établissement de la colonie de la Louisiane, 1717.
43. AC, F 1A 19, f. 280–82, Project of expenditure on Louisiana for 1717.
44. Giraud, *History*, I, 347–48.
45. AC, C 13A 4, f. 783, Bienville, Jan. 20, 1716; AC, C 11A 38, f. 37, Vaudreuil and Bégon, Nov. 6, 1717; f. 101–101v, Vaudreuil, Oct. 12, 1717.
46. AM,B 1 8, f. 274–75, Ramezay and Bégon, Nov. 7, 1715; AC, F 3 9, f. 316, Mémoire du roi au Sr de Ramezay, July 10, 1715; Giraud, *History*, I, 350–54.

Fort Saint Joseph, and the fort among the Miamis, to which was added in 1717 the post among the Ouiatenon (or Wea) on the upper Wabash.[47] While Sieur de Vincennes continued his work of pacification among the Miami tribes, especially the Ouiatenon, of whom he had long experience, Sieur de Louvigny, appointed commander-in-chief of the region, sought to subdue the Fox. In 1716 he obtained their submission and reestablished, for the moment at least, the state of peace in these "upcountry areas" needed for the security of New France.[48]

Native policy there unquestionably followed a coherent program that had no equivalent in Louisiana. The Council of the Navy left Governor Vaudreuil a degree of freedom of action that encouraged his initiatives.[49] The missionaries helped the officers, and the settlers in the Tamaroa and Kaskaskia countries, responding to the officers' appeal, intervened to good effect among the natives. One of them, Bisaillon, raised a large number of Illinois to fight against the Fox.[50] Thanks to the reactivation of the permit system, Canadian traders brought into the area possibilities for trade that were not available in more southerly latitudes. And the gradual elimination of the *coureurs de bois*, many of whom returned to Canada, broke up the centers of indiscipline that had been formed in these parts, often to the detriment of France's interests.[51]

47. AC, C 11A 36, f. 75v, Vaudreuil, Oct. 14, 1716; C 11A 38, f. 164, Vaudreuil, Nov. 11, 1717; C 11E 13, f. 144, Description of the Western posts; C 11E 15, f. 192v, Dupuy on the claims made by La Mothe-Cadillac, January, 1717; AM, B 1 19, f. 81–81v, Vaudreuil and Bégon, Oct. 14, 1716; AE, Mem. & Doc., America, I, f. 46, Bienville, Mémoire sur la Louisiane, 1725; America, 21, f. 80v, 84, Development of the country which the British claim to own and the savage peoples they allege are subject to them, 1761.

48. AC, C 11A 36, f. 75, Vaudreuil, Oct. 14, 1716; f. 117, Vaudreuil, 1716; C 11A 37, f. 324, Louvigny, Oct. 1, 1717; C 11A 38, f. 103–107, Vaudreuil, Oct. 12, 1717; AM, B 1 9, f. 627-31, Proceedings of the Council of the Navy, Dec. 28, 1716; B 1 20, f. 166, Draft of *mémoire* from the king to Vaudreuil and Bégon; B 1 29, f. 4, Vaudreuil, Oct. 20, 1717; AC, B 39, f. 24, to Louvigny, May 31, 1717.

49. AM, B 1 19 f. 81, Vaudreuil and Bégon, Oct. 14, 1716; AC, C 11A 37, f. 344v–45, Vaudreuil, April 20, 1717.

50. AM, B 1 9, f. 627–28, Proceedings of the Council of the Navy, Dec. 28, 1716; Giraud, *History*, I, 352n12.

51. AC, C 11A 36, f. 118, 119, Vaudreuil, 1716; C 11A 37, f. 324–26, Louvigny, Oct. 1, 1717; f. 344v–45, Vaudreuil, April 20, 1717; C 11A 38, f. 85–88, List of thirty permits granted in 1717; AM, B 1 20, f. 165, Draft of *mémoire* from the king to Vaudreuil and Bégon; B 1 29, f. 50, Vaudreuil and Bégon, Nov. 6, 1717, f. 202v–203, Vaudreuil, Oct. 12, 1717; AM, A 1 51, March 28, 1716, Letters patent in the form of an edict granting amnesty to the *coureurs de bois* of New France.

But the British had not given up their plans for penetration, and although New France occupied with some thoroughness the section bordering on the Great Lakes, it had neither the military forces nor the economic weapons needed to withstand the British. The garrisons were still weak, the "stock of gifts," though more liberal than in Louisiana, was nevertheless inadequate, and British commercial competition was the harder to meet because France sought to restrict the sphere of operation of the *"voyageurs* with permits" and the traffic in brandy.[52]

Once again, British traders were trying to get behind the Miamis by using the Iroquois as intermediaries to win over the nations of the Detroit area and the Illinois tribes. If the British succeeded in installing themselves in the lower valley of the Ohio where France kept deferring its own occupation, they would create a permanent threat in northern Louisiana.[53] It was clear that if this happened the posts that depended on New France would not be able to afford effective protection to the establishments in the Illinois country. What the latter needed was a system of defense in the immediate area capable of barring the British from the approaches to the lower Ohio "crossroads." The danger was not so imminent as it was made to appear in Crozat's *mémoires* or Vincennes' reports, since the British had not yet taken up positions on the Ohio.[54] Nevertheless, it was increasingly evident that the security of the settlements in the Illinois country depended to a large extent on occupation of the Wabash crossroads, especially since the building of Fort Toulouse. It was foreseeable that the British, being now deprived of their usual route to the Mississippi,[55] would strive to get through to the

---

52. AC, C 11A 36, f. 97, Vaudreuil, 1716; f. 213–14, Proceedings of the Council of the Navy, March 28, 1716; C 11A 38, f. 109–15, Vaudreuil, Oct. 12, 1717; f. 134v–37, Vaudreuil, Oct. 30, 1717; AM, B 1 8, f. 268v–69v, Ramezay and Bégon, Nov. 7, 1715; f. 513–14, Proceedings of the Council of the Navy, May 17, 1716; B 1 29, f. 78v–79, Vaudreuil, Oct. 12, 1717.

53. AC, C 11A 37, f. 4–5, Vaudreuil, Oct. 14, 1716; f. 378–80, Vaudreuil and Bégon, Oct. 20, 1717; C 11A 38, f. 166–67, Sabrevois, April 8, 1717; AM, B 1 8, f. 291–92, Ramezay, Sept. 16, 1715; B 1 29, f. 26, Vaudreuil, Oct. 12, 1717; AE, Mem. & Doc., America, I, f. 46, Bienville, Mémoire sur la Louisiane, 1725; f. 277v–78, Crozat to the duc de Noailles, Sept. 28, 1716; PRO, CO 5, 324 (10), f. 399–400, the Board of Trade to the king, Sept. 8, 1721.

54. AC, C 11A 36, f. 75, Vaudreuil, Oct. 14, 1716; C 13A 4, f. 505, Mémoire de Crozat, 1716; L. H. Gipson, *Zones of International Friction, 1748–1754* (New York, 1939), 153–54, Vol. IV of *The British Empire Before the American Revolution.*

55. Giraud, *History,* I, map on pp. 74–75.

river by way of the Cherokee territory and the valley of the Tennessee ("the river of the Casquinampo"), which would open the lower course of the Ohio to them. So long as France did nothing about this important confluence, Governor Vaudreuil's policy of maintaining peaceful relations between the Illinois and the Iroquois would not suffice to safeguard the region against incursion by the British.[56]

As Crozat's regime came to an end, the inhabitants of Mobile still saw Britain, despite its weakening position in the southern zone, as the enemy most to be feared. The *rapprochement* between Britain and France effected by the Regent had no significance outside Europe,[57] and in no way did it blunt the sharpness of colonial rivalries. Despite this superficial reconciliation, the British supplanted and despoiled the French Royal Company of the *Asiento* in the Spanish Indies, and on the American mainland the British Board of Trade formally forbade, in accordance with the "treaty of peace and neutrality" signed in 1686, any sort of trade relations between "the English plantations and the French colonies."[58] The absence of an official frontier between them[59] gave rise to conflicts and prevented decisive solutions. The British could thus denounce as "encroachments" the gains their opponents made as a result of the rebellion of 1715, and they persisted in claiming the Alabamas' country as part of their colonial domain.[60] Moreover, though South Carolina was obliged for the moment to restrain its projects for expansion, Virginia was directing its ambitions toward the Mississippi basin and the approaches to the Great Lakes, and to avoid repeating South Carolina's mistakes, it sought to improve its relations with the Indians of the interior by putting an end to free competition

---

56. AC, C 11A 38, f. 125–31v, Vaudreuil, Oct. 24, 1717; AM, B 1 29, f. 107v, Proceedings of the Council of the Navy, Jan. 25, 1718; AE, Mem. & Doc., America, I, f. 205, Bienville, June 10, 1718.

57. PRO, State papers, France, 78, 160, f. 106–106v, Mémoire de Mylord Stair au Duc d'Orléans, Sept. 14, 1715.

58. AC, F 2A 10, To the Council of the Navy, July 5, 1718, Le Cordier to the Council of the Navy, Aug. 20, 1714; the Company of the Indies to the Council of the Navy, May, 1716; PRO, CO 5, 1265, f. 89, The Lords Commissioners . . . to the naval officer and collector of the customs in Pennsylvania, Nov. 25, 1717.

59. Giraud, *History*, I, 330–31.

60. AE, Mem. & Doc., America, I, f. 164v, Mémoire du Sr Le Bartz, 1717; PRO, CO 5, 382, f. 60v, The Council and Assembly . . . of the settlement in South Carolina (to the Board of Trade), Feb. 3, 1719–20.

among the traders and by introducing into its policy a certain concern for bringing the Gospel to the natives.[61]

61. PRO, CO 5, 1317, f. 337, Robert Cary to the Lords Commissioners, June 12, 1716; f. 378–82, Alexander Spotswood to the Board of Trade, May 9, 1716; CO 5, 1318, f. 64, 81, The Virginia Indian Company to the Lords Commissioners; f. 440, A. Spotswood to the Lords Commissioners, Aug. 14, 1718.

XIII Tension Between France and Spain

THE THREAT FROM Spain, which seemed more remote, worried the French colonies less than the threat from the British, yet the years leading up to the arrival of the Company of the West were years of growing tension between France and Spain. In both Europe and America the two nations were moving toward the break that was soon to set them openly against each other. While France tried in vain to obtain a settlement of the debts to the Treasurers of the Navy contracted by the Court of Madrid during the War of the Spanish Succession, her merchants found themselves, when in Spanish ports, exposed to hostility on the part of the local authorities.[1] On the pretext that the documents governing the status of French merchants when in Spanish territory were imprecisely worded, Spanish officials deprived the French of immunities that the French thought were well established and subjected them to a policy of taxation and house-searches that "brought them under the same rules as the natives." The Spaniards even considered banning the French from the Barbary trade for which France had held the exclusive privilege since 1703.[2]

The personal attitudes of the Most Catholic King's ministers were not solely responsible for a situation that to a certain extent expressed the hostile reaction of Spain's merchant circles, which were displeased with the profits French merchants had made as a result of the union of the two crowns. But the conflict in the

1. AM, B 7 31, f. 73–74v, Saint-Aignan to the Council of the Navy, Madrid, Jan. 11, 1717; B 7 32, f. 228–28v, Catalan, Madrid, July 12, 1717; B 7 104, f. 58, 525, 715, Council of the Navy to Sr Partyet and Saint-Aignan, Jan. 28, 1716, September, 1716, Oct. 14, 1717; B 7 270, f. 15–20, Partyet to Catalan, June 20, 1716; B 7, 271, Catalan, Madrid, July 12, 1717.

2. AM, B 7 32, f. 184v–85, Partyet, Cadiz, June 13, 1717; B 7 33, f. 3–3v, 23–23v, Partyet, Cadiz, Aug. 8, 16, 1717; B 7 34, f. 86v, Partyet, Cadiz, Jan. 9, 1718; B 7 270, f. 57, Partyet to Catalan, June 20, 1716; M. Giraud, "Un aspect de la rivalité franco-espagnole au début du XVIIIe siècle," *Revue historique* (April–June, 1957), 250–69.

overseas possessions contributed still more actively to the general tension, for although France had grounds for alleging that authorities in the Spanish colonies showed systematic ill will toward French subjects, France itself provided some justification for the prejudiced attitude for which it blamed the Spanish.

France certainly had legitimate grievances against Spain. The cession of the *Asiento* monopoly to Britain in March, 1713, and the immediate putting into effect of a treaty that was not to have come into force until May 1, 1715, with the resulting advantages for British trade, were seen by the French as grave injustices. Grievances became especially bitter after Britain, not content with ousting the French *Asiento* company, used the pretext of its newly acquired privilege to confiscate the company's property, with the complicity of the Spanish officials, and to subject its director to an internment for which there was no justification.[3]

It is certain, however, that where colonial matters were concerned France often behaved in a way that could only cause resentment among the Spaniards. In 1717, at the suggestion of its ambassador in Madrid, France contemplated demanding that Spain give up its part of St. Domingue as settlement of the "considerable sums" that the Most Catholic King owed to the French Crown. Apparently, this scheme, which Louis XIV had discreetly endeavored to initiate two years earlier, aroused so much opposition that the ambassador decided against discussing it openly. The Spanish government could not consent to an agreement wrested from it under pressure of financial necessities while its officers in St. Domingue, far from accepting the idea of a loss of territory, were themselves putting forward claims for the French areas of the island.[4]

3. AM, B 7 33, f. 27–27v, 270, f. 9–15, Porlier, Teneriffe, June 10, 1717; B 7 34, f. 212ff., Saint-Aignan, Madrid, March 7, 1718; B 7 270, f. 9–15, Partyet to Catalan, June 20, 1716; B 7 270, Catalan, Madrid, June 8, 1716; AN, B III 340, Mémoire des commissaires du Conseil pour les affaires . . . de la nation française en Espagne, March, 1725; AM, B 1 18, f. 123v, Porlier, Teneriffe, June 10, 1717; B 1 27, f. 185–86, Jonchée, June 11, Oct. 21, 1717; B 1 32, f. 187–89, Saint-Aignan, March 7, 1718; AC, F 2A 10, Mémoire anonyme au Conseil de marine, July 5, 1718; Le Cordier to the Council, Aug. 20, 1714; The *Asiento* Company to the Council, May, 1716, May, 1724; AE, Mem. & Doc., America, 24, f. 57–58, Mémoire de Pontchartrain concernant les colonies . . . , Jan. 2, 1712.

4. AN, B III 340, Council of the Navy to Saint-Aignan, Jan. 29, 1719; AM, B 7 31, f. 73–77, Saint-Aignan, Madrid, Jan. 11, 1717; B 7 109, f. 61–62, to Saint-Aignan, Jan. 29, 1719; AM, B 1 17, f. 54–57; B 1 20, f. 367, Saint-Aignan, Madrid, Jan. 11, 1717; B 1 21, f. 109, Chateaumorant, March 8, 1717; f. 134–38, Chateaumorant and Mithon, June 20, June 19, 1717; AC, C 9A 12, Blénac and Mithon, Feb. 10, 1716; C 9A 13, Chateaumorant and Mithon, March 25, 1717.

It is equally clear that the Council of the Navy encouraged French merchants to violate the Spanish Crown's ban on their trading in Spain's American ports. As the council saw things, it was important not to interfere with this clandestine commerce, which provided the French colonies with the specie they needed. All that mattered was that the merchants should behave with sufficient prudence not to risk losing their cargoes.[5] In order to gain admission to harbors "under the rule of Spain," French merchants usually employed the excuse that they needed to repair damage suffered by their ships or to renew their supply of water and wood. When the captain of the *Aimable-Marie* of La Rochelle, Jean Escoubet, tells how he entered the port of Vera Cruz, he does not hide the fact that, under the pretext of careening, he had no aim but to sell his cargo—and he managed in this way to dispose, on "the Spanish coast," of 30,000 piastres' worth of goods.[6] The French government did not hesitate to give protection to the transgressors by supplying them with passports for Mobile, so that they might hide their actual destination from the Spanish authorities. For the administrators of the French West Indies, Louisiana, in this period when there was no commercial activity going on there, was interesting solely as a useful port of call and a means of providing a semblance of legality through which they could gain access to Spanish possessions.[7] Sometimes, even the Council of the Navy associated itself directly with trade that was forbidden by the ordinances of the Most Catholic King. When in 1716 the council sent the frigate the *Bellone* to patrol the seas round the West Indian islands in order to put down piracy, it advised that pilots be taken on board who knew "the coasts of the Spanish Indies," so that the officers might secretly trade in the goods the vessel would be carrying.[8]

Under these conditions, it was inevitable that French ships were received with suspicion in the ports where they requested

---

5. AC, B 40, f. 237, to the chevalier de Feuquières, March 15, 1718; f. 262–62v, to Sr de Silvecanne; f. 406–406v, to Sr Du Clos, March 15, June 22, 1718.

6. AC, C 9A 12, Blénac and Mithon, Léogane, July 2, 1716; C 9A 13, Chateaumorant and Mithon, May 11, 1717; AM, B 1 27, f. 186v–88, Jonchée, June 11, Oct. 21, 1717. On the *Aimable-Marie, cf.* Giraud, *History,* I, 315–18. The ship actually stopped at Dauphin Island to put ashore the deserters it had taken on board at Pensacola.

7. AC, C 9A 13, Chateaumorant and Mithon, May 11, 1717.

8. AM, B 2 246 (1), f. 6v–8, to M. Robert, July 1, 1716; f. 58–59, to Sr. Querquelin, captain of the *Bellone,* July, 1716.

to be allowed to make a stay. Knowing that it was easy for the French to contact Spanish merchants, the local governors in many cases refused to allow them to put in under pretexts too obviously meant to get around official bans.[9] The merchants' behavior eventually aroused so much suspicion that the Spaniards, far from interpreting as a measure of appeasement the French king's decision to prohibit trading activity in the South Pacific (January, 1716), saw in it, groundlessly perhaps, a move intended to promote smuggling operations in the ports of Peru.[10]

Consequently, the situation between the two powers became more and more equivocal. While France and Spain remained "allies" in principle, the Spanish governors, provoked by frequent breaches of the rules by French merchants, caused their ships to be seized, sometimes unreasonably, or even to be stopped and examined on the high seas by "vessels armed as privateers." The Spanish went so far as to organize veritable acts of piracy, to which the governors of the French islands replied by confiscating Spanish ships.[11] All this gave rise to innumerable disputes that would have degenerated into open hostilities if France, concerned not to ruin a trade that was necessary for the prosperity of its colonies, had not ordered its agents to resort to reprisals only with moderation and on their own responsibility: they were to present such actions as measures aimed at the Spanish governors, without involving the Court of Madrid, with the sole purpose of obtaining justice for wrongful confiscations and restoring peaceful relations.[12]

9. AC, C 9A 12, Blénac and Mithon, Léogane, July 2, 1716, and statement by Lescoubet, June 12, 1716; AM, B 7 267, Porlier, Teneriffe, June 26, 1716, (Mémoire concernant le commerce des Anglais aux îles Canaries . . .). See p. 145 above.

10. AE, Correspondance politique, Spain, 263, f. 114–16, 136–37, Mémoire de Cellamare, Dec. 5, 1717, and reply by the Council of the Navy, Dec. 11, 1717.

11. AE, Correspondence politique, Spain, 260, f. 64–64v, Cellamare to M. de La Varenne, April 29, 1717; f. 67, Mémoire pour servir de réponse à celui de Cellamare, Sept. 28, 1717; AE, Mem. & Doc., America, 6, f. 156–62, Extract from the books of the registrar's office . . . of Martinique, July 19, 1715; AM, B 1 29, f. 13v–14v, 17–18, Chateaumorant and Mithon, n.d.; f. 314, M. Charlot, at La Rochelle, March 12, 1718; AM, B 3 247, f. 81v, 85v, Mémoire de Cellamare au Conseil de Marine, n.d.; AC, B 40, f. 63v–64, Decision of Oct. 24, 1718; AC, C 9A 12, Blénac and Mithon, Feb. 10, April 28, 1716, Blénac, May 17, 1716; C 9A 13, Chateaumorant, July 10, 1717. For a more detailed account, see Giraud, "Un aspect de la rivalité franco-espagnole au début du XVIIIe siècle," 250–69.

12. AC, C 9A 12, Blénac and Mithon, April 28, July 1, 1716, Blénac, May 17, 1716; C 9A 13, Petition to the marquis de Chateaumorant, Léogane, Oct. 15,

In Louisiana especially, it seemed opportune to the council to show "circumspection" and "prudence." Spain had grounds for taking offense at the progress of the French occupation, the alliance being formed with the Alabama and the Creek, the threat of encirclement of Spanish coastal positions that would result from this, and the "zeal" shown by the Council of the Navy in strengthening the garrisons of Mobile and Dauphin Island.[13] The Spaniards knew that the council had not given up Louis XIV's claims to Pensacola, and they could fear that the closure of the harbor of Dauphin Island might stimulate France's assertion of these claims to a position that Spain was still determined not to surrender.[14]

At the same time, the policy of mutual aid followed during the war years became itself a cause of misunderstanding. The authorities of Vera Cruz had agreed in those days to advance funds to Louisiana. French ships had on several occasions gone from Dauphin Island to Mexico to inform the viceroy of events in the Spanish zone or to obtain payment for provisions furnished to the garrison of Pensacola. The two sides could not agree on the exact amount of the debts they had incurred to each other, and since the *ordonnateur* of Louisiana considered the claims of the Spanish officials excessive, the moves made to settle this matter led to discussions of a kind not calculated to bring the French and Spanish colonies into friendlier relations.[15] Again, the Council of the Navy feared the consequences of Abbé Jules Alberoni's policy, meaning the unfavorable attitude toward

---

1717; AC, B 39, f. 320, to M. de La Varenne, March 8, 1717; f. 411–12, to Chateaumorant and Mithon, Oct. 31, 1717; AC, B 40, f. 157v–58v, to duc de Saint-Aignan, July 20, 1718; f. 236–37, to chevalier de Feuquières, March 15, 1718; f. 263v, Mémoire pour le Sr de Silvecane, March 15, 1718; f. 401v–402, Mémoire pour Chateaumorant et Mithon, May 17, 1718; AM, B 1 9, f. 152–54, Draft of *mémoire* to Sr de La Varenne; B 1 18, f. 201–202, Petition of Sr Jacques Belin to Council of the Navy; B 1 29, f. 531–33v, Draft of *mémoire* to Chateaumorant and Mithon; B 1 30, f. 12–14v, Chateaumorant and Mithon, March 8, 1718; AM, B 7 106, f. 752–53, to Saint Aignan, Dec. 6, 1717; B 7 270, f. 38, Partyet to Catalan, June 20, 1716; B 7 35, f. 137–37v, Saint-Aignan, June 13, 1718.

13. AC, C 13A 4, f. 76–77, 1041, Mémoire sur la Louisiane porté au Conseil de Régence, Feb. 11, 1716.

14. *Ibid.*, f. 78–9; AC, C 13C 1, f. 83, Hubert to the Council of the Navy, n.d.; AC, B 38, f. 317, Mémoire pour servir d'instruction au Sr de Lépinay, Oct. 20, 1716; AE, Mem. & Doc., America, I, f. 262–63, Mémoire de Le Gendre d'Arménie; AN, AHM 3 JJ 202, Cahier de routes dans le golfe du Mexique.

15. AM, B 1 9, f. 339–46, Duclos, Jan. 15, 1716; AC, B 38, f. 310, Mémoire pour servir d'instructions au Sr Hubert, Oct. 20, 1716.

France that this policy was bound to inspire in the Spanish officials. And indeed, although the Court of Madrid examined in a spirit of equity the complaints addressed to the Council of the Indies and ordered replevin of the property belonging to Bienville and Martin d'Artaguiette that had been confiscated at Vera Cruz in 1710,[16] it nevertheless took up an increasingly hostile stance toward the French positions on the Gulf of Mexico. At the beginning of 1716 Spain increased the garrison of Pensacola, and when France erected Fort Toulouse, Spain took steps to counter French activity among the Alabama and the Creek. With the latter, especially among the Abihka, Spain maintained emissaries who succeeded in winning the allegiance of some influential chiefs.[17]

As the Council of the Navy saw matters, the unfriendliness of the Spanish ministers made it necessary for France to show itself particularly "moderate" and "circumspect" in Louisiana. In its *mémoire* addressed to the Regent in February, 1716, the council emphasized that in view of the harassment being suffered by the French nation in Spain, the French must take care not to provide Spanish officials with any pretext to "do us harm" in the province of the Mississippi, which would arouse their jealousy more and more as it "improved." In order to resume successfully the projects for commercial links with Mexico, the French would have to avoid all excessive "forwardness" and greed, act secretly with Indians as go-betweens, refrain from "making a show," and take care about the quality of French goods being offered. On these conditions alone would the Spanish governors be able to "pretend not to see us" and allow exchanges to take place from which they would be the prime beneficiaries.[18] But the enterprises that were under way west of the Mississippi did not fit into this policy of prudence. Those engaged in them constantly harbored an intention of aggression against the Spanish colonies, and it was inevitable that the latter should strive to contain the French occupation within bounds sufficiently remote for the security of New Spain not to be threatened.

The Viceroy of Mexico, the duke of Linares, had replied to

---

16. *Cf.* Giraud, *History,* I, 198–99. AM, B 1 9, f. 81v, Council of the Navy, July 29, 1716, Request from Sr d'Ibaignette; AM, B 7 269, Partyet, Feb. 17, 1716.

17. AC, C 13A 4, f. 77–79, Mémoire sur la Louisiane porté au Conseil de Régence, Feb. 11, 1716; C 13A 5, f. 117v–18, La Tour to Hubert, from Fort Toulouse, March 17, 1718.

18. AC, C 13A 4, f. 76–79, Mémoire sur la Louisiane porté au Conseil de Régence, Feb. 11, 1716; AC, B 38, f. 346v, to Hubert, Nov. 30, 1716.

Saint-Denis' first expedition by deciding to resume possession of the area beyond the Rio Grande del Norte to which the Spaniards, without assigning to it any definite frontier, gave the name "las Tejas."[19] La Mothe immediately informed the French government. The Spaniard Geraldo Moro, a member of the viceroy's entourage, sent to France a copy of the account of Saint-Denis' journey that he had written for the Court of Madrid, and this document was brought to the knowledge of the Council of the Navy by Sieur Gallut, a former agent of the *Asiento* company who had returned to France after rendering important services in the household of the duke of Linares.[20] The council refrained from taking any precipitate action. Instead, it requested the French consul in Madrid to discover what Spain's real intentions were; it abstained from asserting a claim to "La Salle's bay," so as to safeguard that place against any attempt at occupation by the viceroy; and it called on Hubert and Lépinay to do no more than "obtain information" about the routes toward the "two Mexicos" that had been discovered by Saint-Denis. They were, at most, to send along those routes a few Indians who were loyal to France, laden with goods, but to avoid "using [these routes] to an extent that could stir up any jealousy among the Spaniards."[21]

By the time these instructions reached Louisiana (March, 1717), the duke of Linares, though postponing occupation of La Salle's bay, had made himself master of the interior of Texas. A substantial expedition made up of about sixty persons—missionaries, soldiers, and settlers accompanied by their families—and followed by a herd of cattle had crossed the Rio Grande in April, 1716, under the command of Captain Domingo Ramon. Guided by Saint-Denis, the expedition made its way toward the Red River, setting up as it went four mission centers between the Neches River and the Assinai country.[22] Bienville was at this

---

19. Giraud, *History*, I, 367–69.

20. AM, B 1 9, f. 82v–84, Lusançay, Nantes, July 17, 1716; f. 333–36, Proceedings of the Council of the Navy, Sept. 1, 1716; AM, B 7 104, f. 121, to Saint-Aignan, March 16, 1716; AC, C 11A 36, f. 415, Copy of a letter from Mexico written to M. Gallut, Sept. 20, 1715; f. 418–20, Extract from letter from Geraldo Moro to Crozat, from Mexico, July 18, 1716; AC, C 13A 4, f. 607, La Mothe, June 22, 1716; f. 622, La Mothe, Feb. 7, 1716; C 13C 4, f. 50, Account of Saint-Denis' journey, attached to Gallut's letter, Aug. 1, 1716.

21. AM, B 7 104, f. 499–500, to Sr de Catalan, Sept. 7, 1716; AC, C 13A 4, f. 976, Draft of king's *mémoire* to Lépinay and Hubert.

22. AC, C 11A 36, f. 415, 418–19, Copy of a letter from Mexico written to M. Gallut, Sept. 20, 1715; Henry Folmer, *Franco-Spanish Rivalry in North America, 1564–1763* (Glendale, Calif., 1953), 238–39; C. W. Hackett, "The Marquis of San

time at Fort Saint-Joseph-des-Tunicas, where he had just obtained the submission of the Natchez. It was there that he learned of the Spanish offensive from the Natchitoches Indians who came to sell salt in the Tunicas' village (June, 1716). He immediately resolved to bar Spain from the Red River Valley and dispatched for this purpose a detachment made up of a sergeant and six men, with orders to take up a position in the Natchitoches village, where the French had as yet only a storehouse, and to reconnoiter the mineral possibilities of the region.[23] The little troop got there ten days before the Spaniards. However, the latter made up for this by setting up, at a distance of only seven leagues from the Red River, two new mission centers among the Adai and the Ais—San Miguel de Linares and Nuestra Señora de los Dolores. Unhappy about the close proximity of the two occupation zones, Bienville obtained from the "Reverend Father Missionary" who presided over the creation of these missions (possibly Father Francisco Hidalgo) an assurance that their purposes were purely religious. Nevertheless, from this time onward the Spaniards held, near the French post among the Natchitoches, bases that could block French access to Texas and which they could use if the need arose, and despite the verbal assurance given by the religious, against the French position. Their proximity also lessened the success achieved by Bienville on the Red River.[24]

It does not appear that Saint-Denis, despite his marriage on his return from Mexico to the granddaughter of Captain Diego Ramon[25] and the payment he received for guiding the expedi-

---

Miguel de Aguayo and His Recovery of Texas from the French," *Southeastern Historical Quarterly* (October, 1945), 195; Charmion Clair Shelby, "St. Denis's Declaration Concerning Texas in 1717," *Southwestern Historical Quarterly*, XVII (1924), 190–216. *Cf.* map, p. 166–67, above.

23. AM, B 1 9, f. 463v–64, Mémoire de Crozat presenté au Conseil de marine, Oct. 11, 1716; AC, C 13A 4, f. 804–805, Journal de la première expédition de Bienville aux Natchez en 1716; C 13C 4, f. 47, Mémoire sur les services du Sr de Bienville, [1724 ?]. Du Tisné does not seem to have been with this detachment. Bienville makes no mention of him, and entrusted command of the detachment to a sergeant (La Breuière? See AM, B 1 9, f. 463v–64, Mémoire de Crozat presenté au Conseil de marine, Oct. 11, 1716). This rules out Du Tisné. We cannot say when, exactly, Du Tisné reached Natchitoches. According to Bénard de La Harpe (BN, FF 8989, f. 9), it was in 1717, but Crozat mentions him as having already left in October, 1716, for the Red River (C 13A 4, f. 443).

24. AC, C 13A 6, f. 157, Bienville to the marquis commandant, Fort Louis, Dec. 10, 1721; AE, Mem. & Doc., America, I, f. 23v, 39, Bienville, Mémoire sur la Louisiane, 1725.

25. Giraud, *History*, I, 367.

tion, had any intention of remaining in the service of Spain.[26] As far back as September, 1715, he had informed the authorities at Mobile of the viceroy's plans and asked them to send a boat "to meet him" and a brigantine to La Salle's bay, thus inviting them to oppose the Spanish offensive. As Saint-Denis saw it, the lands of the king of France ought to extend to the Rio Grande.[27] When obliged to go with the Texas expedition, he may have regarded the posts and mission centers he would help to found as so many outlets for French goods or as points where the respective products of the two colonies could be exchanged. The journey that Saint-Denis' father-in-law made to Mobile after the Texas expedition, accompanied by his son-in-law (August, 1716), and the trade in horses that he effected there showed that the French colony would have gained a lot from such exchanges.[28] The Spanish posts in Texas, which were too far from Mexico to receive with ease the articles they needed for their material existence, would also have benefited.

These operations, conducted behind the backs of the Mexican authorities, would not have been contrary to the policy of the Council of the Navy. That was not the case, however, when Saint-Denis decided, with La Mothe's approval, to resume on a larger scale his attempts at trade with Mexico. He returned to Mobile, nominally in order to report on his first journey and subsequent events, sold his land on Bayou St. John, obtained his salary as governor of Biloxy in the form of goods,[29] and in this way assembled a small capital that he invested in his new enterprise. He took as partners some inhabitants of Dauphin Island and Mobile—Graveline, Derbanne, Beaulieu, Joseph Chauvin de Léry, Nicolas Chauvin de La Fresnière—who stocked themselves with an assortment of goods, much of which was advanced to them on credit by Crozat's agents.[30]

Saint-Denis hoped to succeed through his familiarity with Spanish circles and the sympathy and protection his marriage would ensure for him in those quarters. He had apparently

26. BN, FF 8989, f. 9, Bénard de la Harpe, Journal du voyage de la Louisiane; C. C. Shelby, "St. Denis's Declaration Concerning Texas," 190–216; C. C. Shelby, "St.-Denis's Second Expedition from Louisiana to the Rio Grande," *Southwestern Historical Quarterly*, XXVI (1932), 165–83.

27. AC, C 13A 4, f. 622–23, La Mothe, Feb. 7, 1716.

28. BN, FF 8989, f. 9, Bénard de la Harpe, Journal; Shelby, "St. Denis's Declaration Concerning Texas."

29. Giraud, *History*, I, 216.

30. BN, FF 8989, f. 9, Bénard de la Harpe, Journal; AC, C 13C 4, f. 56v, Extract from a letter from Chauvin de Léry and Chauvin de La Fresnière, Fort Louis, end of June, 1718; Folmer, *Franco-Spanish Rivalry in North America*, 243.

made some useful arrangements in preparation for his undertaking even before he went to Mobile. This would explain how it was that two Spanish religious were awaiting the expedition at the Natchitoches post, where it arrived in November, 1716, with sixty mules for transporting the goods—these mules having perhaps been made available through the cooperation of the commandant of the Assinai post.[31] In order to make sure of this officer's goodwill, Crozat's directors had told Saint-Denis and his partners not to refuse him any material aid he might need. And in fact they did contribute from their personal stocks to the feeding of the Spanish garrison. Saint-Denis even made several trips between the Spanish mission centers and the Natchitoches post to fetch maize for the missions.[32] Subsequently, having failed to obtain payment for what they had advanced, Saint-Denis and his partners had reason to regret their obliging conduct, but they had won the protection of the commandant, and thanks to him, their goods were conveyed without hindrance to the Assinai country.[33]

However, it was not long before difficulties arose between Saint-Denis and his partners. The latter hesitated to venture into Spanish territory, and Saint-Denis' proposal that he pretend to be the sole owner of the goods, so as to prevent their being confiscated, caused his partners to suspect that he meant to claim all the profits.[34] Their mistrust increased when, on arriving among the Assinai, they observed that all danger of confiscation had not been removed. Despite Saint-Denis' arguments and the good relations that he claimed to enjoy with the Spanish merchants, his partners refused to risk everything in an enterprise the outcome of which they could not foresee. Consequently, they left some of their property at the Assinai post when they set off for the Rio Grande in March, 1717.[35]

31. AC, C 13C 4, f. 39, Mémoire de M. Derbanne au sujet du canton des Natchitoches, New Orleans, Oct. 22, 1723; C 13C 4, f. 56, Extract from a letter from Chauvin de Léry and Chauvin de La Fresnière. Folmer, basing himself on the Mexican records, gives a different version, according to which the mules were provided by Captain Diego Ramon, commandant of the fort on the Rio Grande.

32. AC, C 13C 4, f. 39, Mémoire de M. Derbanne . . . , Oct. 22, 1723; Shelby, "St. Denis's Declaration Concerning Texas."

33. AC, C 13C 4, f. 39, Mémoire de M. Derbanne . . . , Oct. 22, 1723.

34. AC, C 13C 4, f. 56, Extract from a letter from Chauvin de Léry and Chauvin de La Fresnière.

35. Ibid., f. 56–57. The expedition set out from the Natchitoches post in December, 1716, but did not reach the Assinai post until January, 1717, because of bad weather (C 13C 4, f. 40–40v, Journal d'un voyage que M. Derbanne a fait au Mexique; BN, FF 8989, f. 9–10, Bérnard de la Harpe, Journal).

They reached the "fort on the River of the North" several days later than Saint-Denis, who had left them at the most dangerous point in their journey when they were exposed to attack by Indians. But his kinship with Captain Diego Ramon was not enough to prevent the seizure of his goods, and when his companions arrived seals were placed on their baggage as well. Convinced now of Saint-Denis' bad faith, even though he was equally victim of the confiscation ordered by the commandant, La Fresnière and de Léry accused him of having planned this betrayal.[36] Actually, the commandant of the fort did not want to confiscate the goods: desirous not to get into trouble through showing too much indulgence toward the French, he waited before taking this step for instructions from the viceroy of Mexico, the marquis of Valero, successor to the duke of Linares. With the Spanish missionaries' help, moreover, Saint-Denis' partners succeeded in concealing some of their goods, thereby saving them from confiscation, and disposing of them on the spot—an operation that brought them no profit, if we are to believe the statement of Bénard de La Harpe, who says they failed to receive payment for the goods they sold.[37]

Saint-Denis himself went to Mexico to try to win the favor of the viceroy. He spoke of the services he had rendered to Spain and said that he intended to sell his goods in order to live in the place where his marriage gave him the right to reside. His arguments, which justified his original plan to claim that he was the owner of all the goods that he and his partners had brought into Spanish territory, might have convinced the marquis of Valero if the viceroy had not been warned of the pro-French sympathies of the Ramon family, of the help they were accused of giving to Saint-Denis' smuggling activities, and especially of the harmful consequences that would ensue for New Spain if communication were to be established between the Red River and the Rio Grande.[38] The viceroy put Saint-Denis in prison, and when the news of his arrest reached his partners they fled from the Span-

---

36. AC, C 13C 4, f. 56–57, Extract from a letter from Chauvin de Léry and Chauvin de La Fresnière.

37. BN, FF 8989, f. 11, Bérnard de la Harpe, Journal; AC, C 13C 4, f. 57, Extract from a letter from Chauvin de Léry and Chauvin de La Fresnière; C 13A 5, f. 124v, Hubert, Dauphin Island, Nov. 27, 1717; Shelby, "St. Denis's Declaration Concerning Texas."

38. BN, FF 8989, f. 11, Bénard de la Harpe, Journal; Shelby, "St. Denis's Declaration Concerning Texas"; Folmer, *Franco-Spanish Rivalry in North America*, 243–44.

ish fort, returning to Mobile via the Assinai and Natchitoches countries (September, 1717). The missionaries helped them to escape by providing the horses they needed. At the Assinai post they succeeded, though not without difficulty, in recovering the goods they had left there.[39]

As for Saint-Denis, after telling his judges that he intended to take Spanish nationality, he managed after some months to obtain his freedom and the restitution of his property, which he sold in Nuevo León.[40] He would probably then have entered the Spanish service if a well-paid position had been offered him. Irritated, however, by the slowness of the authorities in meeting his requests, he provoked them with excessive outspokenness and eventually, realizing that he was in danger again, fled back into French territory, where thenceforth he devoted himself to defending the Natchitoches outpost. This "turbulent" spirit, hostile to all "subordination," became, despite the suspicions his marriage and his gestures toward defection had aroused among his compatriots,[41] one of the best helpers of the cause of France in this border region.

The failure of Saint-Denis' enterprise proved once again the impossibility of establishing by land the regular relations with New Spain that Crozat had been unable to achieve by sea. From the experience of Saint-Denis' companions it emerged that only a "semi-official" sort of trade was practicable, using the protection offered by the religious and by the commandants of Spanish posts. The governor of the province of "las Tejas," Don Martín de Alarcón himself, would perhaps not have refused to connive with Saint-Denis if the latter had behaved more thoughtfully toward him.[42] Officially, however, the venture had ended in defeat. Crozat's company suffered a heavy loss—more than 30,000 livres worth of goods. On this account it passed on to the Company of the Indies a claim on Saint-Denis and his partners that the latter were called upon to settle in 1741.[43] Saint-Denis, being

---

39. AC, C 13C 4, f. 43v, Journal d'un voyage que M. Derbanne . . . ; f. 57, Extract from a letter from Chauvin de Léry and Chauvin de La Fresnière.

40. BN, FF 8989, f. 11, Bénard de la Harpe, Journal; Shelby, "St. Denis's Declaration Concerning Texas."

41. AC, C 13A 6, f. 317v, Leblond de La Tour, May 17, 1722.

42. AC, C 13C 4, f. 57, Extract from a letter from Chauvin de Léry and Chauvin de la Fresnière; BN, FF 8989, f. 11, Bénard de la Harpe, Journal.

43. AE, Mem. & Doc., America, I, f. 227–28, Mémoire de Crozat [?], May 14, 1717; f. 265–65v, Mémoire de Le Gendre d'Arménie; LSHM, Extract from the registers of the hearings by the royal commissioners . . . , May 5, 1741.

now too compromised to risk entering the Spanish zone again, was unable to consider another attempt, and the attitude of the Spaniards seemed to rule out any hope of success at a later date. In July, 1717, a Frenchman who had served in the retinue of the duke of Linares, Sieur du Bourg, informed the Council of the Navy of the viceroy's decision to reinforce without delay his garrisons in Texas. There were twenty-five soldiers already at the Assinai post, and the Spaniards proposed to double this number. Also, they seemed once more to want to give their inland positions the support of a base on the coast from which provisions could be brought in, and the site for this would be "the river of Monsieur de La Salle."[44]

The viceroy might seem to have exaggerated the danger to Spanish power implied by the arrival of a few Frenchmen on the Rio Grande frontier, but in fact the desire for territorial expansion that Saint-Denis' adventure stimulated in the French colony fully justified his fears. When Derbanne returned from the Rio Grande he advised that France should reoccupy La Salle's bay so as to expand its trading area and win the alliance of the natives, who had little liking for the Spaniards. The latter were not "fortified in their lands," so it should be possible to proceed to the conquest of their mining districts. Transmitting Derbanne's account to the Council of the Navy, Hubert wrote similarly of the usefulness of "La Salle's bay." Once there, he said, the French would be "in a position to become masters of the mines of New Mexico," which confirmed La Mothe's view that the French would find there a base nearer to the Spanish mines than Vera Cruz.[45] The conviction became more and more firmly held that this bay belonged by right to France, and increasingly the desire to occupy it merged with the idea of territorial expansion that was expressed so often in the correspondence of Crozat, Bienville, and Le Maire. As the financier saw it, increased population in Louisiana should give the colony the means to drive the Spaniards out of Mexico. Bienville perceived in the post that he wanted established on the Arkansas River a base for an attack on New Mexico. For the missionary Le Maire, if France should

44. AM, B 1 32, f. 63–63v, Sr du Bourg, Mexico, July 16, 1717; AC C 13C 4, f. 40, 42–43, Journal d'un voyage que M. Derbanne . . . ; Nov. 1, 1717; BN, FF 8989, f. 9v–10, Bénard de la Harpe, Journal.
45. AC, C 13C 4, f. 43–43v, Journal d'un voyage que M. Derbanne . . . ; C 13A 4, f. 622–23, La Mothe, Feb. 7, 1716; C 13A 5, f. 123–24, Hubert, Nov. 27, 1717; AM, B 1 30, f. 91–92, reproduces Hubert's letter; AE, Mem. & Doc., America, I, f. 138v, Hubert, Mémoire au sujet de l'établissement de la Louisiane.

break with Spain, the Mississippi colony would make possible the conquest of a rich province not guarded by any "fortress."[46]

Faced with intentions that were so often affirmed, it was logical that the marquis of Valero should take defensive measures which, to be effective, must presume an immediate extension of Spanish authority up to the Red River. As Derbanne had discovered, the Spaniards were aware of the fragility of their position on the borders of Mexico.[47] Saint-Denis' expedition proved that, despite their precautions, the road to New Spain was still open and that the French were in a position to "take it from the rear," as this was put in a *mémoire* written during Saint-Denis' captivity, probably by Geraldo Moro.[48] Consequently, the event assumed very serious importance. It seemed to show that France was no longer confining its ambitions to Pensacola but was getting ready to advance on Mexico, disregarding the rights that the Spaniards had acquired in Texas through their rapid action.

In his numerous *mémoires*, Le Maire assigns to Louisiana borders that include the area between the Rio Grande and the Red River. He does not consider the disproportion between the forces at the French posts and those at the Spanish posts. The Natchitoches post could not take on the Assinai *presidio*. Its sole defense was an "entrenchment with stakes," "without cannon or gun for firing stones" and destined soon to fall into ruin, and it was manned by a very small garrison. It was not long before Le Maire agreed that this did not justify the name of "establishment."[49] Nevertheless, since he thought the Spaniards incapable of protecting the territory they occupied, he claimed for Louisiana the province of "las Tejas," including La Salle's bay, and also the zone to the east of Mobile as far as the Florida Peninsula, for, he said, the fort of Pensacola was "too slight a thing" to set a bound to French territory. This was also the view taken by the

46. AC, F 3 241, f. 227, Ordinance authorising the Company of the West . . . , Nov. 16, 1718; AC, C 13C 2, f. 155v, Mémoire de Le Maire, 1718; C 13A 5, f. 233v, Mémoire pour faire connaître . . . (Crozat), Jan. 11, 1717; AE, Mem. & Doc., America, I, f. 182v, Crozat, Mémoire sur la Louisiane (1717); f. 205, Bienville, June 10, 1718; BN, FF 12105, f. 14, Le Maire, Mémoire sur la Louisiane, March 1, 1717.

47. AC, C 13C 4, f. 43v, Journal d'un voyage que M. Derbanne . . . , Nov. 1, 1717; C 11A 36, f. 418–19, Geraldo Moro to Crozat, from Mexico, July 18, 1716.

48. AC, C 13A 4, f. 1001ff.

49. AC, C 13A 5, f. 344, Proceedings of the Council of Trade, Dauphin Island, Oct. 26, 1719; AN, AHM 3 JJ 200 4, Le Maire, May 13, 1718; BN FF 8989, f. 9, Bénard de la Harpe, Journal.

Native Peoples of the Missouri Country   Map by John Snead

ordonnateur Hubert.[50] West of the Mississippi, the missionary thought, France had the right to advance as far as it chose above the northern border of New Mexico, which he placed at the 37th or 38th degree of latitude.[51] Everything here would depend on the discoveries that might be made as the Missouri route—which was engaging more and more attention because of the growing importance given in France and in Louisiana to investigation of the continent's mineral resources—became better known.

By the end of the first years of Crozat's regime it was certain, through the prospecting carried out by La Mothe and the stories told by *voyageurs,* that the land on the banks of the Missouri River contained mineral deposits. The observations that Etienne Véniard de Bourgmont had made filled in with more detail the knowledge already possessed concerning the regions through which the river ran and their population. In his "Exacte description de la Louisianne," Bourgmont completed the purely topographical data of the "way to be followed in going up the Missouri River."[52] He recorded the locations of the tribes who lived along the river and its chief tributaries—the Missouri, Osage, Kansas, Oto or "Maquetantata," Pawnee and Pawnee-Omaha, Ayowest (Iowa), White Omaha, Paducah, and Aricara. He described the Missouri country, in which "the prairies . . . are like seas, and are filled with wild beasts . . . in such great numbers as are beyond imagination," as well as the river itself, "the water of which is always muddy," and its tributary the Niobrara, "the smoky river," with its "flying sand, like smoke."[53] His knowledge of the Aricara meant that the limit to which the Missouri country had been explored could now be extended as far as the Cheyenne River.[54] Furs, the superior quality of which was guaranteed by the cold climate, seemed to him likely to be the great resource of these regions. At the same time, however, Bourgmont emphasized that the Spanish mining areas were not far off

50. AC, C 13C 2, f. 153v–55, Le Maire, Mémoire sur la Louisiane, 1718; AE, Mem. & Doc., America, I, f. 138v, Hubert, Mémoire au sujet de l'établissement de la . . . Louisiane, 1717; AN, AHM 3 JJ 200 4, Le Maire, May 13, 1718.

51. AC, C 13C 2, f. 154, Le Maire, Mémoire sur la Louisiane, 1718; C 13A 4, f. 991, Crozat, Mémoire sur la Louisiane [1715 ?]; BN, FF 12105, Le Maire, March 1, 1717.

52. Giraud, *History,* I, 364n26; AC, C 13C 1, f. 346–56 (V. de Bourgmont), Exacte description de la Louisianne.

53. *Ibid.,* f. 353–55.

54. Marc de Villiers du Terrage, *La Découverte du Missouri et l'histoire du fort d' Orléans* (Paris, 1925), 63–64.

and that it would be possible to trade with them along the Missouri and its tributaries, following the example of the Pawnee-Omaha. The Spaniards, he wrote, were, according to the Indians, "very rich in mines in these parts." He thus raised afresh the question of communications between the Missouri and New Mexico and confirmed what had already been said by Le Maire and by Martin d'Artaguiette d'Iron.[55]

It has been customary, since the work of Marc de Villiers du Terrage, to give the date 1717 to Véniard de Bourgmont's "Description" and to assign to it a decisive role in the revival of interest in the Missouri that became marked at that time.[56] Close examination of the text, however, enables us to name 1714 as the year when it was written. There are several reasons for rejecting Marc de Villiers' date. The importance ascribed by Bourgmont to the roadstead of Dauphin Island, where between fifteen and twenty ships could drop anchor "with ease, and well sheltered from any wind," and to its access channel, practicable even though narrow, and the fact that he presents the island's harbor as being quite without defense works express a state of affairs that went back to 1715, at latest.[57] When he mentions the presence of the Taensa Indians on the Mississippi and says that the French colony had "no trade" with the Creeks (Conchaques and Abihkas), he is describing a situation earlier than 1715, because in that year the Taensa left the river and settled near Mobile, and the rebellion of the Indians against the British, also in that year, was followed by a commercial *rapprochement* between the French and the Creek tribes, a fact to which Bourgmont makes no allusion.[58] Furthermore, the reference to Saint-Denis' journey contained in the document permits us to give 1714 as the date of its composition. By the Red River, Bourgmont writes, "went the Frenchmen whom Monsieur de La Mothe . . . sent there last year, in the month of July, to try to engage in some trade with the Spaniards."[59] Neither of Saint-Denis' journeys took place in July: both began in the autumn (September–October, 1713, and

55. AC, C 13C 1, f. 354v (V. de Bourgmont), Exacte description de la Louisianne; Giraud, *History*, I, 362–63.
56. De Villiers, *La Découverte du Missouri*, 64.
57. AC, C 13C 1, f. 347 (V. de Bourgmont), Exacte description de la Louisiane. *Cf.* pp. 107 and 137 above.
58. *Cf.* pp. 165, 170 above. Giraud, *History*, I, 329–30; AC, C 13C 1, f. 348–48v, 349v (V. de Bourgmont), Exacte description de la Louisianne.
59. *Ibid.*, f. 350.

October, 1716). But Bourgmont can only mean the first of the two journeys, because he depicts the Natchez as "allies and friends of the French, very good, hard-working people," an opinion he could not have expressed in 1716 after the attacks that provoked the first Natchez war.[60] Again, the illusions he cherishes concerning Crozat's regime and the hope he voices that the inhabitants of Mobile, after the disappointments they had suffered, "will enjoy the mildness" of the "company *that has been formed*" can apply only to the beginning of the monopoly. He would have written differently in 1717.[61]

By the light of this document we can, moreover, fill in the rather sketchy picture that Marc de Villiers gave us of Véniard de Bourgmont's career. We learn from it that he took part in Juchereau de Saint-Denis' enterprise on the lower Ohio in 1702, that he was present at the construction of the fort set up to provide protection for the tannery, and that he lived for eighteen months among the Mascoutins and the Miamis in order to obtain the skins needed as raw material for this tannery.[62] We learn especially that before he went up the Missouri in 1714 he made a long journey through Louisiana that took him right down to the coast. His description of Dauphin Island and its garrison, Mobile, Ship Island, the mouths of the Mississippi, the Biloxi ("Bilocchy") portage, and of the native tribes living along the shore of the Gulf of Mexico, on the lower Mississippi, and on the Red River is the result of his travels in these various parts in 1713: "I tell of what I have seen," he says. "This is how [these nations] were *last year, when I was there.*"[63]

After all these peregrinations, Bourgmont returned to the Illinois country, and at the beginning of 1714 his conduct brought upon him once more the reprobation of the missionaries.[64] Then in the spring of that year he began his journey up the Missouri River, the purely topographical data from which appear in his "Routte qu'il faut tenir pour remonter la rivière de Missoury,"

60. *Ibid. Cf.* p. 78 above.
61. *Ibid.*, f. 347.
62. *Ibid.*, f. 351v–52. On Juchereau de Saint-Denis' tannery, *cf.* Giraud, *History,* I, 51.
63. AC, C 13C 1, f. 346v, 349v (V. de Bourgmont), Exacte description de la Louisianne.
64. AC, B 36 (Iles), f. 198v, Pontchartrain to Father Le Tellier, June 10, 1714; AC, C 11A 36, f. 356v, Ramezay to the Minister, Sept. 18, 1714; Giraud, *History,* I, 347.

while the ethnological and geographical observations he made are included in his "Exacte description."[65] The two documents belong to the same year and consequently relate to the same journey. As the former has come down to us in an incomplete state, it is the "Exacte description" that enables us to reconstitute fully the course followed in 1714 by Véniard de Bourgmont, who, far from finishing at the Platte River, which is where the "Routte qu'il faut tenir" finishes, actually went as far as the Aricaras' country at the confluence of the Cheyenne River.[66] It was only in this year that, as Claude de l'Isle formally states, Bourgmont returned to the Missouri. De l'Isle adds that he lived there until 1719, but he cannot have remained there all the time, since in 1715 he is mentioned as being "among the Illinois and the Wabash."[67]

If, then, the Missouri became from 1717 onward the theme of more and more *mémoires*, it is not in the "Exacte description de la Louisianne," a document already old by that time, that we must seek the cause of this interest. The policy of the Council of the Navy, the encouragement it was giving to exploration of the mineral resources of Louisiana, and the curiosity aroused by the question of access to the "Western Sea" were the reasons for the attention now being focused on the Missouri. The pur-

---

65. Giraud, *History*, I, 363–64. Bourgmont, who in the autumn of 1713 was in southern Louisiana, where he learned of Saint-Denis' departure, would not have had time to ascend the Missouri at the end of that year and be back in the Illinois country at the beginning of 1714. For a more detailed discussion of this question, see Giraud, "L'Éxacte description de la Louisianne' de Véniard de Bourgmont," *Revue historique* (January–March, 1957), 29–41.

66. De Villiers, *La Découverte du Missouri*, 63–64, basing himself on the distances given by Bourgmont and on the location of the Aricaras in the time of Lewis and Clark, speculates that he may have got as far as the Little Missouri. If so, we must identify the Little Missouri with the river Nidejaudegé. However, from the description given by Bourgmont and the placing of the White Omahas, this river must be the Niobrara. Bourgmont places the Aricaras on the Niobrara, not on the Missouri. (Marc de Villiers deliberately altered Bourgmont's text: "Higher up in the Missouri country we find three villages called Aricaras." The original does not mention the Missouri country [C 13C 1, f. 354v].) However, as there is nothing to show that the Aricaras were settled on the Niobrara, we can presume a slip of the pen on Bourgmont's part.

The account I gave of Bourgmont's journeys in Volume I of my *History of French Louisiana* (pp. 363–64) was unfortunately based upon the work of Marc de Villiers. Study of the "Exacte description," which led to my dating the document differently, has compelled me to take a different view.

67. AN, AHM 3 JJ 201 17, Manuscript notes by Claude de l'Isle at the end of Routte qu'il faut tenir . . . ; AC, B 37, f. 201v, Pontchartrain to M. de Ramezay, July 13, 1715.

pose of the *mémoires* of 1717 was to supply the Council of the Navy with information that, by emphasizing the interesting aspects of the river and its future possibilities, would perhaps induce the council to give active backing to enterprises of discovery and exploitation.

Le Maire, in his report of March 1, 1717, repeated what he had already written in 1714, namely, that the upper course of the Missouri led to regions that abounded in precious metals, since the "caravans of Spanish adventurers" coming from New Mexico crossed the river not far from its sources in order to gather "yellow iron" in the regions lying to the west and northwest of the Missouri. And because he thought the sources of the Rio Grande (Rio Bravo) were close to those of the Missouri, he wrote as though there were possibilities of communication between the two that would make New Mexico easily accessible.[68] This was also what the *ordonnateur* Hubert was saying in the *mémoire* he drew up in October, 1717, for the Council of the Navy: by going up the Missouri as far as its source, one would arrive at mineral deposits just as rich as those of New Mexico, while also coming close to the latter.[69] In both cases the idea that emerges is that the Missouri would enable the French to penetrate into Spanish territory, just as the lower course of the Rio Grande, according to Hubert, would easily carry them there once they were in possession of La Salle's bay.[70]

Consequently, the *ordonnateur* proposed to the Council of the Navy that the upper Missouri country be occupied by the French. This would amount, of course, to a considerable undertaking that would require some fifty soldiers together with a body of Canadians, blacks, and miners needed to row the pirogues, carry on trade and reconnaissance, and begin the mining work. However, Hubert, "having already some knowledge of the prospecting and exploitation of minerals," offered to assume responsibility for the undertaking himself.[71] France would then possess an establishment that could be used to prospect for minerals. This would also be a center for trade with the "caravans" that crossed the Missouri, and it would serve as a military

---

68. BN, FF 12105, f. 7, Le Maire, March 1, 1717; AC, C 13C 2, f. 160, Le Maire, Mémoire sur la Louisiane, 1718.

69. AC, C 13A 5, f. 143–44, Hubert, October, 1715.

70. AC, C 13A 5, f. 123–23v, Hubert, Nov. 27, 1717; f. 233–33v, Crozat, Mémoire pour faire connaître . . . , Jan. 11, 1717.

71. AC, C 13A 5, f. 121, 143–143v, Hubert, Mémoire sur la colonie de la Louisiane, October, 1717.

base against New Mexico, which the French, helped by Indians, would take over whenever they wished.⁷² Through it, moreover, France would make sure of reaching the "Western Sea," because a river that ran into that sea rose not far from the sources of the Missouri and was perhaps only a "branch" of it. Simplifying to excess a problem of which he had probably been given a quick survey by Le Maire, Hubert contemplated the formation in the near future of trade relations with the Far East.⁷³ More boldly still, he imagined that by conquering New Mexico the domain of Louisiana could be extended, regardless of latitude, to the extreme edge of the continent. He thus went further than the missionary's imperialistic idea. Had his projects been put into effect, they would have created, as Gallut's correspondent predicted in 1715, a new zone of conflict between the French and Spanish empires.⁷⁴

To the moderate policy of the Council of the Navy Hubert thus counterposed notions that could only revive the mistrust between the possessions of France and Spain that had prevailed in previous years. Coming on top of Saint-Denis' enterprises and the fear the Spaniards felt as they watched the progress of France's domination in Louisiana, this expression of desire to expand the sphere of French rule at the expense of that of the Most Catholic King spread through the Spanish empire the feeling that war between the colonies was imminent. At Havana and in the Canaries Spanish officers were saying in 1717 that the viceroy of Mexico was preparing to drive out "the French established on the Mississippi."⁷⁵

On the surface, there was still unity between the two powers. From time to time Spanish officers still demonstrated confidence in their French counterparts. In 1717 the governor of Havana did not hesitate to entrust to the captain of the *Paon*, on his return to France from Dauphin Island, "important mail" addressed to the king of Spain.⁷⁶ But the purposes of the colonial policy of the Council of the Navy, the schemes of its subordinates, the enterprises launched in the colonies, all contradicted too overtly the

72. AC, C 13A 5, f. 143–44, Hubert, October, 1715.
73. *Ibid.*, f. 144–45.
74. *Ibid.*, f. 144; AC, C 11A 36, f. 415–16, Copy of a letter from Mexico, Sept. 20, 1715, . . . written to M. Gallut.
75. AC, C 13C 1, f. 84v, Hubert, n.d.; AM, B 1 18, f. 123v, Porlier, at Teneriffe, June 10, 1717.
76. AC, C 13C 2, f. 151; AM, B 1 21, f. 11v, Du Sault, on board the *Paon*, Aug. 29, 1717.

prudent instructions issued by the council for them not to aggravate the divisions that contact between the two empires made inevitable. These divisions became acute in Louisiana as well as in the islands and furnished the Spanish ministers with more and more grievances against the French "nation," which were certainly not unconnected with the ill will of which the French were the object in Spain itself. Soon, moreover, the creation of the Company of the West and fear lest the Company should undertake more vigorous action on behalf of Louisiana were to provoke in Spain a resentment that would result in revived hostility toward France. It would then no longer be possible to avoid the conflict of which there had been so many premonitions during the years of transition. And that would be, for the progress of Louisiana, an impediment all the more injurious because the break with Spain happened at the very beginning of the colonizing activity launched by the Company of the Indies.

Bibliography

THE BIBLIOGRAPHY differs little from the one given in the first volume of this work. The documents used are mainly in the Archives des Colonies.

ARCHIVES DES COLONIES

Series A, Acts of the sovereign power, Registers 22 and 23.
Series B, Orders of the king and dispatches concerning the colonies, Registers 38–40.
Series C, General correspondence: C 13A, Registers 4–5, C 13B, Register 1, C 13C, Registers 1–4.
Series D 2C, Troops in the colonies, Register 51.
Series F: F 1A, Accounts; F 2A, Trading companies; F 2C, Colonies generally; F 3, Canada and Louisiana.
Dépôt des Fortifications des Colonies (Depository of records of the fortifications in the colonies [maps, plans, *mémoires*]): The series relating to Canada, C 11A and C 11E, and to St. Domingue, C 9A, were most used, together with the series G 1 412 (Censuses), G 1 464 (Censuses and passenger lists), G 1 465 (Concessions), although these chiefly concern the period after 1717.

All of the documents included in the Archives des Colonies have recently been transferred from Paris to Aix-en-Provence. However, a great many of them are still available in the building of the Archives Nationales, where they have been microfilmed.

ARCHIVES DE LA MARINE

The Archives de la Marine are, as ever, the indispensable complement to the colonial series.
Series A 1 51, Acts of the sovereign power, Navy.
Series B 1, Proceedings of the Council of the Navy.
Series B 2, Letters from the Council of the Navy to the port administrators.
Series B 3, Letters from the port administrators to the Council of the Navy.
Series B 7, Foreign countries.

Archives Hydrographique de la Marine: This series of naval maps has been transferred to the Archives Nationales. Registers 67, 67², 115 IX, 115 X, and 115 XI, are now shelf-marked 3 JJ 200, 201, 386, 387, and 388, respectively.

ARCHIVES NATIONALES

To be added to the above are the following series in the Archives Nationales.
G 7 1830, Navy, and 1849, Proceedings of the Council of Finance.
K, Boxes 1232 and 1374, Historical monuments.
B III, Foreign Affairs.

ARCHIVES DU MINISTÈRE DES AFFAIRES ETRANGÈRES

Mémoires et documents, America and France.
Correspondance politique, Spain.

BIBLIOTHÈQUE NATIONALE

The manuscripts in the Bibliothèque Nationale have been more fully utilized in this volume. Besides François Le Maire's Mémoire sur la Louisiana (FF 12105), Pénigaut's Relation, and Bénard de la Harpe's Journal du voyage de la Louisiane (FF 8989), the following documents in the Fond Français have been drawn upon: the registers relating to the Council of the Navy (11329), the Council of Finance (6930), and the Regency Council (23663, 23664, 23672, 23673); the correspondence of the Regent and the duc de Noailles (6931–33); the collections of edicts and declarations on financial matters (7220, 7221); John Law's Histoire des finances pendant le Régence (10361; duplicate of the manuscript in FFNA 1431); the regulations concerning the Navy and the colonies (11332), the correspondence of the intendants (11370, 11371, 11372, 11375, 11378, 11379); and the correspondence of the comte de Toulouse (16731, 16732).

ARCHIVES DE LA CHARENTE-MARITIME

This collection was relevant to the present volume only in the case of the records of the notaries Rivière and Soullard.

PUBLIC RECORD OFFICE, LONDON

The colonial series in the Public Records Office, London, was consulted with advantage.
CO 5, 323 (7), 324 (10), Colonies, general.
CO 5, 382, 383, 387, 1265, 1266, 1293, Board of Trade, correspondence.
CO 5, 1317, 1342, 1418, Virginia.
State papers, France, 78, 160.

OTHER SOURCES

The records of the Séminaire Laval, Quebec, contain little of interest for the period 1715 to 1717. This is true also of the documents held in the United States, with the single exception of the parish register of Mobile (Bishopric of Mobile, Alabama). The records in the Louisiana State Historical Museum, New Orleans, do not start until 1717.

As for the bibliography of printed works, it will be enough to add to the list given in Volume I a few detailed studies concerning the history of France under the Regency or which discuss points of the local history of Louisiana.

Buvat, Jean. *Gazette de la Régence.* Paris, 1887 (extract from Ms 20 in the Royal Library, The Hague).

———. *Journal de la Régence.* Edited by Campardon. Vol. I. Paris, 1865.

Brunet, M. G., trans. *Correspondence complète de Madame, duchesse d'Orléans.* 2 vols. Paris, 1904.

Dangeau, Philippe de Courcillon, Marquis de. *Journal du marquis de Dangeau, avec les additions inédites du duc de Saint-Simon.* Edited by E. Soubié and L. Dussieux. Vol. XVI. Paris, 1858.

Dunne, Peter Masten. "Lower California an Island." *Mid-America* (January, 1953), 37–67.

Folmer, Henry. "Contraband Trade Between Louisiana and New Mexico in the 18th Century." *New Mexico Historical Review* (1941), 249–74.

———. "Etienne Véniard de Bourgmond in the Missouri Country." *Missouri Historical Review* (1942), 279–99.

———. *Franco-Spanish Rivalry in North America, 1564–1763.* Glendale, Calif., 1953.

Gipson, L. H. *Zones of International Friction, 1748–1754.* New York, 1939. Vol. IV of *The British Empire Before the American Revolution.*

Hackett, Charles W. "The Marquis of San Miguel de Aguayo and His Recovery of Texas from the French." *Southwestern Historical Quarterly* (October, 1945).

La Mothe, known as La Hote. *La Vie de Philippe d'Orléans, petit-fils de France.* 2 vols. London, 1736.

Le Jau, Francis. *The Carolina Chronicle of Dr. Francis Le Jau, 1706–1717.* Edited by Frank J. Klingberg. University of California Publications in History, LIII. 1956.

McDowell, W. L. *Journals of the Commissioners of the Indian Trade, September 20, 1710–August 29, 1718.* The Colonial Records of South Carolina, Series 2. Columbia, S.C., 1955.

Portré-Bobinski, G. *French Civilization and Culture in Natchitoches.* 1941.

Shelby, Charmion Clair. "St-Denis's Declaration Concerning Texas in 1717." *Southwestern Historical Quarterly,* XVII (1924), 190–216.

———. "St.-Denis's Second Expedition from Louisiana to the Rio Grande." *Southwestern Historical Quarterly,* XXVI (1932), 165–83.

Villette, Marquis de. *Mémoires.* Paris, 1844.

Index

Académie des Sciences, 11–13, 17, 22
Académie Française, 11
Agriculture, 6, 132–35
Aimable-Marie, 182
Alain-Emmanuel, marquis de Coëtlogon, 1
Alarcón, Don Martín de, 191
Alberoni, Abbé Jules, 184–85
Alcohol use, 129
Alexandre, Jean, 124
Arkansas country, 160
Artaguiette Diron, Jean-Baptiste Martin d', 24, 81, 105, 106, 185, 196
Artaguiette d'Itouralde, Chevalier d', 105
Artus, Sieur, 13–14, 85, 104, 106, 108, 109, 119
Asiento monopoly, 178, 181, 186
Astronomy, 12

Bajot, aide, 106, 107, 109
Barbu, 168
Baudreau, Jean-Baptiste, 135
Beauharnais, 102, 107
Beaulieu, 188
Bécard de Grandville, Sieur Louis, 137
Béchameil, Louis, sieur de Nointel, 1
Bégon, Michel, 32
Bellisle, Gotteville, 8
Bellone, 182
Benoist, Sieur, 86
Bernard, Jean-Frédéric, 25
Bienville: charges against, 36–37; and Indians, 37, 77–80, 154–55, 164, 165, 168, 171–72, 186–87; payments to, 54, 85, 96; conflicts with Crozat, 75, 81; supporters of, 76; in Natchez territory, 77–80, 154; as provisional commander of Louisiana, 82, 91; conflicts with Lépinay, 90–93; inland command of, 90–93, 152, 175; purchase of ship by, 94; and Canadians, 121; and slavery, 130; interest in Horn Island, 135; confiscation of property of, 185; and territorial expansion, 192
Bignon, Abbé Jean-Paul, 13, 16
Bignon, Jérôme, 105
Biloxi, 153, 188, 197
Bisaillon, 176
Blacks: as slaves, 130–31, 132. *See also* Slavery
Bobé, Jean, 15, 16, 19–24
Bochard, Antoine, comte de Champigny, 1
Bodin-Miragouenne, Nicolas, 135
Boisrenaud de Roisneau, Marie-Françoise de, 124–25
Bonnille, Sieur de, 103–104, 121
Botany, 15–17
Bourbon, Louis Alexandre de. *See* Toulouse, comte de
Bourbon-Condé, Louis Henri de, 120
Bourdon, 158
Bourgmont, Etienne Véniard de, 158, 195–98, 198n
Broutin, engineer, 156
Buache, Philippe, 13, 14
Burel, Geneviève, 124

Cadillac, sieur de. *See* La Mothe, Antoine de, sieur de Cadillac
Canada, 12, 13, 25, 32, 39, 63, 81, 89, 94, 114, 118, 120–21, 162–63
Canadian traders, 78, 154, 155, 158, 176
Canary Islands, 12, 13, 145, 200
Cap Français, 45, 57, 64, 81, 121
Cape Breton Island, 13, 14, 33, 88, 136

Capsole, Abbé, 126
Capuchins, 159–60
Cartography, 13–15
Cassini, Dominique-Jean, 13
Castelain, 145
Catherine, 143–44
Cattle, 133–34, 136
Cayenne, 34, 63
Charlevoix, Father, 22
Chastelain, clerk, 86
Chateaugué, Sieur de, 37, 83, 91, 96, 120–21, 134
Chauvin, Jacques, 124
Chauvin, Joseph, 124, 188
Chavanne de Richebourg, Captain, 154
Christopher, Catherine, 124
Churches, 127–28
Code Noir, 130–31
Colonies. *See* Council of the Navy; Louisiana; and names of other colonies
Company of Saint-Domingue, 57, 66
Company of the Indies, 15, 34, 133, 201
Company of the West, 25, 68, 70, 82, 89, 93, 95, 109, 118, 201
Conseil Supérieur, 87–88, 96–98, 120, 125, 131
Council of Finance, 1, 5, 61, 94
Council of State, 84
Council of the Indies, 185
Council of the Navy: composition of, 1; governance of colonies by, 1–10, 27–37, 88, 200–201; expectations of, 3; trade policy of, 6–7, 56–58, 140–42, 147, 182; and frigates sent to Mississippi River, 7–8; and indentured servants, 8; and military defense, 9, 101–106, 107, 108, 110–13, 184; and scientific movement, 12, 13; and discovery of Western Sea, 19, 20–23, 198–99; interest in Louisiana, 24; Indian policy of, 30–31, 162–79; emigration policy for colonies, 31–34, 46–47, 115–18; on Bienville, 36–37; Crozat on, 39; and Crozat's plans for Louisiana, 41–47; and changes in Crozat's recommendations on Louisiana, 47–49; and financial difficulties, 51–52, 144–46;

establishment of, 56; and Crozat, 58–62; and Crozat's resignation, 67–68; and Company of the West, 68; and Raujon, 72–73; and Crozat's criticisms of Louisiana government, 76; and La Mothe, 79–80, 82; and Lépinay, 86, 89–90; and Bienville, 90–92; and Hubert, 92–93, 95; and notarial records in Louisiana, 97; and supplies for colonies, 122; and agriculture in Louisiana, 132–34; and land tenure system in Louisiana, 135; and improvements in Louisiana, 149; and occupation of interior of Louisiana, 151–61; and relations with Spain, 184–85
Council of Trade, 1, 89
Couturier, 96–97, 119
Crozat: and Council of Trade, 1; and comte de Toulouse, 3; and Mississippi trade, 6–7; and discovery of Western Sea, 19; importance of, 25; and emigration policy, 34, 42–44, 120–23; on Bienville, 36; royal approval of, 38, 235; views and influence of, 38–49; reasons of Louisiana's importance to France, 39–41; and military defense, 41–42, 103, 104, 106, 107, 108, 109; plans for Louisiana, 41–47; and supplies and food for Louisiana, 45, 52–55, 59–61, 63–64; changes made by Council of the Navy on recommendations of, 47–49; authority of, 55; end of monopoly of, 56–71; monopoly of, 57–58, 85–86, 140–41, 149, 197; payments made by, 58–62; price policy of, 64–65, 86; resignation of, 65–67, 109, 111, 113, 115; failure to make payments after resignation, 66–67, 111; gains from monopoly in Louisiana, 68–71; criticisms of Louisiana government, 72–82; and Lépinay and Hubert, 85–86; and Bienville, 91; and sawmill in Louisiana, 142; and trade, 146–47, 162; and wealth of Louisiana, 151; and missionaries, 159–60, 161; and territorial expansion, 192
Cuba, 133–34, 145–46, 200

Dardenne, Gilbert, 124
Dauphin Island: uncertainties of inhabitants of, 7; cartography of, 13–14; fortification of, 45, 80, 106–10, 184; and Crozat's monopoly, 56–58; supplies for, 63–65, 112; missionaries in, 77, 127; and Conseil Supérieur, 87; Hubert's headquarters on, 90; hospital established on, 93, 110, 148; Raguet's settlement on, 97; emigrants to, 119, 126–28, 130; church on, 127; animals on, 134; land concessions on, 136; possibility of abandonment of, 137–40, 148; storehouse on, 142–43; navigation confined to, 144; and trade, 146; relations with Illinois country, 159; importance of, 196; Saint-Denis' description of, 197
Dauphine, 16, 64, 66, 69, 72, 90, 115, 126
Davion, Father Antoine, 126, 161
De Boisbriant, Major Pierre Dugué, 24, 54, 100
De La Tour, Lt., 172
De Lause de Villemarets, Captain, 101, 104, 114, 125–26, 126*n*
De Lery Chauvin, Joseph, 188, 190
De l'Isle, Claude, 11, 17–19, 21, 198
De l'Isle, Guillaume, 12–15, 17, 19–20, 23–25
De l'Isle, Joseph-Nicolas, 12, 13
De Louvigny, Sieur, 176
De Ville, Father Louis, 158, 175
De Vincennes, Sieur, 176
Derbanne, François, 78–79, 86, 137, 154, 188, 192
Derigoin, Basque, 24, 72, 75
Descoublan de Gillan, François, 105
Deslauriers, Clairin, 96
Desmaretz, Nicolas, 38
Desplaces, Sieur, 60, 66
Du Bourg, Sieur, 192
Du Mouchel de Villainville, 105
Du Sault, chevalier, 8
Du Sault, Lt. Simon, 14, 138, 146
Dubreuil, Vincent, 120, 147
Duché, Jean-Baptiste, 22, 58, 61, 103, 106, 151, 153, 160
Duclos, Jean Baptiste du Bois: on Indian policy, 31, 53, 153; failure to investigate Bienville, 36; and military defense, 53, 107; request for increased funds by, 53; recall of, 54, 80, 81, 87; and Crozat, 72, 75, 86; and Raujon, 74–75; appointment to St. Domingue, 81; compared with Hubert, 89, 90, 92; salary of, 90; inventory assigned to, 94–95; and employment of Raguet, 96; interest in inhabitants' opinions, 98, 149; and slaughtering of animals, 133

Education, 124–25
Emigration policy, 31–34, 46–47, 115–31
Escoubet, Captain Jean, 57–58, 182
Estrées, Marshal d', 1, 3, 11, 15, 19, 23, 30, 33, 45–48, 51, 58, 68, 121, 135

Fabvre, Jean, 124
Fay, Anthony, 126
Feuillée, Louis, 12, 13
Fishing, 134
Fleury, Charles, 144
Follart, Chevalier Jean-Charles de, 104, 151
Fort Bourbon, 20
Fort Crèvecoeur, 175
Fort Green, 20
Fort Louis, 87, 109, 110, 126, 128, 129, 140, 147, 153, 157, 161, 164, 165, 171
Fort Rosalie, 77, 155–57, 168
Fort Saint Joseph, 176
Fort Saint-Joseph-des-Tunicas, 187
Fort Toulouse, 157, 170–71, 174
France: colonies of, 1–10, 25, 27–37, 88, 181, 200–201; scientific movement in, 11–26; explorations of, 18–19; Crozat's views on importance of Louisiana to, 39–41; financial difficulties of, 50–55; and trade, 140–42; Indian policy of, 162–79; tensions with Great Britain, 162–79; tensions with Spain, 180–201. *See also* Council of the Navy

Gallut, Sieur, 186, 200
Gauvry, Captain Joachim de, 101, 104
Geography, 12–15

209

Index

Granville, Sublieutenant, 48
Graveline, Jean-Baptiste Baudreau, 94, 125, 135, 188
Great Britain, 35–36, 39–42, 46, 130, 147, 153, 162–79, 181
Guadeloupe, 118
Guénot de Tréfontaine, Philippe, 120, 147, 174
Guénot de Tréfontaine, Pierre, 120, 147, 174
Guérin, Louis, 86

Hennepin, Father Louis, 18, 25
Hersent, Lieutenant, 106, 119
Heureux, 144
Hidalgo, Father Francisco, 187
Hubert, Marc-Antoine: on increased interest in Louisiana, 3; reports requested from, 6–7; and Bienville, 36, 92–93; and price policy, 48; appointment of, 81; on La Mothe, 82–83; and Crozat, 85–86; and Lépinay, 89–90, 92; residence on Dauphin Island, 90; salary of, 90; responsibility for liquidation of notes and orders-to-pay, 93–96; on Artus, 109; and discontent of military, 111–13; on food supplies, 112; on emigration policy, 122; discouragement of, 129, 137, 147–49; on licentious life in Louisiana, 129; and slavery, 131; and Indians, 132, 172–73, 175; and Dauphin Island, 139, 140; and Saint-Denis expedition to Mexico, 186; on La Salle's bay, 192; and territorial expansion, 195; on Missouri River, 199–200
Huché, Antoine, 124
Huvé, Alexandre, 126
Hydrography, 12

Ibaignette, Sieur d', 105
Iberville, Governor, 14, 17, 35, 37
Illinois country, 74, 151–52, 158–60, 175–78, 197–98
Indentured servants, 8, 32, 117, 119, 121–22
Indians: Le Maire's report on, 17, 30–31; French policy toward, 30–31, 162–79, 184, 185; and Bienville, 37, 77–80, 154–55, 164, 165, 168, 171–72, 186–87; British policy toward, 41, 162–79; trade with, 64, 65, 90, 120, 132, 143, 146–47, 162, 196; and Lépinay, 92, 163–64, 168–69, 171; education of, 125; as slaves, 129–30; as supplier of maize for colonists, 134; French military posts among, 151–57; missionary activity among, 157–61, 175; Canadians' marriages with, 158; decline in, 165, 168; Spanish policy toward, 185; Natchez war, 197
Isnard, Danty d', 16

Jappie, Captain Elie, 56, 119, 122
Jérémie, Nicolas, 20
Jesuits, 158–61. *See also* Missionaries
Journal des Savants, 12, 25
Justice, 71

La Chapelle, Henri de Besset de, 1, 29
La Combe, Sieur de, 62, 67
La Fresnière, Nicolas Chauvin de, 96, 188, 190
La Galissonnière, Marquis de, 104–105
La Harpe, Bénard de, 190
La Hontan, baron de, 20
La Loire des Ursins, Sieur de, 78
La Longueville, Chevalier de, 105, 114
La Morandière, Sieur Etienne Rocbert de, 105, 113–14
La Mothe, Antoine de, sieur de Cadillac: and botany, 16; as traveler, 20; unfavorable views of Louisiana, 24; and mineral resources, 40, 195; complaints by and about, 72–82, 86; recall of, 72, 82, 87; return to favor by, 82–84; interest in colony of Detroit, 83–84; working jointly with Duclos, 89, 92; salary of, 90; cliques during time of, 93; and Conseil Supérieur, 96, 97; interest in inhabitants' opinions, 98; and military defense, 107, 153; authority of, 125; and slaughtering of animals, 133; land policy of, 136; and trade with Spanish colonies, 145, 196; pricing policy of, 148; on wealth of Louisiana, 151; Indian

policy of, 164; and Saint-Denis expedition, 186, 188; and La Salle's bay, 192
La Salle, 18, 36, 40
La Tardière, Vaucher de, 105
La Tour Vitral, Lieutenant de, 76, 86
La Vente, Henry Roulleaux de, 31
Land tenure system, 135–36
Law, John, 50, 94
Le Bart, Sieur, 68, 73, 86, 129
Le Boullenger, Father Jean, 128, 160–61
Le Compte, Jacques, 124
Le Maire, François: on increased interest in Louisiana, 3; information on Louisiana provided by, 14–17, 151; on Indians, 17, 30–31, 165; on Western Sea, 20–23, 200; on Bienville, 36; on Crozat, 48; on Raujon, 74; on Conseil Supérieur, 96; on military fortifications, 108; on population policy, 122; as missionary, 126–30; on agriculture, 133; on Jesuits, 161; and La Salle's bay, 192; on France's relation with Spain, 192–93; on Missouri country, 196, 199
Le Moine de Longueil, Charles, 37
Le Roux, Jacques, 124, 138
Le Sueur, Charles, 124
Le Sueur, Pierre-Charles, 14, 18, 20, 76
Legac, Charles, 109, 133
Lépinay, Sieur de: command of frigates going to Louisiana, 8; advice on weapons by, 59; on supplies and food for Louisiana, 63; appointment as governor of Louisiana, 81; arrival in Louisiana, 82; as governor of Louisiana, 85–99; and military defense, 110–11; and emigration policy, 118, 119; authority of, 125; and churches, 127; and alcohol use, 129; on hunting and fishing, 134; and Indians, 147, 162–64, 168–69, 171; and trade, 147, 149; and improvements on Dauphin Island, 148; and mineral resources, 151; and interior of Louisiana, 159; and Saint-Denis expedition to Mexico, 186

Lerondière, Gabaret de, 13
Lesterier, Sieur, 120
L'Hermitte, Jacques de, 13, 14
Linares, duke of, 185–86
Loches, Father Alexis de, 159–60
Louis XIV, 1, 4, 31, 37, 51, 95, 103, 141, 151, 181, 184
Louisiana: supplies and food for, 7, 45, 52–55, 59–61, 63–64, 112–13, 122, 132–35, 142–43, 148; cartography of, 13–15; botany of, 15–17; and discovery of Western Sea, 17–23; Indians in, 17, 30–31, 162–79; general interest on, 23–26; unfavorable opinions on, 24–25; importance of, to France, 39–41, 68; and trade, 40, 120–21, 140–47; mineral resources in, 40–41, 151–52, 198; Crozat's plans for, 41–47; military defense of, 41–42, 59–60, 100–14; emigration and, 42–44, 46–47, 115–31; price policy in, 48, 64–65, 86; economic situation in, 50–55, 132–50; salaries in, 54, 90, 106, 110–11; end of Crozat's monopoly in, 56–71; Crozat's monopoly in, 57–58; and payments made by Crozat, 58–62; Council of Trade in, 65, 86; Crozat's gains from, 68–71; government of, 72–99; La Mothe as governor of, 72–84; Lépinay as governor of, 81, 82, 85–99, 163–64, 168–69, 171; Conseil Supérieur of, 87–88, 96–98, 120, 125, 131; claims to payment in, 94–96; Canadians in, 121, 124, 154, 155, 158, 176; hierarchical social structure of, 123–26; population statistics on, 123, 123n; education in, 124–25; religion in, 126–29; agriculture in, 132–35; land tenure system in, 135–36; monetary situation in, 144–46; prices in, 148–49; occupation of interior of, 151–61; territorial expansion of, 192–93, 195
Loyard, Father Guillaume, 128, 160–61
Ludlow, 7–8, 52–53, 63, 65, 85, 106, 115, 121, 122, 138, 145, 146

Magin, Jean, 13
Magin, Nicolas, 13

211

Index

Magnou, Commodore du, 105
Mandeville, Captain François, 24, 76, 100
Marest, Father, 25
Maret de La Loge, François, 120
Maret de Lugé, Louis, 120
Marguerite, 94, 144
Martinique, 118
Massy, Jean-Baptiste, 120, 147
Merchants, 2, 8, 27, 31–32, 52, 56, 119–20, 125, 141, 142, 146–47, 183. *See also* Trade
Mermet, Father Jean, 158, 175
Mexico, 185–92, 193
Michiele, Jean. *See* Lépinay, Sieur de
Military defense: and the Council of the Navy, 9–10; and uniforms for soldiers, 9–10; voluntary enlistments of soldiers or midshipmen, 28; soldiers sent to colonial garrisons, 33; of Louisiana, 41–42, 100–14, 151–57; salaries of military, 54, 106, 110–11; uniforms for soldiers, 59–60, 113; weapons for, 59, 62–63; new recruits sent to Louisiana, 101–106; workmen for, 102–103; medical personnel for, 103; officers for, 103–105; fortifications for, 106–10, 184; food supply for troops, 112–13; complaints of troops, 113–14; social status of officers, 125– 26; posts in interior of Louisiana, 151–57
Mineral resources, 40–41, 151–52, 192, 195–96, 198
Miscegenation, 31, 129, 158
Missionaries, 30–31, 126–29, 157–63, 175, 187. *See also* names of specific missionaries
Missouri country, 14, 195–99
Mobile, 7, 56, 87, 90, 96, 97, 106, 107, 109, 110, 126, 127, 129, 130, 134, 143, 145, 147, 153, 159, 171, 178, 184, 197
Mobile Bay, 139, 140, 143, 144
Monceaux, Charles d'Auteuil de, 100
Montespan, Madame de, 125
Moro, Geraldo, 186, 193

Native Americans. *See* Indians
Navy, French, 51
Nevis affair, 35, 37
New Mexico, 192, 195, 199, 200

New Orleans, 42, 139
Noailles, duc de, 3, 5, 40, 48, 50, 55, 61, 70
Notre-Dame-de-la-Trappe, 57

Olivier, 125
Orléans, Chevalier d', 38
Orléans, duc d', 2–3, 11, 22, 23, 37, 38, 48, 83–84

Pailloux de Barbezan, Sieur, 100, 155, 156
Paix, 56, 69, 119, 122
Paon, 7–8, 52–53, 63, 65, 82, 106, 115, 121, 122, 138, 200
Pénigaut, André-Joseph, 124
Pensacola, 184, 185, 193
Peter the Great, Tsar, 22
Physics, 12
Poirier, Sieur, 86
Pont, Paul de, 59
Pontchartrain, comte de, 1, 4, 27–29, 31, 33, 35–38, 42, 51, 80, 84, 133, 151–53
Portugal, 42
Price policy: in Louisiana, 48, 64–65, 86
Prices: in Louisiana, 148–49
Protestant colonists, 34–35

Raguet, 97
Ramon, Captain Diego, 187–88, 190
Ramon, Captain Domingo, 186
Raudot, Antoine-Denis, 15, 16, 20
Raujon, 72–75, 77, 86, 119, 134
Reform projects, 2–3
Regency Council, 1, 30, 34–35, 56, 57, 58, 135
Religion, 2–3, 126–29. *See also* Missionaries
Remonville, 137, 141, 143
Renaut, Bernard, 1
Richebourg, Captain Chavagne de, 76
Rossard, Michel, 97
Rouille du Coudray, 103
Roy, Jean, 24–25, 124

Saint-Clair, Benoist de, 76, 86
Saint-Denis, Louis Juchereau de, 14, 39, 40, 46, 145, 186–92, 193, 196, 197, 200
St. Domingue, 28, 34, 35, 45, 64, 69,

72, 81, 89, 96, 118, 121, 134, 142, 143, 144, 181
Saint-Julien, Chevalier de, 105
Saint Michel, 152
Saint Sulpice, Monsieur de, 54
Salaries, 54, 90, 106, 110–11
Samslack, 7
Sarrazin, Sieur Michel, 12
Saussier, Jean, 124
Savary, Gabrielle, 124
Scientific movement: and Council of the Navy, 11–13; geography, 12–13; cartography, 13–15; botany, 15–16; discovery of Western Sea, 17–23
Seminary of Foreign Missions, 31, 127–30, 159–61. *See also* Missionaries
Sérigny, 37
Ship Island, 139, 140, 197
Ships. *See* names of specific ships
Slavery, 28–30, 56, 98, 129–31, 132
South Carolina, 169–74, 178
Spain and Spanish colonies: explorations of, 18; trade with, 39, 40, 68, 137, 145–46, 150, 182–83; tensions with France, 180–201; colonial policy of, 181; Indian policy of, 185; mineral resources of, 192, 195–96
Spaniards Island, 137, 138

Taxation, 3
Ternan, Ensign Terrisse de, 76
Terre Blanche, 155
Tisné, Ensign François du, 39, 78–79
Tonty, Henri de, 20
Toulouse, comte de: as member of Council of the Navy, 1, 3–6, 27; personal qualities of, 3–4, 56; and military defense of the colonies, 9–10; and cartography, 15; and forced emigration, 32; Crozat on, 38; and resources of Louisiana, 40; and policies for Louisiana, 47, 48; and financial difficulties, 51; and Crozat, 61; Crozat's criticism of Louisiana government to, 72, 74; and La Mothe, 80, 83; and emigration policy, 121
Tournefort, Joseph Pitton de, 16
Trade: Crozat on, 6–7; and Toulouse, 27; with Spain and Spanish colonies, 39, 40, 68, 137, 145–46, 150, 182–83; and Louisiana, 40, 120–21, 140–47; and Council of the Navy, 56–58; with Indians, 64, 65, 120, 132, 143, 146–47, 162, 196; Canadian traders, 78, 154, 155, 158, 176; British traders, 153, 177–78, 178, 181
Trépanier, Claude, 124
Trousset de Valincourt, Jean-Baptiste du, 4
Turpin, Alexandre, 20
Tusseau, Chevalier de, 105

Vallemont, Abbé Pierre Le Lorrain, 23–24
Varlet, Father, 157–58
Vaudreuil, Governor, 22–23, 84, 114, 176, 178
Verville, Jean-François de, 13
Villiers du Terrage, Marc de, 196, 197

War of the Spanish Succession, 9, 38, 50, 77, 144
West Indies, 12, 25, 27, 28, 141, 182. *See also* names of specific islands
Western Sea: discovery of, 17–23, 198–200
Windward Islands, 89
Women: Indian women, 31, 129–30; as immigrants, 33–34, 44, 47, 115, 117–19, 124; education of girls, 125

Yamasee War, 169